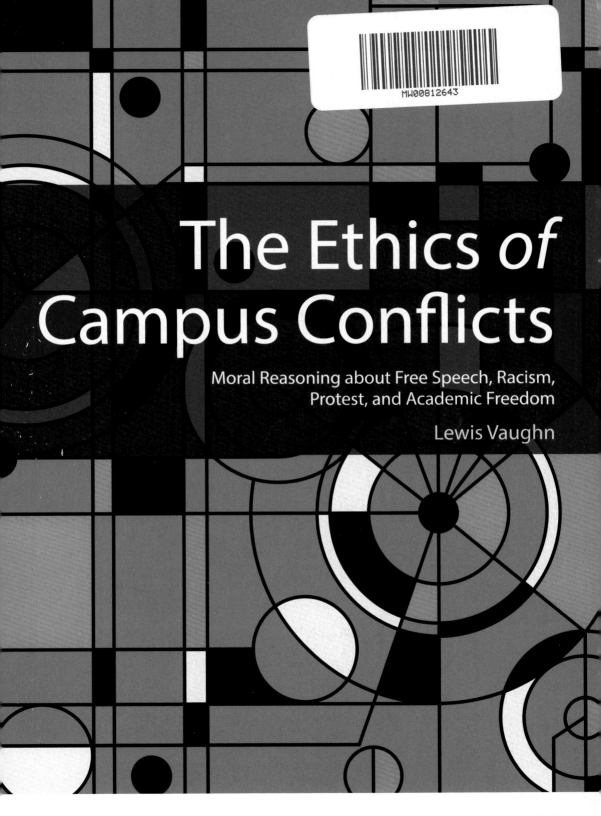

The Ethics *of* Campus Conflicts

Moral Reasoning about Free Speech, Racism, Protest, and Academic Freedom

Lewis Vaughn

New York   Oxford

OXFORD UNIVERSITY PRESS

Oxford University Press is a department of the University of Oxford.
It furthers the University's objective of excellence in research, scholarship,
and education by publishing worldwide. Oxford is a registered trade mark of
Oxford University Press in the UK and certain other countries.

Published in the United States of America by Oxford University Press
198 Madison Avenue, New York, NY 10016, United States of America.

© 2022 by Oxford University Press

For titles covered by Section 112 of the US Higher Education
Opportunity Act, please visit www.oup.com/us/he for the latest
information about pricing and alternate formats.

All rights reserved. No part of this publication may be reproduced, stored in
a retrieval system, or transmitted, in any form or by any means, without the
prior permission in writing of Oxford University Press, or as expressly permitted
by law, by license, or under terms agreed with the appropriate reproduction
rights organization. Inquiries concerning reproduction outside the scope of the
above should be sent to the Rights Department, Oxford University Press,
at the address above.

You must not circulate this work in any other form
and you must impose this same condition on any acquirer.

CIP data is on file at the Library of Congress
978–0–19–755011–3

9 8 7 6 5 4 3 2 1
Paperback printed by Quad/Mexico, Mexico

Contents

Readings discussed: Louis D. Brandeis, Susan Benesch, Nadine Strossen, Ulrich Baer, Lee C. Bollinger, Greg Lukianoff, Jonathan Haidt, Sigal R. Ben-Porath, Jeremy Waldron, Maxime Lepoutre, the AAUP, PEN America, the ACLU, Erwin Chemerinsky, Howard Gillman, Pamela Paresky, Justice Louis Brandeis, University of Chicago, Dangerous Speech Project, Susan Benesch, Richard Delgado, Jean Stefancic, Harper's Magazine letter, Michelle Goldberg, Thomas Chatterton Williams, Jonathan Zimmerman.

CHAPTER 3   Hate Speech and Speech Codes   93

Readings discussed: Foundation for Individual Rights in Education, Henry Louis Gates, Jr., Nadine Strossen, Erwin Chemerinsky, Howard Gillman, Mari J. Matsuda, University of Michigan, University of Wisconsin, University of the Virgin Islands, Azhar Majeed, Glenn Greenwald, Richard Stengel, Conor Friedersdorf

CHAPTER 4   Academic Freedom   109

Readings discussed: Jennifer Lackey, John Stuart Mill, John Dewey, Michael P. Lynch, Jennifer Saul, Michele Moody-Adams, Mary Kate McGowan, Jonathan Zimmerman, Ann Franke, Benjamin Daniels, Catherine Baiocchi, Cary Nelson, Sigal R. Ben-Porath, Colleen Flaherty, Divya Kumar, Michael Levenson, Joy Karega, Steven Salaita, Charles Negy, Inside Higher Ed, Tampa Bay Times, New York Times, Michele Moody-Adams, Michael S. Roth, Ruth Simmons, Robert Mark Simpson, Amia Srinivasan, Barack Obama

CHAPTER 5   Race, Racism, and Justice   137

Readings discussed: Randall Kennedy, Lawrence Blum, Maria Golash-Boza, Naomi Zack, American Anthropological Association, Michaels James, Hasan Kwame Jeffries, Eduardo Bonilla-Silva, Shannon Sullivan, Radley Balko, Conor Friedersdorf, Michele Moody-Adams, Kevin Nadal

CHAPTER 6   The Ethics of Protest   167

Readings discussed: American Civil Liberties Union (ACLU), The Foundation for Individual Rights in Education (FIRE), Martin Luther King, Jr., Kimberley Brownlee, Peter Suber, Martha C. Nussbaum, Charles Watson, Sarah Holtman, Candice Delmas

CHAPTER 7   The Ethics of Belief Online   187

Readings discussed: W. K. Clifford, Sabrina Tavernise, Guy Harrison, Walter Sinnott-Armstrong

Preface

Not since the campus protests of the 1960s have colleges and universities endured such intense political and ideological conflict. The political polarization, intolerance, partisan extremism, and clashes of values that afflict the national discourse have flooded into the academy. Students, faculty, and administrators have grappled with competing moral demands about racism, rights, speech, academic freedom, protests, equality, rights, and truth. The coronavirus pandemic may have dampened some skirmishes and muffled some demands, but disagreements still persist over hate speech, trigger warnings, microaggressions, safe spaces, no platforming, speech codes, minority rights, women's rights, LGBTQ rights, civility, the right to protest, civil disobedience, uncivil disobedience, and more.

Meanwhile, conservative critics have denounced universities as "left-wing indoctrination mills" where "political correctness" has strangled free speech and students are coddled lest different ideas upset them. Administrators have heard their institutions accused of racism, bigotry, and insensitivity, while minority students have condemned universities for failing to counter hostile environments rife with racist speech, microaggressions, and bigoted behavior. And faculty members have raised concerns about the adverse effects that challenges to established norms and standards may be having on academic freedom.

Commentators on these disputes have focused on issues of law, policy, and political philosophy, and they have produced some valuable work. But as far as I know, there is no textbook available that helps students think about the *ethics* of so many of these controversies—that is, about the right and wrong and the good and bad that is always at stake in these fights. This textbook is an attempt to fill this need. It shows students how to apply critical thinking and moral reasoning to the questions that are at the heart of campus controversies—that is, how to identify and evaluate the moral arguments involved, distinguish between good and bad arguments, grasp the relevance of moral principles and theories, and detect and avoid fallacies in moral thinking. This book, then, is an applied ethics text focused on issues that students likely already have a stake in.

The Ethics of Campus Conflicts tries to do two things well: (1) emphasize the habits of mind that are prerequisites for making sense of today's campus controversies and (2) develop these dispositions by showing students how to apply moral reasoning deliberately and carefully to the tough questions that they confront.

The habits of mind fostered here include the following:

- Metacognition—the ability to reflect critically on one's own thinking and values
- Overview perspective—the willingness to evaluate claims and ideas in the context of all relevant information and viewpoints
- Openness—the readiness to consider ideas different from one's own and to try to understand opposing views
- Intellectual humility—the tendency to recognize one's own limitations, be aware of the likelihood of error, and suspend judgment until all relevant information is understood
- Reasonable skepticism—the habit of refusing to accept a claim unless there are legitimate reasons for doing so and resisting the temptation to believe automatically
- Responsibility—the recognition that one's beliefs and actions have consequences online and off

The skills that exemplify these attitudes are explained and demonstrated throughout the text, illustrated with real-world examples, and reinforced and tested in chapter exercises and writing assignments. The general approach is to first give students the basics of moral reasoning (Chapter 1) and then provide the following key elements in each of the subsequent chapters:

1. Background on each controversy—the facts behind it, why it has generated so much heat, how it has played out at different institutions, and what values are at stake.
2. Expositions of the views of the most outspoken and articulate participants.
3. Close analysis of arguments (conservative, liberal, and moderate) laid out in clear premise-conclusion format, with plausible assessments of the truth of premises and the soundness of the reasoning.

The overall objective here is not to advocate a particular point of view but to explain and model good moral reasoning so students can come to their own well-considered conclusions about campus conflicts. The idea is to provide a framework that students can use to think and talk about these issues productively instead of shouting about them.

The Ethics of Campus Conflicts covers most of the contentious issues that have provoked confrontations and inflamed rhetoric in classrooms, on the quad, and in the wider culture. Both the large battles and the small skirmishes are covered in chapters on free speech, equality, and harm; hate speech and speech codes; academic freedom; race, racism, and justice; the ethics of protest; and the ethics of belief online.

Chapter 1 ends with both study and review questions. Chapters 2 through 7 have study questions and writing prompts asking students to articulate what they believe about the issue at hand and why. Text boxes in each chapter highlight important points and compelling cases on campus and in the news. All this is supplemented by an end-of-book bibliography, a glossary, and an appendix featuring guidelines for writing argumentative essays.

Ethics of Campus Conflicts comes with digital teaching and learning resources to help students understand the material. For more information, visit www.oup.com/he/vaughn-campus-conflicts.

Many thanks to all the people who have helped make this book possible. At the top of the list are the Editorial staff at Oxford University Press who worked on this title—most notably, Andy Blitzer and Rachel Boland. Thank you also to all the reviewers who helped shape this book by providing their invaluable feedback:

Robert Arp, *Johnson County Community College*
C. Tabor Fisher, *Le Moyne College*
William Hartmann, *Maryville University*
Albert Spencer, *Portland State University*
Jay Valentine, *Troy University*
Lisa Yount, *Savannah State University*

Moral Reasoning on Campus 1

On campuses across the country, political and ideological battles have been fought over a host of bewildering issues with an intensity that has not been seen since the campus protests of the 1960s. Students, faculty, and administrators have been buffeted by the crosswinds of competing moral demands about racism, speech, freedom, equality, rights, and truth. Clashes have occurred over hate speech, trigger warnings, microaggressions, safe spaces, no platforming, political correctness, speech codes (speech-restricting regulations or policies), minority rights, women's rights, LGBTQ rights, civility, academic freedom, civil disobedience, and more. Meanwhile, conservative critics have denounced universities as "left-wing indoctrination mills," where "political correctness" has strangled free speech and students are coddled lest different ideas upset them. Administrators have heard their institutions accused of racism, bigotry, and insensitivity, while minority students have condemned universities for failing to counter hostile environments rife with racist speech, microaggressions, and bigoted behavior. And faculty members have raised concerns about the adverse effects that challenges to established norms and standards may be having on academic freedom.

News reports and social media posts have obsessed over these events but rarely provided any guidance on how to think about them. Some of the more recent flashpoints:

- Dozens of campuses have enacted speech codes to try to eradicate hate speech, variously defined as racist, stigmatizing, demeaning, obscene, or otherwise offensive. A widespread idea is that there must be limits to free speech to protect vulnerable students. As an editorial in a student newspaper put it, "While it is important for students to challenge each other's opinions, this should not come at the expense of students' mental well-being or safety." Supporters of the codes say they are needed because hate speech causes psychological and physical harm and are an affront to the dignity of persons who are targeted. But courts have consistently declared such codes unconstitutional. Critics argue that hate speech laws violate fundamental principles of free speech and equality, are ineffective, and can actually be harmful. Because the laws are necessarily vague and overbroad, they argue, they can be (and have been) used to punish people for their political views as well as the very people the laws are meant to protect.

- On several campuses, controversial speakers have been blocked or disinvited (not merely protested) because of their moral or political views. As scholars have observed, "Recent examples of people targeted for disinvitation by left-wing activists include former Secretary of State Madeline Albright, on the grounds of war crimes, former New York Mayor Rudolph Giuliani, on grounds of anti-black racism, anti-F.G.M. [female genital mutilation] campaigner Ayaan Hirsi Ali, on grounds of Islamophobia, and Indian Prime Minister Narendra Modi, on grounds of human rights

Fig. 1.1 Notre Dame students protest an event featuring Charles Murray, a controversial conservative speaker, writer, and academic, outside McKenna Hall.

abuses. Disinvitation campaigns have also sometimes been mounted by conservative groups, targeting people like Angela Davis for anti-capitalist views, or Cornel West for criticism of Israel."[1]

- Trigger, or content, warnings are statements from teachers alerting students to course material that might be traumatizing, stigmatizing, offensive, or disturbing. Some students have insisted that trigger warnings are needed to shield vulnerable students from harmful expression. Many faculty members have thought it reasonable when covering violent content to warn students who have been victims of sexual assault or other violence (such as soldiers who suffer from posttraumatic stress disorder [PTSD]). And many teachers issue trigger warnings about disturbing content so students can prepare themselves to be exposed to it. But most faculty members strongly object to being required to use them and regard them as threats to their academic freedom and as restraints on their ability to teach a subject properly. Professors have also been concerned that trigger warnings treat adult students like children who need to be shielded from harsh realities. Some students have demanded trigger warnings on *any* content that might be offensive or traumatic, objecting to material on sex, rape, addiction, suicide, racism, sexism, homophobia, blood, spiders, literary works (Ovid's *Metamorphoses* and F. Scott Fitzgerald's *The Great Gatsby*, for example), and more. They also have mistakenly conceived of content warnings as a demand that they not experience anything that might disturb, upset, or offend them—an attitude that detractors have seized on as more proof of how college students are being intellectually "coddled."

- Some students have been demanding "safe spaces" on campus, which they define as learning environments where they are not exposed to offensive, demeaning, or hateful words or ideas. They contend that such expression violates students' right to equal educational opportunity, makes them feel uncomfortable and thus unsafe, or causes psychological trauma. In the spirit of safe spaces, students have insisted that all offensive or hateful speech be banned from campus, including objectionable ideas expressed by controversial speakers and campus newspapers. Fuming critics assert that students who demand safe spaces are whiney "snowflakes" who are afraid to engage with scary ideas. More thoughtful commentators argue that it's possible to create an inclusive, respectful environment without curtailing serious debate and intellectual freedom. According to one observer, "[W]e should support well thought-out efforts to make all students feel welcome in, and valued by, the institutions they attend. But being welcome in college or university is not the same thing as being 'at home.' When the university is purged of every form of expression that may cause discomfort, the only thing it will be 'safe' for is the worst excesses of the 'new tribalism.'"[2]

- Members of the Sigma Alpha Epsilon fraternity at the University of Oklahoma were videoed on a bus "chanting a song whose lyrics included racial slurs boasting that there would never be an African-American member. The song also referred to lynching, with the words 'You can hang 'em from a tree.' The videos were recorded on Saturday night as fraternity members and their dates rode a bus to a formal event celebrating the national organization's Founders Day." Two of the SAE students were expelled for "leading a racist song that sparked outrage across the country."[3]
- Northwestern professor Laura Kipnis, who identified herself as a feminist, wrote an article for the *Chronicle of Higher Education* criticizing rules that prohibit professor–student romantic relationships, denouncing them as instances of "sexual paranoia" that arose from the "melodramatic imagination's obsession with helpless victims and powerful predators . . . The result? Students' sense of vulnerability is skyrocketing." Students staged a protest over the essay, and two women students filed a complaint against the professor, alleging that her article had created a hostile learning environment, a Title IX violation. For several months the professor was investigated but in the end was cleared of any wrongdoing.[4]

Fig. 1.2 University of Oklahoma students rally outside the now closed University of Oklahoma's Sigma Alpha Epsilon fraternity house during a rally in Norman, Oklahoma. The university's president expelled two students Tuesday after he said they were identified as leaders of a racist chant captured on video during a fraternity event. A moving truck can be seen at the rear. Fraternity members were given a midnight Tuesday deadline to be moved out of the house.

- The University of Connecticut attempted to expel two students from college housing for publicly using racist insults. According to the *New York Times*, "Two white students at the University of Connecticut were arrested by the campus police on Monday night, 10 days after they were captured on video repeatedly shouting a racist slur outside student apartments, the university said. The students . . . were charged with ridicule on account of creed, religion, color, denomination, nationality or race. Their arrests came after the widely shared video drew outrage and calls by students for the administration to take action. . . . The investigation by the UConn Police Department found that the men were playing a game in which they yelled vulgar words. As they walked through the parking lot, witnesses heard two of the men switch to shouting a racial epithet, the police said."[5]
- At Yale, administrators warned students not to wear Halloween costumes that signified racism, cultural appropriation, or misrepresentation (for example, wearing turbans, blackface, or war paint), or that held people up to ridicule. In response, Erika Christakis, a lecturer, wrote an email expressing concern about students letting an institution dictate their Halloween costume preferences. "Is there no room anymore for a child or young person to be a little bit obnoxious," she wrote, "a little bit inappropriate or provocative or, yes, offensive?" After furious students demanded that she resign, and after intense media coverage, she announced that she would no longer teach at Yale.[6]
- Princeton students have demanded the removal of Woodrow Wilson's name from campus buildings, pointing out that Wilson, president of both Princeton and the United States, was an ardent segregationist and advocate for the Ku Klux Klan. Students at other schools have also protested the presence of symbols they believe are racist, segregationist, or white supremacist, including statues of Thomas Jefferson at the University of Missouri at Columbia and the College of William and Mary, the statue of a Confederate soldier at the University of Mississippi, a Confederate statue at the University of North Carolina at Chapel Hill, the family crest of a ruthless slaveholder at Harvard Law School, and a statue of Robert E. Lee at the University of Texas at Austin. As a result, many such symbols have been removed, a process that was hastened by massive anti-racist protests after George Floyd, a forty-six-year-old black man, was killed by a Minneapolis police officer who was later convicted of murder.

Such incidents have provoked dismay, disgust, rage, fear, and confusion. They have also prompted countless serious, worthwhile questions. Some are *legal* questions (for example, "Is this campus speech code constitutional?" "Is this campus protest lawful?"). Some are *policy* questions ("Should the university require professors to issue trigger warnings?"). Some are *political* questions ("What do my favorite politicians or political commentators have to say about

Fig. 1.3 The first and largest piece of the remnants of a Confederate statue known as "Silent Sam" is lifted before being transported to the bed of a truck early Tuesday, January 15, 2019, on the campus of the University of North Carolina in Chapel Hill. The last remnants of the statue were removed at the request of UNC-Chapel Hill Chancellor Carol Folt, who also announced her resignation in a move that increases pressure on the system's board of governors to give up on plans to restore the monument.

this?" "What does my political tribe believe?") But the more fundamental and more important questions are the ones that arise from **morality** and give point to the other questions. Morality is part of the unavoidable, bittersweet drama of being persons who think and feel and choose. Morality concerns beliefs regarding morally *right and wrong actions* and morally *good and bad persons or character.* Whether we like it or not, we seem confronted continually with the necessity to deliberate about right and wrong, to judge someone morally good or bad, to agree or disagree with the moral pronouncements of others, and to accept or reject the moral outlook of our culture or community.

Moral issues are thus inescapable—including those that result from the competing claims and conflicts of values now roiling college campuses. Whatever policies, politicians, or laws say, we must still ask—and seek answers to—the tough moral questions. We must ask ourselves, do speech codes violate students' rights to free speech? Is it unjust to expel a student for posting a racial slur online? Should speech that undermines the dignity of minorities be permitted on campus? When, if ever, are students justified in interfering with the speech of others? Do teachers have a right to say whatever they want in class? Is violence against controversial speakers immoral? Is it wrong to display a swastika or hangman's noose on campus? Is public incivility toward individuals you disagree with ever justified? Do students have a right not to be offended? Whatever our view of these questions, there is little doubt that they matter immensely. Whatever answers we give will surely have weight, however they fall.

The good news is that reasonable answers to such questions are possible through ethics. **Ethics** (also called moral philosophy) is the study of morality using the methods of philosophy. The moral issues that confront us are often difficult, contentious, and complex, yet ethics holds out the hope of making headway even in these turbulent waters. Through careful reflection, critical assessment of the relevant facts, and the close examination of moral arguments, we can often make good progress.

Morality consists mostly of our moral judgments, principles, values, and theories; and ethics is the careful, philosophical examination of them. There are many ways to study morality, but the deepest and most enlightening is the philosophical way. Philosophy is the systematic exploration of life's big questions using critical thinking and logical argument. Using its methods, we can examine the heart of moral issues, judge the worth of moral judgments or principles, and—above all—work to ensure that our moral beliefs rest on the solid ground of good reasons.

Our distinction between morality and ethics seems clear enough, but everyday language sometimes blurs it. People often use *morality* and *ethics* as synonyms for moral beliefs or practices in general (as in "Morality is the foundation of civilization" or "Ethics cannot be ignored"). Or they may use the words to refer to the moral beliefs or practices of specific groups or persons (e.g., "Muslim morality," "Chinese ethics," or "the ethics of John Stuart Mill"). They may maintain our distinction and use the adjective forms *moral* and *ethical* accordingly. Or they may consider these terms equivalent to *right* or *good* ("That was the ethical thing to do") and use *immoral* or *unethical* as synonyms for *wrong* or *bad* ("abortion is immoral," "cheating on an exam is unethical").

The answers we find through ethics may or may not be to our liking; they may confirm or confute our preconceived notions; they may take us far or not far enough. But, as the following pages will show, the trail has more light than shadow—and thinking critically and carefully about the problems can help us see our way forward.

The way forward, however, is too often obscured or even blocked by partisan passion and prejudice, both on campus and in the larger arena of national politics. This is an era when some politicians—across the political spectrum—lie with impunity and maintain the lie even when confronted with evidence to the contrary. It is a time when, in many quarters, feelings outweigh facts, and facts from knowledgeable sources with excellent credentials are called fake news. Some leaders who think with their gut and forgo appeals to reason and evidence are treated as sages. In too many cases, politicians are admired not because they are wise, virtuous, or truthful, but because they say what people want to hear, regardless of the facts. Such uncritical thinking has always plagued society, but now its prevalence and potential for harm seem greater than in other times in recent memory. To many people, facts and well-reasoned arguments are obstacles that get in the way of preferred subjective beliefs. For them, willful ignorance is the default position, and their commitment to their partisan tribe, leader, or cause can be all-consuming. The journalist Amanda Taub describes this kind of outsized fervor:

> Partisan bias now operates more like racism than mere political disagreement, academic research on the subject shows. And this widespread prejudice could have serious consequences for American democracy. . . .
>
> Americans' deep bias against the political party they oppose is so strong that it acts as a kind of partisan prism for facts, refracting a different reality to Republicans than to Democrats. . . .
>
> Today, political parties are no longer just the people who are supposed to govern the way you want. They are a team to support, and a tribe to feel part of. And the public's view of politics is becoming more and more zero-sum: It's about helping their team win, and making the other team lose.[7]

This means that too often, when partisans disagree, they are not really disagreeing about the facts. They are simply showing support for their tribe. They may share fake news not because they believe it, but because they want to strike a blow for their side. They may deny (or affirm) their belief in campus free speech or LGBTQ rights not because they really accept or reject the idea, but because they want to show solidarity with their fellow partisans.

The worst scenario is disagreement (whether about facts or tribes) coupled with intense hate, in which the other side is thought to be not just wrong or misinformed, but evil, beyond the pale, irredeemable. And because they are evil, they can be shunned, ignored, or savaged.

Such partisan fever widens the gap between opposing sides, prevents intelligent discussion of the issues, puts a stop to any semblance of intelligent disagreement, substitutes invective and dishonest polemics for rational argument, and causes mistakes, misunderstanding, and confusion. Ethics as a disinterested search for moral knowledge is our best bet for overcoming this kind of intellectual and moral blindness.

So now you know this book is not about *winning* moral arguments or *defeating* (or humiliating) your opponent in moral debates. It is not about pointless back-and-forth exchanges of unsupported assertions, or tense attacks and counterattacks of words, which at their worst degrade into accusations, name-calling, ridicule, and rage. Online, these sorts of exchanges are the bailiwick of trolls, baiters, harassers, bullies, narcissists, sadists, and other toxic players. They are the domain of those who naively believe they prove a proposition simply by boldly stating it. Or by screaming it in ALL CAPS. This kind of "arguing" has very little to do with critical thinking and logical argument and nothing to do with a search for moral insight.

Rational debates and logical arguments are a search for truth, or at least for what's reasonable to believe. They go something like this: someone offers a real argument—that is, they give reasons that they think logically support a conclusion—and then there is a genuine discussion about that argument, focusing on whether the logic is solid and the reasons given are true. Then someone might offer a counterargument—another set of reasons supporting a conclusion—and there is a discussion about those reasons and conclusion. In such a give and take—if it is conducted with open minds and mutual respect—there is a far better chance of arriving at justified opinions than in any pseudo-intellectual free-for-all.

The eminent philosopher Walter Sinnott-Armstrong says that too many people think arguments are fights or competitions. But such verbal wrestling matches, he says, will not help you win in any way that really matters. As he sees it,

> If you see a conversation as a fight or competition, you can win by cheating as long as you don't get caught. You will be happy to convince people with bad arguments. You don't mind interrupting them. You can call their views crazy, stupid, silly or ridiculous, or you can joke about how ignorant they are, how short they are or how small their hands are. None of these tricks will help you understand them, their positions or the issues that divide you, but they can help you win—in one way.

But things will turn out better, he says, if you engage in argument in the critical thinking sense:

> [S]uppose you give a reasonable argument: that full-time workers should not have to live in poverty. Then I counter with another reasonable argument: that a higher minimum wage will force businesses to employ less people for less time. Now we can understand each other's positions and recognize our shared values, since we both care about needy workers.
>
> What if, in the end, you convince me that we should increase the minimum wage because there are ways to do so without creating unemployment or underemployment? Who won? You ended up in exactly the position where you started, so you did not "win" anything, except perhaps some minor fleeting joy at beating me. On the other side, I gained a lot: more accurate beliefs, stronger evidence and deeper understanding of the issues, of you and of myself. If what I wanted was truth, reason and understanding, then I got what I wanted. In that way, I won. Instead of resenting you for beating me, I should thank you for helping me. That positive reaction undermines the common view of arguments as fights or competitions, while enhancing our personal relationships.[8]

Ethics and the Moral Life

Morality, then, is a normative, or evaluative, enterprise. It concerns moral norms or standards that help us decide the rightness of actions, judge the goodness of persons or character, and prescribe the form of moral conduct. There are, of course, other sorts of norms we apply in life—*nonmoral* norms. Aesthetic norms help us make value judgments about art; norms of etiquette about polite social behavior; grammatical norms about correct use of language; prudential norms about what is in one's interests; and legal norms about lawful and unlawful acts. But moral norms differ from these nonmoral kinds. Some of the features they are thought to possess include the following.

Normative dominance

In our moral practice, moral norms are presumed to dominate other kinds of norms, to take precedence over them. Philosophers call this characteristic of moral norms overridingness because moral considerations so often seem to override other factors. A maxim of prudence, for example, may suggest that you should steal if you can avoid getting caught, but a moral prohibition against stealing would overrule such a principle. An aesthetic (or pragmatic) norm implying that homeless people should be thrown in jail for blocking the view of a beautiful public mural would have to yield to moral principles demanding more humane treatment of the homeless. A law mandating brutal actions against a minority group would conflict with moral principles of justice and would therefore be deemed illegitimate. We usually think that immoral laws are defective, that they need to be changed, or that, in rare cases, they should be defied through acts of civil disobedience.

Universality

Moral norms (but not exclusively moral norms) have universality: Moral principles or judgments apply in all relevantly similar situations. If it is wrong for you to tell a lie in a particular circumstance, then it is wrong for everyone in relevantly similar circumstances to tell a lie. Logic demands this sort of consistency. It makes no sense to say that Maria's doing action A in circumstances C is morally wrong, but John's doing A in circumstances relevantly similar to C is morally right. Universality, however, is not unique to moral norms; it's a characteristic of all normative spheres.

Impartiality

Implicit in moral norms is the notion of impartiality—the idea that everyone should be considered equal, that everyone's interests should count the same. From the perspective of morality, no person is any better than any other. Everyone should be treated the same unless there is a morally relevant difference between persons. We probably would be completely baffled (or outraged) if someone seriously said something like "Murder is wrong . . . except when committed by myself," when there was no morally relevant difference between that person and the rest of the world. If we took such a statement seriously at all, we would likely not only reject it but also would not even consider it a bona fide moral statement.

The requirement of moral impartiality prohibits discrimination against people merely because they are different—different in ways that are not morally relevant. Two people can be different in many ways: skin color, weight, gender, income, age, occupation, and so forth. But these are not differences relevant to the way they should be treated as persons. However, if there are morally relevant differences between people, then we may have good reasons to treat them differently, and this treatment would not be a violation of impartiality. This is how philosopher James Rachels explains the point:

> The requirement of impartiality, then, is at bottom nothing more than a proscription against arbitrariness in dealing with people. It is a rule that forbids us from treating one person differently from another *when there is no good reason to do so.* But if this explains what is wrong with racism, it also explains why, in some special kinds of cases, it is not racist to treat people differently. Suppose a film director was making a movie about the life of Martin Luther King, Jr. He would have a perfectly good reason for ruling out Tom Cruise for the starring role. Obviously, such casting would make no sense. Because there would be a good reason for it, the director's "discrimination" would not be arbitrary and so would not be open to criticism.[9]

Reasonableness

To participate in morality—to engage in the essential, unavoidable practices of the moral life—is to do moral reasoning. If our moral judgments are to have any weight at all, if they are to be anything more than mere personal taste or knee-jerk emotional response, they must be backed by the best of reasons. They must be the result of careful reflection in which we arrive at good reasons for accepting them, reasons that could be acknowledged as such by any other reasoning persons.

Both logic and our commonsense moral experience demand that the thorough sifting of reasons constitutes the main work of our moral deliberations—regardless of our particular moral outlook or theory. We would think it odd, perhaps even perverse, if someone asserted that physically assaulting someone whose views they dislike is always morally permissible—and then said she has no reasons at all for believing such a judgment but *just does*. Whatever our views on physical assault, we would be justified in ignoring her judgment, for we would have no way to distinguish it from personal whim or wishful thinking. Likewise, she herself (if she genuinely had no good reasons for her assertion) would be in the same boat, adrift with a firm opinion moored to nothing solid.

Our feelings, of course, are also part of our moral experience. When we ponder a moral issue we care about (hate speech or racism, for example), we may feel anger, sadness, disgust, fear, irritation, or sympathy. Such strong emotions are normal and often useful, helping us empathize with others, deepening our understanding of human suffering, and sharpening our insight into the consequences of our moral decisions. To make fully informed moral decisions, we have to listen to our feelings and to those of others. But our feelings can mislead us by reflecting not moral truth but our own psychological needs, our own personal or cultural biases, or our concern for personal advantage. Throughout history, some people's feelings led them to conclude that women should be burned for witchcraft, that whole races should be exterminated, that black men should be lynched, and that adherents of a different religion were evil. Critical reasoning can help restrain such terrible impulses. It can help us put our feelings in proper perspective and achieve a measure of impartiality. Most of all, it can guide us to moral judgments that are trustworthy because they are supported by the best of reasons.

What about our conscience—can we trust it? Our conscience is conditioned by our upbringing, cultural background, and other influences. At times, it seems to speak to us in an imaginary though authoritative voice, telling us to do or not do something. But conscience is like our feelings in that it may be the result of irrelevant influences and is therefore no infallible indicator of moral truth. In the name of conscience, people have done noble deeds—and committed horrible acts. Like our feelings, the voice of conscience should not be ignored; it can often alert us to something of moral importance—something that we need to submit to critical examination. Only through critical thinking can we rise above our feelings, our conscience, and our personal interests to see with moral clarity.

The moral life, then, is about grappling with a distinctive class of norms marked by normative dominance, universality, impartiality, and reasonableness. As we saw earlier, these norms can include moral principles, rules, theories, and judgments. We should notice that we commonly apply these norms to two distinct spheres of our moral experience—to both moral *obligations* and moral *values*.

Moral obligations concern our duty, what we are obligated to do. That is, obligations are about conduct, how we ought or ought not to behave. In this sphere, we talk primarily about *actions*. We may look to moral principles or rules to guide our actions, study a moral theory that purports to explain right actions, or make judgments about right or wrong actions.

Moral values, however, generally concern those things that we judge to be morally good, bad, praiseworthy, or blameworthy. Normally we use such words to describe persons (as in "He is a good person" or "She is to blame for hurting them"), their character ("He is virtuous"; "She is honest"), or their motives ("She did wrong but did not mean to"). Note that we also attribute *nonmoral* value to things. If we say that a book or bicycle or vacation is good, we mean good in a nonmoral sense. Such things in themselves cannot have *moral* value.

Strictly speaking, only actions are morally *right* or *wrong*, but persons are morally *good* or *bad* (or some degree of goodness or badness). With this distinction we can acknowledge a simple fact of the moral life: A good person can do something wrong, and a bad person can do something right. A Gandhi can tell a lie, and a Hitler can save a drowning man.

In addition, we may judge an action right or wrong depending on the motive behind it. If John knocks a stranger down in the street to prevent her from being hit by a car, we would deem his action right (and might judge him a good person). But if he knocks her down because he dislikes the color of her skin, we would believe his action wrong (and likely think him evil).

The general meaning of *right* and *wrong* seems clear to just about everyone. But we should be careful to differentiate degrees of meaning in these moral terms. *Right* can mean either "obligatory" or "permissible." An obligatory action is one that would be wrong *not* to perform. We are obligated or required to do it. A permissible action is one that is permitted. It is not wrong to perform it. *Wrong* means "prohibited." A prohibited action is one that would be wrong to

MORALITY AND THE LAW

Some people confuse morality with the law, or identify the one with the other, but the two are distinct though they may often coincide. Laws are norms enacted or enforced by the state to protect or promote the public good. They specify which actions are *legally* right or wrong. But these same actions can also be judged *morally* right or wrong, and these two kinds of judgments will not necessarily agree. Lying to a friend about a personal matter, deliberately trying to destroy yourself through reckless living, or failing to save a drowning child (when you easily could have) may be immoral—but not illegal. Racial bias, discrimination based on gender or sexual orientation, slavery, spousal rape, and unequal treatment of minority groups are immoral—but, depending on the society, they may not be illegal.

Much of the time, however, morality and the law overlap. Often what is immoral also turns out to be illegal. This is usually the case when immoral actions cause substantial harm to others, whether physical or economic. Thus, murder and embezzlement are both immoral and illegal, backed by social disapproval and severe sanctions imposed by law. Controversy often arises when an action is not obviously or seriously harmful but is considered immoral by some who want the practice prohibited by law. The contentious notion at work is that something may be made illegal solely on the grounds that it is immoral, regardless of any physical or economic harm involved. This view of the law is known as *legal moralism*, and it sometimes underlies debates about the legalization of abortion, euthanasia, pornography, contraception, and other practices. Many issues in ethics have both a moral and legal dimension, and it is important not to confuse the two. Sometimes the question at hand is a moral one; whether a practice should be legal or illegal, then, is beside the point. Sometimes the question is about legality. And sometimes the discussion concerns both. A person may consider physician-assisted suicide morally acceptable but argue that it should nevertheless be illegal because allowing the practice to become widespread would harm both patients and the medical profession.

perform. We are obligated or required *not* to do it. A *supererogatory* action is one that is "above and beyond" our duty. It is praiseworthy—a good thing to do—but not required. Giving all your possessions to the poor is generally considered a supererogatory act.

Moral Relativism

The commonsense view of morality and moral standards is this: There are moral norms or principles that are valid or true for everyone. This claim is known as **moral objectivism**, the idea that at least some moral standards are objective. Moral objectivism, however, is distinct from **moral absolutism**, the belief that objective moral principles allow no exceptions or must be applied the same way in all cases and cultures. A moral objectivist can be absolutist about moral principles, or she can avoid absolutism by accepting that moral principles are *prima facie*—that is, applying in all cases unless an exception is warranted (as when two moral principles conflict and one must be given more weight than the other). Most people probably assume some form of moral objectivism and would not take seriously any claim implying that valid moral norms can be whatever we want them to be.

But moral objectivism is directly challenged by a doctrine that some find extremely appealing and that, if true, would undermine ethics itself: **moral relativism**. According to this view, moral standards are not objective but are relative to what individuals or cultures believe. There simply are no *objective* moral truths, only *relative* ones. An action is morally right if endorsed by a person or culture and morally wrong if condemned by a person or culture. So affirmative action is right for person A if he approves of it but wrong for person B if she disapproves of it, and the same would go for cultures with similarly diverging views on the subject. In this way, moral norms are not discovered but made; the individual or culture makes right and wrong. Moral relativism pertaining to individuals is known as **subjective relativism**, more precisely stated as the view that right actions are those sanctioned by a person. Moral relativism regarding cultures is called **cultural relativism**, the view that right actions are those sanctioned by one's culture.

In some ways, subjective relativism is a comforting position. It relieves individuals of the burden of serious critical reasoning about morality. After all, determining right and wrong is a matter of inventorying one's beliefs, and any sincerely held beliefs will do. Morality is essentially a matter of personal taste, which is an extremely easy thing to establish. Determining what one's moral views are may indeed involve deliberation and analysis—but neither of these is a necessary requirement for the job. Subjective relativism also helps people short-circuit the unpleasantness of moral debate. The subjective relativist's familiar refrain—"That may be *your* truth, but it's not *my* truth"—has a way of stopping conversations and putting an end to reasoned arguments.

The doctrine, however, is difficult to maintain consistently. On issues that the relativist cares little about (the moral rightness of gambling, say), she may be content to point out that moral norms are relative to each individual and that "to each his own." But on more momentous topics (such as genocide in Africa or the Middle East), she may slip back into objectivism and declare that genocide is morally wrong—not just wrong for her but wrong *period*.

Such inconsistencies hint that there may be something amiss with subjective relativism, and indeed there is: It seems to conflict violently with commonsense realities of the moral life. For one thing, the doctrine implies that each person is morally infallible. An action is morally right for someone if he approves of it—if he sincerely believes it to be right. His approval makes the action right, and—if his approval is genuine—he cannot be mistaken. His believing it to be right makes it right, and that's the end of it. If he endorses infanticide as a method of population control, then infanticide is morally permissible. His sincere approval settles the issue, and he cannot be in error. But our commonsense moral experience suggests that this relativist account is absurd. Our judgments about moral matters—actions, principles, and people—are often wide of the mark. We are morally fallible, and we are rightly suspicious of anyone who claims to be otherwise.

There is a more disturbing way to frame this point. Suppose former Iraqi leader Saddam Hussein approved of slaughtering thousands of Iraqis during his reign. Suppose Hitler approved of killing millions of Jews during World War II. Suppose American serial killer and cannibal Jeffrey Dahmer approved of his murdering seventeen men and boys. Then, by the lights of subjective relativism, all these mass killings were morally right because their perpetrators deemed them so. But we would find this conclusion almost impossible to swallow. We would think these actions morally wrong whether the killers approved of their own actions or not.

Subjective relativism also implies that another commonplace of the moral life is an illusion: moral disagreement. Consider: Hernando tells Sophia that allowing seriously impaired infants to die is morally right. Sophia replies that allowing seriously impaired infants to die is morally wrong. We may think that Hernando and Sophia are having a straightforward disagreement over an important moral issue. But according to subjective relativism, no such disagreement is happening or could ever happen. In stating his approval of the

Fig. 1.4 Pro-choice demonstrators are confronted by pro-life advocates as they rally outside the Supreme Court. Moral relativism implies that moral disagreements like this are not possible.

actions in question, Hernando is essentially expressing his personal taste on the issue, and Sophia is expressing her personal taste. He is saying he likes something; she says she does not like it—and they could both be correct. Subjective relativism implies that they are not uttering conflicting claims at all—they are discussing different subjects, their own personal feelings or preferences. But this strange dance is not at all what we think we are doing when we have a moral disagreement. Because subjective relativism conflicts with what we take to be a basic fact of the moral life, we have good reason to doubt it.

Cultural relativism seems to many to be a much more plausible doctrine. In fact, many people think it obviously true, supported as it is by a convincing argument and the common conviction that it is admirably consistent with social tolerance and understanding in a pluralistic world. The argument in its favor goes like this:

1. If people's moral judgments differ from culture to culture, moral norms are relative to culture (there are no objective moral standards).
2. People's moral judgments do differ from culture to culture.
3. Therefore, moral norms are relative to culture (there are no objective moral standards).

Is this a good argument? That is, does it provide us with good reason to accept the conclusion (statement 3)? For an argument to be good, its conclusion must follow logically from the premises, and the premises must be true. In this case, the conclusion does indeed follow logically from the premises (statements 1 and 2). The truth of the premises is another matter.

Let us look first at premise 2. All sorts of empirical evidence—including a trove of anthropological and sociological data—show that the premise is in fact true. Clearly, the moral beliefs of people from diverse cultures often do differ drastically on the same moral issue. Some societies condone infanticide; others condemn it. Some approve of the killing of wives and daughters to protect a family's honor; others think this tradition evil. Some bury their dead; others cremate them. Some judge the killing of one's elders to be a kindly act; others say it is cold-hearted murder. Some think polygamy morally permissible; others believe it deplorable. Some consider it a solemn duty to surgically remove the clitorises of young girls; others say this is immoral and cruel. Some commend the killing of people who practice a different religion; others believe such intolerance is morally reprehensible. We are forced to conclude that diversity of moral judgments among cultures is a reality.

But what of premise 1—is it also true? It says that because cultures have different moral beliefs, they must also have different moral standards, which means morality is relative to cultures. If diverse moral standards arise from each culture, then morality cannot be objective, applying to all people everywhere. There is no objective morality, just *moralities*.

Premise 1, however, is false. First, from the fact that cultures have divergent moral beliefs on an issue, it does not logically follow that there is no objective moral truth to be sought, that there is no opinion that is objectively correct. People may disagree about the existence of biological life on Mars, but the disagreement does not demonstrate that there is no fact of the matter or that no statement on the subject could be objectively true. Disagreements on a moral question may simply indicate that there is an objective fact of the matter but that someone (or everyone) is wrong about it.

Second, a conflict between moral beliefs does not necessarily indicate a fundamental conflict between basic moral norms. Moral disagreements between cultures can arise not just because their basic moral principles clash, but because they have differing nonmoral beliefs that put those principles in a very different light. From the annals of anthropology, for example, we have the classic story of a culture that sanctions the killing of parents when they become elderly but not yet enfeebled. Our society would condemn such a practice, no doubt appealing to moral precepts urging respect for parents and for human life. But consider: This strange (to us) culture believes that people enter heaven when they die and spend eternity in the same physical condition they were in when they passed away. Those who kill their parents are doing so because they do not want their elders to spend eternity in a state of senility but rather in good health. This culture's way is not our way; we are unlikely to share these people's nonmoral beliefs. But it is probable that they embrace the same moral principles of respect for parents and life that we do. According to some anthropologists, diverse cultures often share basic moral standards while seeming to have little or nothing in common.

The argument we are considering, then, fails to support cultural relativism. Moreover, many considerations count strongly against the view. Specifically, the logical implications of the doctrine give us substantial reasons to doubt it.

Like subjective relativism, cultural relativism implies moral infallibility, a very hard implication to take seriously. As the doctrine would have it, if a culture genuinely approves of an action, then there can be no question about the action's moral rightness: It is right, and that's that. Cultures make moral rightness, so they cannot be mistaken about it. But is it at all plausible that cultures cannot be wrong about morality? Throughout history, cultures have approved of ethnic cleansing, slavery, racism, holocausts, massacres, mass rape, torture of innocents, burning of heretics, and much more. Is it reasonable to conclude that the cultures that approved of such deeds could not have been mistaken?

Related to the infallibility problem is this difficulty: Cultural relativism implies that we cannot legitimately criticize other cultures. If a culture approves of its actions, then those actions are morally right—and it does not matter one bit whether another culture disapproves of them. Remember, there is no objective moral code to appeal to. Each society is its own maker of the moral law. It makes no sense for society X to accuse society Y of immorality, for what society Y approves of *is* moral. Some may be willing to accept this consequence of cultural relativism, but look at what it would mean. What if the people of Germany approved of the extermination of millions of Jews, Gypsies, and others during World War II? Then the extermination was morally right. Suppose the people of Libya approved of the terrorist bombing of Pan Am flight 103 over Lockerbie, Scotland, killing 270 people (a tragedy for which the Libyan government eventually took responsibility). Then the bombing was morally right, and those who placed the bomb on board did no wrong. But all this seems very much at odds with our moral experience. We think it makes perfect sense sometimes to condemn other cultures for morally wrong actions.

Now consider the notion of moral progress. We sometimes compare what people did in the past with what they do now, noting that current practices are morally better than they used to be. We no longer countenance such horrors as massacres of native peoples, slavery, and lynchings, and we think that these changes are signs of moral progress. But cultural relativism implies that there cannot be any such thing as moral progress. To claim legitimately that there has been moral progress, there must be an objective, transcultural standard for comparing cultures of the past and present. But according to cultural relativism, there are no objective moral standards, just

Fig. 1.5 American slaves at the Cassina Point plantation of James Hopkinson on Edisto Island, South Carolina, in 1862. The fact that we no longer condone slavery seems like an obvious case of moral progress, but cultural relativism cannot countenance any progress in our moral views.

norms relative to each culture. However, if there is moral progress as we think there is, then there must be objective moral standards.

Cultural relativism also has a difficult time explaining the moral status of social reformers. We tend to believe they are at least sometimes right and society is wrong. When we contemplate social reform, we think of such moral exemplars as Martin Luther King, Jr., Mahatma Gandhi, Mary Wollstonecraft, and Rosa Parks, all of whom agitated for justice and moral progress. But one of the consequences of cultural relativism is that social reformers could *never* be morally right. By definition, what society judges to be morally right is morally right, and since social reformers disagree with society, they could not be right—ever. But surely on occasion it's the reformers who are right and society is wrong.

There is also the serious difficulty of using cultural relativism to make moral decisions. Cultural relativism says that moral rightness is whatever a culture or society approves of, but determining which culture or society one truly belongs to seems almost impossible. The problem is that we each belong to many social groups, and there is no fact of the matter regarding which one is our "true" society. Suppose you are an African American Catholic Republican living in an artists' colony in Alabama and enjoying the advantages of membership in an extremely large extended family. What is your true society? If you cannot identify your proper society, you cannot tell which cultural norms apply to you.

Some people may be willing to overlook these problems of cultural relativism because they believe it promotes cultural tolerance, an attitude that seems both morally praiseworthy and increasingly necessary in a pluralistic world. After all, human history has been darkened repeatedly by the intolerance of one society toward another, engendering vast measures of bloodshed, pain, oppression, injustice, and ignorance. The thought is that because all cultures are morally equal, there is no objective reason for criticizing any of them. Tolerance is then the best policy.

Cultural relativism, however, does not necessarily lead to tolerance and certainly does not logically entail it. In fact, cultural relativism can easily justify either tolerance or intolerance. It says that if a society sanctions tolerance, then tolerance is morally right for that society. But if a society approves of intolerance, then *intolerance* is morally right for that society—and the society cannot be legitimately criticized for endorsing such an attitude. According to cultural relativism, intolerance can be morally permissible just as tolerance can. In addition, though moral relativists may want to advocate universal tolerance, they cannot consistently do so. To say that all cultures should be tolerant is to endorse an objective moral norm, but cultural relativists insist that there are no objective moral norms. To endorse universal tolerance is to abandon cultural relativism.

Ethics and Religion

How is ethics related to religion? One obvious connection is that historically religion has always had moral content—mostly in the form of moral precepts, codes, or commandments to guide the conduct of adherents. In Western civilization, this content has been so influential in moral (and legal) matters that many now take for granted that religion is the fundamental basis of morality. Secular or nontheistic systems of ethics (for example, the ethics of Stoicism, Confucianism, Buddhism, utilitarianism, and contractarianism) have also shaped how we think about morality. But for millions of people, religion is the fountainhead of the moral law.

An important query in ethics is whether this view of morality is correct: whether morality depends fundamentally on religion, whether—to state the question in its traditional form—the moral law is constituted by the will of God. The view that morality does have this kind of dependence is known as the **divine command theory**. It says that right actions are those commanded by God, and wrong actions are those forbidden by God. God is the author of the moral law, making right and wrong by his will.

But many people—both religious and nonreligious—have found this doctrine troubling. Philosophers have generally rejected it, including some famous theistic thinkers such as Thomas Aquinas (1225–1274), Gottfried Leibniz (1646–1710), and Immanuel Kant (1724–1804).

The problem is that the theory presents us with a disconcerting dilemma first spelled out in Plato's *Euthyphro*. In this dialogue, Socrates asks a penetrating question that is often expressed like this: Are actions morally right because God commands them, or does God command them because they are morally right? In the first option, God creates the moral law (the divine command theory); in the second, the moral law is independent of God's will so that even God is subject to it. Critics of the divine command theory have argued that the first option implies the moral law is entirely arbitrary. The second option denies the theory.

The arbitrariness is thought to arise like this: If actions are morally right just because God commands them to be so, then it is possible that any actions whatsoever could be morally right. The murder and rape of innocents, the oppression of the weak, the abuse of the poor—these and many other awful deeds would be morally permissible if God so willed. There would be no independent standard to judge that these acts are wrong, no moral reasons apart from God's will to suggest that such deeds are evil. God would be free to establish arbitrarily any actions whatsoever as morally right.

Defenders of the divine command theory have replied to the arbitrariness charge by saying that God would never command something evil because God is all good. But critics point out that if the theory is true, the assertion that God is all good would be meaningless, and the traditional religious idea of the goodness of God would become an empty notion. If God makes the moral law, then the moral term *good* would mean "commanded by God." But then "God is good" would mean something like "God does what God commands" or even "God is what God is," which tells us nothing about the goodness of God. Likewise, "God's commands are good" would translate as "God's commands are God's commands." This attempt to escape the charge of arbitrariness seems to have intolerable implications.

Theists and nontheists alike find this horn of Socrates's dilemma—the idea of an arbitrary, divinely ordained morality—incredible. They therefore reject the divine command theory and embrace the other horn, the view that right and wrong are independent of God's will. Moral standards are external to God, binding on both God and mortals. If there are divine commands, they will conform to these independent moral norms. The religious may then claim that God is good—good because he abides perfectly by the moral law and guides the conduct of believers accordingly.

If moral standards are not grounded in the divine will, if they are logically independent of religion, then morality is a legitimate concern for the religious and nonreligious alike, and everyone has equal access to moral reflection and the moral life. The best evidence for the latter is ethics itself. The fact is that people *do ethics*. They use critical reasoning and experience to determine moral norms, explore ethical issues, test moral theories, and live a good life. The results of these explorations are moral outlooks and standards founded on good reasons and arguments and assented to by reflective people everywhere.

In ethics, the informed opinions of religious people are as relevant as those of secularists. But all parties must be willing to submit their views to the tests and criteria of critical reasoning and evidence.

But even if ethics does not have this independent status, there are still good reasons for religious believers to know how to use the critical tools that ethics offers. First, like many secular moral rules, religious moral codes are often vague and difficult to apply to conflicts and issues. Getting around this problem requires interpreting the codes, and this task involves consideration of broader norms or theories, a typical job for ethics. Second, like everyone else, believers must deal with moral conflicts of all sorts—including clashes between the moral beliefs of religious adherents, religious leaders, and religious traditions. What is often needed is a neutral standard and critical analyses to arrive at a resolution—tools that ethics can easily provide. Third, public debate on ethical issues in a diverse society requires ground rules—chief among them being that positions must be explained and reasons must be given in their support. Unexplained assertions without supporting reasons or arguments are likely to be ignored. In this arena, ethics is essential.

Argument Fundamentals

Critical thinking, or reasoning, is something we employ every time we carefully and systematically assess the truth of a statement or the merits of a logical argument. We ask: Are there good reasons for believing this statement? Is this a good argument—does it prove its case? These sorts of questions are asked in every academic field and in every serious human endeavor. Wherever there is a need to acquire knowledge, to separate truth from falsity, and to come to a reliable understanding of how the world works, these questions are asked and answers are sought. Ethics is no exception. Critical thinking in ethics—called moral reasoning—employs the same general principles of logic and evidence that guide the search for truth in every other field. So we need not wonder whether we use critical reasoning in ethics but whether we use it well.

Most critical thinking is concerned in one way or another with the construction or evaluation of arguments. As we've seen, here *argument* denotes not an altercation but a patterned set of assertions: at least one statement providing support for another statement. We have an argument when one or more statements give us reasons for believing another one. The supporting statements are *premises*, and the supported statement is the *conclusion*. In critical thinking, the term *statement* also has a technical meaning. A statement (or claim) is an assertion that something is or is not the case and is therefore the kind of utterance that is either true or false.

You need to understand at the outset that *argument* in this sense is not synonymous with *persuasion*. An argument provides us with reasons for accepting a claim; it is an attempted "proof" for an assertion. But persuasion does not necessarily involve giving any reasons at all for accepting a claim. To persuade is to influence people's opinions, which can be accomplished by offering a good argument but also by misleading with logical fallacies, exploiting emotions and prejudices, dazzling with rhetorical gimmicks, hiding or distorting the facts, threatening or coercing people—the list is long. Good arguments prove something whether or not they persuade. Persuasive ploys can change minds but do not necessarily prove anything.

So we formulate an argument to try to show that a particular claim (the conclusion) should be believed, and we analyze an argument to see if it really does show what it purports to show. If the argument is good, we are entitled to believe its conclusion. If it is bad, we are not entitled to believe it.

Consider these two simple arguments:

Argument 1
Law enforcement in the city is a complete failure. Incidents of serious crime have doubled.

Argument 2
It's wrong to take the life of an innocent person. Abortion takes the life of an innocent person. So abortion is wrong.

In argument 1, the conclusion is "Law enforcement in the city is a complete failure," which is supported by the premise "Incidents of serious crime have doubled." The conclusion of argument 2 is "abortion is wrong," and it is backed by two premises: "It's wrong to take the life of an innocent person" and "Abortion takes the life of an innocent person." Despite the differences between these two passages (differences in content, the number of premises, and the order of their parts), they are both arguments because they exemplify basic argument structure: a conclusion supported by at least one premise.

Though the components of an argument are usually apparent, people often fail to distinguish between arguments and strong statements that contain no arguments at all. Suppose we change argument 1 into this:

Law enforcement in the city is a complete failure. Nothing seems to work anymore. This situation is intolerable.

Now there is no argument, just an expression of annoyance or anger. There are no statements giving us reasons to believe a conclusion. What we have are some unsupported assertions that may merely *appear* to make a case. If we ignore the distinction between genuine arguments and nonargumentative material, critical reasoning is undone.

Consider this example from Twitter:

> I choose these words carefully because I mean them sincerely: Guns are disgusting, despicable creations of human engineering, and ownership of them is creepy and disturbing.

This is not an argument. It proves nothing. It's merely an assertion of beliefs. Often such assertions of opinion are just a jumble of unsupported claims. Search high and low and you will not find an argument anywhere. A writer or speaker of these claims gives the readers or listeners no grounds for believing the claims.

Assuming we can recognize an argument when we see it, how can we tell if it is a good one? Fortunately, the general criteria for judging the merits of an argument are simple and clear. A good argument—one that gives us good reasons for believing a claim—must have (1) solid logic and (2) true premises. Requirement (1) means that the conclusion should follow logically from the premises, that there must be a proper logical connection between supporting statements and the statement supported. Requirement (2) says that what the premises assert must in fact be the case. An argument that fails in either respect is a bad argument.

There are two basic kinds of arguments—deductive and inductive—and our two requirements hold for both of them, even though the logical connections in each type are distinct. **Deductive arguments** are intended to give *logically conclusive* support to their conclusions so that if the premises are true, the conclusion absolutely must be true. Argument 2 is a deductive argument and is therefore supposed to be constructed so that if the two premises are true, its conclusion cannot possibly be false. Here it is with its structure laid bare:

Argument 2
1. It's wrong to take the life of an innocent person.
2. Abortion takes the life of an innocent person.
3. Therefore, abortion is wrong.

Do you see that, given the form or structure of this argument, if the premises are true, then the conclusion has to be true? It would be very strange—illogical, in fact—to agree that the two premises are true but that the conclusion is false.

Now look at this one:

Argument 3
1. All dogs are mammals.
2. Rex is a dog.
3. Therefore, Rex is a mammal.

Again, there is no way for the premises to be true while the conclusion is false. The deductive form of the argument guarantees this.

So a deductive argument is intended to have this sort of airtight structure. If it actually does have this structure, it is said to be *valid*. Argument 2 is deductive because it is intended to provide logically conclusive support to its conclusion. It is valid because, as a matter of fact, it does offer this kind of support. A deductive argument that fails to provide conclusive support to its conclusion is said to be *invalid*. In such an argument, it is possible for the premises to be true and the conclusion false. Argument 3 is intended to have a deductive form, and because it actually does have this form, the argument is also valid.

An elementary fact about deductive arguments is that their validity (or lack thereof) is a separate issue from the truth of the premises. Validity is a structural matter, depending entirely on how an argument is put together. Truth concerns the nature of the claims made in the premises and conclusion. A deductive argument is supposed to be built so that *if* the premises are true, the conclusion must be true—but in a particular case, the premises might *not* be true. A valid argument can have true or false premises and a true or false conclusion. (By definition, of course, it cannot have true premises and a false conclusion.) In any case, being invalid or having false premises dooms a deductive argument.

Inductive arguments are supposed to give *probable* support to their conclusions. Unlike deductive arguments, they are not designed to support their conclusions decisively. They can establish only that, if their premises are true, their conclusions are probably true (more likely to be true than not). Argument 1 is an inductive argument meant to demonstrate the probable truth that "law enforcement in the city is a complete failure." Like all inductive arguments (and unlike deductive ones), it can have true premises and a false conclusion. So the sole premise—"incidents of serious crime have doubled"—can be true while the conclusion is false.

If inductive arguments succeed in lending very probable support to their conclusions, they are said to be *strong*. Strong arguments are such that if their premises are true, their conclusions are very probably true. If they fail to provide this very probable support, they are termed *weak*. Argument 1 is a weak argument because its premise, even if true, does not show that more likely than not law enforcement in the city is a complete failure. After all, even if incidents of serious crime have doubled, law enforcement may be successful in other ways, or incidents of serious crime may be up for reasons unrelated to the effectiveness of law enforcement.

But consider this inductive argument:

Argument 4
1. Eighty-five percent of the students at this university are Republicans.
2. Sonia is a student at this university.
3. Therefore, Sonia is probably a Republican.

This argument is strong. If its premises are true, its conclusion is likely to be true. If 85 percent of the university's students are Republicans, and Sonia is a university student, she is more likely than not to be a Republican, too.

When a valid (deductive) argument has true premises, it is a good argument. A good deductive argument is said to be *sound*. Argument 2 is valid, but we cannot say whether it is sound until we determine the truth of the premises. Argument 3 is valid, and if its premises are true, it is sound. When a strong (inductive) argument has true premises, it is also a good argument. A good inductive argument is said to be *cogent*. Argument 1 is weak, so there is no way it can be cogent. Argument 4 is strong, and if its premises are true, it is cogent.

Checking the validity or strength of an argument is often a plain, common-sense undertaking. Using our natural reasoning ability, we can examine how the premises are linked to the conclusion and can see quickly whether the conclusion follows from the premises. We are most likely to make an easy job of it when the arguments are simple. Many times, however, we need some help, and help is available in the form of methods and guidelines for evaluating arguments.

Having a familiarity with common argument patterns, or forms, is especially useful when assessing the validity of deductive arguments. We are likely to encounter these forms again and again in ethics as well as in everyday life. Here is a prime example:

Argument 5
1. If the surgeon operates, then the patient will be cured.
2. The surgeon is operating.
3. Therefore, the patient will be cured.

This argument form contains a *conditional* premise—that is, a premise consisting of a conditional, or if-then, statement (actually a compound statement composed of two constituent statements). Premise 1 is a conditional statement. A conditional statement has two parts: the part beginning with *if* (called the *antecedent*) and the part beginning with *then* (known as the *consequent*). So the antecedent of premise 1 is "If the surgeon operates," and the consequent is "then the patient will be cured."

The best way to appreciate the structure of such an argument (or any deductive argument, for that matter) is to translate it into traditional argument symbols in which each statement is symbolized by a letter. Here is the symbolization for argument 5:

1. If *p*, then *q*.
2. *p*.
3. Therefore, *q*.

We can see that *p* represents "the surgeon operates," and *q* represents "the patient will be cured." But notice that we can use this same symbolized argument form to represent countless other arguments—arguments with different statements but having the same basic structure.

It just so happens that the underlying argument form for argument 5 is extremely common—common enough to have a name, *modus ponens* (or affirming the antecedent). The truly useful fact about *modus ponens* is that any argument having this form is valid. We can plug any statements we want into the formula and the result will be a valid argument, a circumstance in which if the premises are true, the conclusion must be true.

Another common argument form is *modus tollens* (or denying the consequent). For example:

Argument 6
1. If it's raining, the park is closed.
2. The park is not closed.
3. Therefore, it's not raining.
1. If *p*, then *q*.
2. Not *q*.
3. Therefore, not *p*.

Modus tollens is also a valid form, and any argument using this form must also be valid.

There are also common argument forms that are invalid. Here are two of them:

Affirming the consequent
Argument 7
1. If the mind is an immaterial substance, then ESP is real.
2. ESP is real.
3. Therefore, the mind is an immaterial substance.
1. If *p*, then *q*.
2. *q*.
3. Therefore, *p*.

Denying the antecedent
Argument 8
1. If Einstein invented the steam engine, then he is a great scientist.
2. Einstein did not invent the steam engine.
3. Therefore, he is not a great scientist.
1. If *p*, then *q*.
2. Not *p*.
3. Therefore, not *q*.

The advantage of being able to recognize these and other common argument forms is that you can use that skill to determine readily the validity of many deductive arguments. You know, for example, that any argument having the

VALID AND INVALID ARGUMENT FORMS

Valid Forms

AFFIRMING THE ANTECEDENT
> (*Modus Ponens*)
> Example:
> If Spot barks, a burglar is in the house.
> Spot is barking.
> Therefore, a burglar is in the house.
> If p, then q.
> p.
> Therefore, q.

DENYING THE CONSEQUENT
> (*Modus Tollens*)
> Example:
> If it's raining, the park is closed.
> The park is not closed.
> Therefore, it's not raining.
> If p, then q.
> Not q.
> Therefore, not p.

Invalid Forms

AFFIRMING THE CONSEQUENT
> Example:
> If Donald Trump owns Paris, then he's rich.
> Donald Trump is rich.
> Therefore, he owns Paris.
> If p, then q.
> q.
> Therefore, p.

DENYING THE ANTECEDENT
> Example:
> If Joe Biden was born in California, then he's an American.
> Joe Biden was not born in California.
> Therefore, he is not an American.
> If p, then q.
> Not p.
> Therefore, not q.

same form as *modus ponens* or *modus tollens* must be valid, and any argument in one of the common invalid forms must be invalid.

Inductive arguments also have distinctive forms, and being familiar with the forms can help you evaluate the arguments. Let's look at three common forms of inductive arguments.

In **enumerative induction**, we arrive at a generalization about an entire group of things after observing just some members of the group. (Thus, enumerative induction represents the basic logic behind opinion polls.) Here are some typical enumerative inductive arguments:

Argument 9
Every cell phone I have bought from the computer store is defective.
Therefore, all cell phones sold at the computer store are probably defective.

Argument 10
All the hawks in this wildlife sanctuary that I have observed have had red tails.
Therefore, all the hawks in this sanctuary probably have red tails.

Argument 11
Sixty percent of the Bostonians I have interviewed in various parts of the city are pro-choice.
Therefore, 60 percent of all Bostonians are probably pro-choice.

As you can see, enumerative induction has this form:
X percent of the observed members of group *A* have property *P*.
Therefore, X percent of all members of group *A* probably have property *P*.

The observed members of the group are simply a sample of the entire group. So based on what we know about this sample, we can generalize to all the members. But how do we know whether such an argument is strong? Everything depends on the sample. If the sample is large enough and representative enough, we can safely assume that our generalization drawn from the sample is probably an accurate reflection of the whole group of members. A sample is representative of an entire group only if each member of the group has an equal chance of being included in the sample. In general, the larger the sample, the greater the probability that it accurately reflects the nature of the group as a whole. Often common sense tells us when a sample is too small. Reasoning from a sample that's too small results in a *hasty generalization* .

We do not know how many cell phones from the computer store are in the sample mentioned in argument 9. But if the number is several dozen and the cell phones were bought over a period of weeks or months, the sample is probably sufficiently large and representative. If so, the argument is strong. Likewise, in argument 10 we don't know the size of the sample or how it was obtained.

But if the sample was taken from all the likely spots in the sanctuary where hawks live, and if several hawks were observed in each location, the sample is probably adequate—and the argument is strong. In argument 11, if the sample consists of a handful of Bostonians interviewed on a few street corners, the sample is definitely inadequate and the argument is weak. But if the sample consists of several hundred people, and if every member of the whole group has an equal chance of being included in the sample, then the sample would be good enough to allow us to accurately generalize about the whole population. Typically, selecting such a sample of a large population is done by professional polling organizations.

In the argument form known as **analogical induction** (or argument by analogy), we reason in this fashion: Two or more things are similar in several ways; therefore, they are probably similar in one further way.

Argument 12
Humans can walk upright, use simple tools, learn new skills, and devise deductive arguments.
Chimpanzees can walk upright, use simple tools, and learn new skills.
Therefore, chimpanzees can probably devise deductive arguments.

This argument says that because chimpanzees are similar to humans in several respects, they probably are similar to humans in one further respect.

Here's an argument by analogy that has become a classic in philosophy:

Argument 13
A watch is a complex mechanism with many parts that seem arranged to achieve a specific purpose—a purpose chosen by the watch's designer. In similar fashion, the universe is a complex mechanism with many parts that seem arranged to achieve a specific purpose. Therefore, the universe must also have a designer.

We can represent the form of an argument by analogy in this way:

X has properties $P1$, $P2$, $P3$ plus the property $P4$.
Y has properties $P1$, $P2$, and $P3$.
Therefore, Y probably has property $P4$.

The strength of an analogical induction depends on the relevant similarities between the two things compared. The more relevant similarities there are, the greater the probability that the conclusion is true. In argument 12, several similarities are noted. But there are some unmentioned dissimilarities. The brain of a chimpanzee is smaller and more primitive than that of a human, a difference that probably inhibits higher intellectual functions such as logical argument. Argument 12, then, is weak. A common response to argument 13 is that the argument is weak because, although the universe resembles a watch in some ways, in other ways it does not resemble a watch. Specifically, the universe also resembles a living thing.

The third type of inductive argument is known as **inference to the best explanation**, a kind of reasoning that we all use daily and that is at the heart of scientific investigations. Recall that an argument gives us reasons for believing *that* something is the case. An *explanation*, however, states *how* or *why* something is the case. It attempts to clarify or elucidate, not offer proof. For example:

1. Megan definitely understood the material, for she could answer every question on the test.
2. Megan understood the material because she has a good memory.

Sentence 1 is an argument. The conclusion is "Megan definitely understood the material," and the reason (premise) given for believing that the conclusion is true is "for she could answer every question on the test." Sentence 2, however, is an explanation. It does not try to present reasons for believing something; it has nothing to prove. Instead, it tries to show why something is the way it is (why Megan understood the material). Sentence 2 assumes that Megan understood the material and then tries to explain why. Such explanations play a crucial role in inference to the best explanation.

In this type of inductive argument, we begin with premises about a phenomenon or state of affairs to be explained. Then we reason from those premises to an explanation for that state of affairs. We try to produce not just any old explanation but the best explanation among several possibilities. The best explanation is the one most likely to be true. The conclusion of the argument is that the preferred explanation is indeed probably true. For example:

Argument 14
Tariq flunked his philosophy course. The best explanation for his failure is that he didn't read the material. Therefore, he probably didn't read the material.

Argument 15
Ladies and gentlemen of the jury, the defendant was found with the murder weapon in his hand, blood on his clothes, and the victim's wallet in his pocket. We have an eyewitness putting the defendant at the scene of the crime. The best explanation for all these facts is that the defendant committed the murder. There can be very little doubt—he's guilty.

Here's the form of inference to the best explanation:

Phenomenon *Q*.
E provides the best explanation for *Q*.
Therefore, it is probable that *E* is true.

In any argument of this pattern, if the explanation given is really the best, then the argument is inductively strong. If the explanation is not the best, the argument is inductively weak. If the premises of the strong argument are true, then the argument is cogent. If the argument is cogent, then we have good reason to believe that the conclusion is true.

The biggest challenge in using inference to the best explanation is determining which explanation is the best. Sometimes this feat is easy. If our car has a flat tire, we may quickly uncover the best explanation for such a state of affairs. If we see a nail sticking out of the flat, and there is no obvious evidence of tampering or of any other extraordinary cause (that is, there are no good alternative explanations), we may safely conclude that the best explanation is that a nail punctured the tire.

In more complicated situations, we may need to do what scientists do to evaluate explanations, or theories—use special criteria to sort through the possibilities. Scientists call these standards the *criteria of adequacy*. Despite this fancy name, these criteria are basically just common sense, standards that you have probably used yourself.

One of these criteria is called *conservatism*. This criterion says that, all things being equal, the best explanation or theory is the one that fits best with what is already known or established. For example, if a Facebook friend of yours says— in all seriousness—that she can fly to the moon without using any kind of rocket or spaceship, you probably wouldn't believe her (and might even think she needs psychiatric help). Your reasons for doubting her would probably rest on the criterion of conservatism—that what she says conflicts with everything science knows about space flight, human anatomy, aerodynamics, laws of nature, and much more. It is logically possible that she really can fly to the moon, but her claim's lack of conservatism (the fact that it conflicts with so much of what we already know about the world) casts serious doubt on it.

Here is another useful criterion for judging the worth of explanations: *simplicity*. Other things being equal, the best explanation is the one that is the simplest—that is, the one that rests on the fewest assumptions. The theory making the fewest assumptions is less likely to be false because there are fewer ways for it to go wrong. In the example about the flat tire, one possible (but strange) explanation is that space aliens punctured the tire. You probably wouldn't put much credence in this explanation because you would have to assume too many unknown entities and processes—namely, space aliens who have come from who knows where using who knows what methods to move about and puncture your tires. The nail-in-the-tire theory is much simpler (it assumes no unknown entities or processes) and therefore is much more likely to be true.

When you are carefully reading an argument (whether in an essay or some other context), you will be just as interested in whether the premises are true as in whether the conclusion follows from the premises. If the writer is conscientious, he or she will try to ensure that each premise is either well supported or in no need of support (because the premise is obvious or agreed to by all parties). The needed support will come from the citing of examples, statistics, research, expert opinion, and other kinds of evidence or reasons. This arrangement means that each premise of the primary argument may be a conclusion supported in turn by premises citing evidence or reasons. In any case, you as the reader will have to carefully evaluate the truth of all premises and the support behind them.

When you are trying to make a good argument, the story will be much the same. You will want to provide good reasons to your readers for accepting the premises, for you understand that simply explaining your premises is not enough. You will have to provide support for each premise requiring it and ensure that the support is adequate and reliable.

THREE MENTAL OBSTACLES TO CRITICAL THINKING

Three of the most common psychological impediments to critical thinking—and among the hardest to overcome—are the following. They are hindrances that affect humans in every endeavor, from personal judgments and moral deliberations to high-stakes decision-making in business, government, politics, social networks, and even scientific research.

To define them, we need a correct understanding of the concept of **evidence**. In its most general sense, *evidence is something that makes a statement more likely to be true.* It does not mean "something that I feel or perceive is true." Evidence that there's a tree in the quad is your unimpaired, clear perception of such a tree (and your confidence that there is no reason to doubt your perception). Evidence that most Republicans (or most Democrats) drink alcohol is a scientific opinion survey (done by a reputable, unbiased polling organization) showing the alcohol drinking habits of those groups. Evidence that a measles vaccine does not cause autism in young children is a growing body of scientific research showing no connection between autism and a measles vaccine (and the discrediting and nonreplication of a study that once tied those two together). The mere fact that you strongly believe a statement, or have a friend who strongly believes it, or have read Twitter posts by people swearing that it's true, or hear from your favorite YouTube personality that it's so—*such things do not, by themselves, constitute evidence.* They do not, by themselves, make a statement more likely to be true. They may, however, give you good reason to start looking for evidence.

Denying Contrary Evidence

An all-too-human tendency is to try to deny or resist evidence that flies in the face of our cherished beliefs. We may deny evidence, or ignore it, or reinterpret it so it fits better with our prejudices. Denying evidence may be psychologically comforting (for a while, anyway), but it thwarts any search for knowledge and stunts our understanding.

It's shockingly easy to find examples of the blatant denial of evidence. Scientific research and commonsense experience show that the practice permeates all walks of life. A political activist may refuse to consider evidence that conflicts with his party's principles. A scientist may be so committed to her theory that she refuses to take seriously any data that undermine it. An administrator of a grand program may insist that it is a huge success despite all evidence to the contrary.

Often our resistance to contrary evidence takes a subtle form. If we encounter evidence against our views, we frequently don't reject it outright. We simply apply more critical scrutiny to it than we would to evidence in favor of our views, or we seek out additional confirming information, or we find a way to interpret the data so it doesn't conflict with our expectations.

There is no cure for our tendency to resist opposing evidence. The only available remedy is to *make a conscious effort to look for opposing evidence*. Don't consider your evaluation of a statement or argument finished until you've carefully considered *all the relevant reasons*. Ask yourself, "What is the evidence or reasons against this statement?" This approach is at the heart of science. A basic principle of scientific work is not to accept a favored theory until competing (alternative) theories are thoroughly examined.

Looking for Confirming Evidence

We often not only resist conflicting evidence but also seek out and use only confirming evidence—a phenomenon known as **confirmation bias**. When we go out of our way to find only confirming evidence, we can end up accepting a claim that's not true, seeing relationships that aren't there, and finding confirmation that isn't genuine.

In scientific research on confirmation bias, when subjects are asked to assess a claim, they often look for confirming evidence only, even though disconfirming evidence may be just as revealing. Sometimes we look for confirming evidence even when disconfirming evidence is more telling. For example, take this claim: All swans are white. You can easily find confirming instances; white swans are plentiful and ubiquitous. But even your seeing thousands of white swans will not conclusively confirm that all swans are white because there may be swans in places where you haven't looked. But all you have to do is find one black swan to conclusively show that the claim is false. (People used to believe that the claim was absolutely true— until black swans were discovered in Australia.) In such cases, confirmation bias can lead us way off course.

The pull of confirmation bias is insidious and potent. It is an incredibly strong tendency to cherry-pick evidence while we think we're being perfectly fair and reasonable. It makes false statements seem not only true, but irrefutable. It gives the deluded social media gadfly, who touts the reality of the nonexistent and the obvious evil of everyone in the opposing party, supreme confidence in the truth of the absurd and incredible.

The moral to this story is that when we evaluate claims, we should look for disconfirming as well as confirming evidence. Doing so requires a conscious effort to consider not only the information that supports what we want to believe but also the information that conflicts with it. We have to seek out disconfirming evidence just as we keep an eye out for confirming evidence— an approach that goes against our cognitive grain. We naturally gravitate to people and policies we agree with, to the books that support our views, to the magazines and newspapers that echo our political outlook. Acquiring a broader, smarter, more critical perspective takes effort—and guts.

Preferring Available Evidence

Another common mistake in evaluating evidence is the **availability error**. We commit this blunder when we rely on evidence not because it's trustworthy but because it's memorable or striking—that is, psychologically available. In such cases, we put stock in evidence that's psychologically impressive or persuasive, not necessarily logically acceptable. You fall for the availability error if you vote to convict a murder suspect because he looks menacing, not because the evidence points to his guilt; or if you decide that a Honda Civic is an unsafe vehicle because you saw one get smashed in a highway accident; or if, just because you watched a TV news report about a mugging in your city, you believe that the risk of being mugged is extremely high.

Being taken in by the availability error can lead to some serious misjudgments about the risks involved in various situations. Some people (are you one of them?) believe that air travel is more dangerous than many other modes of transportation, so they shun travel by airplane in favor of the automobile. Their conclusion is based on nothing more than a few vivid media reports of tragic plane crashes. But research shows that per mile traveled, flying is far safer than automobile travel. Your chances of dying in a plane crash in 2001 were 1 in 310,560, but the odds of your dying in a car accident were only 1 in 19,075. The fact is, there are plenty of less vivid and less memorable (that is, psychologically unavailable) things that are much more dangerous than air travel: falling down stairs, drowning, choking, and accidental poisoning.

Moral Arguments

A moral argument, like any other kind of argument, has premises and a conclusion. The premises (and sometimes the conclusion) may be implied, not stated, and they may be simple or complex—just as in other arguments. Moral arguments, however, differ from nonmoral ones in that their conclusions are moral statements. In general, a **moral statement** is a statement asserting that an action is right or wrong (moral or immoral) or that something (such as a person or motive) is good or bad. Here are some moral statements:

- Serena should keep her promise to you.
- It is wrong to treat James so harshly.
- Abortion is immoral.
- We ought to protect Liu from the angry mob.
- My father is a good man.

Moral statements are plainly different from nonmoral, or descriptive, statements. Nonmoral statements do not assert that something is right or wrong, good or bad—they simply describe a state of affairs without giving it a value one way or the other. Compare these nonmoral statements with the moral statements just given:

- Serena did not keep her promise to you.
- James was treated harshly.
- Some people think abortion is immoral.
- Liu was protected from the angry mob.
- My father tried to be a good man.

The standard moral argument is a mixture of moral and nonmoral statements. At least one premise is a moral statement that asserts a general moral principle or moral standard. At least one premise makes a nonmoral claim. And the conclusion is a moral statement, or judgment, about a particular case (usually a particular kind of action). For example:

Argument 16
1. It is wrong to inflict unnecessary pain on a child.
2. Spanking inflicts unnecessary pain on a child.
3. Therefore, spanking is wrong.

In this simple argument, premise 1 is a moral statement, affirming a general moral principle. Premise 2 is a nonmoral statement describing the nature of a specific kind of action. And the conclusion is the moral statement that the argument is intended to establish. It is about a specific kind of action.

A standard moral argument has this form for good reason. In a moral argument, we simply cannot establish the conclusion (a moral statement) without a moral premise. A moral argument with only nonmoral premises does not work. To put it another way, we cannot infer what *should be* or *ought to be* (in the conclusion) from statements about *what is*. Suppose the previous argument reads like this (and there are no missing premises):

> Spanking inflicts unnecessary pain on a child.
> Therefore, spanking is wrong.

The premise doesn't say anything about right or wrong; it just makes a descriptive claim. The conclusion, though, does assert something about right or wrong. So the conclusion is not supported by the premise; it does not follow from the descriptive statement.

Here's another example:

> Torturing prisoners of war is a case of intentional mistreatment.
> Prisoners of war should not be tortured.

This argument fails because the moral premise is missing. We need a moral premise to connect the nonmoral premise to the conclusion, like this:

Argument 17
No prisoner of war should ever be intentionally mistreated.
Torturing prisoners of war is a case of intentional mistreatment.
Prisoners of war should not be tortured.

In the standard moral argument, we also need a nonmoral premise. Remember that the conclusion is a moral statement (judgment) about a particular kind of action. The moral premise, however, is a statement expressing a general moral principle about a much broader class of actions. In order to infer the narrower conclusion from a much broader premise, we need a nonmoral statement to bridge the gap. For example, from the general moral principle that "no prisoner of war should ever be intentionally mistreated," we cannot conclude that "prisoners of war should not be tortured" unless there is a nonmoral premise stating that torturing prisoners of war is a type of intentional mistreatment. Likewise from the general moral principle that "murder is wrong," we cannot conclude that "abortion is wrong" unless there's a factual premise telling us that abortion is murder.

Now, very often when you encounter moral arguments, they are abbreviated and missing the moral premise (the general moral principle), like the arguments discussed earlier:

> Spanking inflicts unnecessary pain on a child.
> Therefore, spanking is wrong.

> Torturing prisoners of war is a case of intentional mistreatment.
> Prisoners of war should not be tortured.

Usually, the moral premise is missing because it's implicit. In such cases, to make sense of the argument, you must supply the implicit premise. Sometimes

you may automatically add the implicit premise in your head without bothering to fill out the argument properly. But if you want to carefully evaluate moral arguments, it's best to spell out any missing premises. Implicit moral premises are often dubious and need to be studied closely. General moral principles that are taken for granted may turn out to be unfounded or incomplete. Also, laying everything out on the table like this is essential if you want to improve the argument—an important exercise if you care that your positions on moral issues are well supported.

The simplest approach to identifying implicit premises is to treat moral arguments as deductive. (Notice that arguments 16 and 17 are valid deductive arguments.) Your task, then, is to supply plausible premises that will make the argument valid. Consider this argument:

> Cloning humans is unnatural.
> Therefore, cloning humans is morally wrong.

As it stands, this argument is not valid, and we can see right away that the missing premise is a general moral principle. A plausible premise to make this argument valid, then, is "Anything unnatural is morally wrong," a general moral principle. The revised version is:

Argument 18
Anything unnatural is morally wrong.
Cloning humans is unnatural.
Therefore, cloning humans is morally wrong.

Here's another incomplete argument:

> Meg lied to her sister for no good reason.
> Therefore, Meg should not have lied to her sister.

To make this argument valid and to supply a general moral principle, we can add this premise:

Argument 19
One should not lie without good reason.
Meg lied to her sister for no good reason.
Therefore, Meg should not have lied to her sister.

Another advantage to treating moral arguments as deductive (and to supplying explicit premises that will make the arguments valid) is ease of analysis. Generally, moral arguments are easier to appraise and modify when they are deductive. And if they are deductively valid, you know that any flaws in the arguments will likely be the result of false premises. For example, if you have a deductively valid argument, and the conclusion is false, you know that at least one of the premises is false.

In good arguments the inferences are valid or strong and the premises—whether nonmoral or moral—are true. This latter stipulation means that to make good arguments, you must ensure that the premises are backed by good reasons and are not simply assumed without warrant. To evaluate arguments, you must check the premises for these same qualities. Accurately assessing the truth of nonmoral premises depends mostly on your knowledge of the subject matter, including the results of relevant scientific research, the analyses of reliable experts, and the content of your background information. Gauging the truth of moral premises (moral principles) mostly involves examining the support they get from three sources: (1) other moral principles, (2) moral theories, and (3) considered moral judgments.

The appeal to another moral principle (usually a more general or higher level principle) is probably the most common way to support a moral premise. Often the more general principle is extremely credible or accepted by all parties so that further support for it is unnecessary. Sometimes it is controversial so that it, too, is in need of support. Suppose the moral premise in question is as follows: "A dying patient in intolerable and untreatable pain should be allowed to commit suicide with a physician's help." Some would say that this claim is derived from, or is based on, the higher (and more widely accepted) principle of autonomy—the notion that a person has an inherent right of self-determination, a right to make autonomous choices about his or her own life and death. Others would support the premise by appealing to the principle of beneficence, or mercy: If we are in a position to relieve the severe suffering of another without excessive cost to ourselves, we have a duty to do so. They would interpret this principle as sanctioning the physician's role in helping a competent, hopelessly ill patient to die. To try to show that the premise is false, someone might appeal to a sanctity-of-life principle, asserting that human life is sacred and should be preserved at all costs. When such higher principles are brought in, the truth of the original premise often becomes clear—or not. They cannot be the court of final appeal in ethics, for they, too, can be tested by reasoned argument showing why they should or should not be believed.

Reasons for accepting or rejecting a moral premise can also come from a *moral theory*, a general explanation of what makes an action right or what makes a person or motive good (see the next section). For example, traditional utilitarianism is a moral theory asserting that right actions are those that produce the greatest happiness for all concerned. To support the assisted suicide premise, you could appeal to the theory, arguing that the least amount of unhappiness (pain and suffering) for all concerned (patient, physician, and family) would result if the physician helped the patient die. To counter your argument, someone would need to show that your happiness calculations were incorrect (for example, that assisted suicide actually causes more unhappiness in the long run), or that utilitarianism itself is an inadequate theory, or that other theories or considerations are more important or relevant than utilitarian factors.

A moral premise can also be supported or undermined by our *considered moral judgments*. These are moral judgments that we consider credible after we carefully and dispassionately reflect on them. Pertaining to either specific cases or general statements, they constitute what philosophers have called our moral common sense. They are not infallible guides to morality, but unless we have good reasons for doubting their soundness, we are entitled to trust them. Some of our considered judgments may seem undeniable, even self-evident—for example: "Inflicting unnecessary, undeserved suffering on someone is wrong"; "Torturing children for the fun of it is immoral"; "Treating people harshly merely because of the color of their skin is unjust."

Moral principles, theories, and judgments relate to one another in interesting ways. For now, it's enough to note that we can evaluate moral premises by seeing if they conflict with principles, theories, or judgments that we have good reason to trust. Specifically, we can assess a moral premise the same way we might assess any other kind of universal generalization—by trying to think of counterexamples to it. Consider this deductively valid argument, a modified version of argument 18:

Argument 18
1. The medical cloning of humans is unnatural because it is something that would not occur without human intervention.
2. All actions that are unnatural and that are not done for religious reasons should not be done.
3. The medical cloning of humans is never done for religious reasons.
4. Therefore, cloning humans should not be done.

Premise 2 is the general moral principle here. Is it true? At the very least it is questionable. We know that it's questionable because we can think of counterexamples to it. That is, we can think of instances in which the principle seems not to hold. For example, what about the use of antibiotics to treat infections? The use of antibiotics is unnatural as defined in the argument (they are a good example of human intervention in the natural course of illness), and few would claim that antibiotics are employed for religious reasons. (The term "for religious reasons" is vague, but we will assume for the sake of this example that it means something like "as an integral part of established religious practice.") But despite its unnaturalness, the use of antibiotics seems to be morally acceptable to almost everyone. At any rate, it is difficult to imagine what a plausible argument against antibiotics would be like. So premise 2 appears to be false. We could probably refute premise 2 by using many other counterexamples, such as wearing clothes, drinking bottled water, and riding a bicycle.

COMMON FALLACIES IN MORAL REASONING

The world is full of bad arguments. Many of them occur again and again in different guises and contexts, being so common that they have been given names and are studied by those who wish to avoid such mistakes. These common, defective arguments are called *fallacies*. Here are a few that often crop up in moral reasoning.

Straw Man

The straw man fallacy is the misrepresentation of a person's views so they can be more easily attacked or dismissed. Suppose you argue that because an immunization program will save the lives of thousands of children and will likely cause the death of only 1 child out of every 500,000, we should fund the immunization program. But then your opponent replies that you think the life of a child isn't worth much. Thus, your point has been distorted, made to look extreme or unsavory, and is now an easier target. The straw man fallacy, of course, proves nothing, though many people fall for it every day.

Appeal to the Person

Closely related to the straw man fallacy is appeal to the person (also known as the *ad hominem* fallacy). Appeal to the person is the rejecting of a statement on the grounds that it comes from a particular person, not because the statement, or claim, itself is false or dubious. For example:

> *You can safely discard anything that Susan has to say about abortion. She's a Catholic. Johnson argues that our current health care system is defective. But don't listen to him— he's a liberal.*

These arguments are defective because they ask us to reject a claim because of a person's character, background, or circumstances—things that are generally irrelevant to the truth of claims. A statement must stand or fall on its own merits. The personal characteristics of the person espousing the view do not necessarily have a bearing on its truth. Only if we can show that someone's dubious traits somehow make the claim dubious are we justified in rejecting the claim because of a person's personal characteristics. Such a circumstance is rare.

Appeal to Ignorance

As its name implies, this fallacy tries to prove something by appealing to what we don't know. The appeal to ignorance is arguing either that (1) a claim is true because it has not been proven false or (2) a claim is false because it has not been proven true. For example:

No one has proven that a fetus is not a person, so it is in fact a person.
It is obviously false that a fetus is a person because science has not proven that it is a person.

The first argument tries to prove a claim by pointing out that it has not been proven false. The second argument tries to prove that a claim is false because it has not been proven true. Both kinds of arguments are bogus because they assume that a lack of evidence proves something. But a lack of evidence can prove nothing. Being ignorant of the facts does not enlighten us. Notice that if a lack of evidence could prove something, then you could prove just about anything you wanted. You could reason, for instance, that since no one can prove that horses cannot fly, horses must be able to fly.

Begging the Question

The fallacy of begging the question is trying to prove a conclusion by using that very same conclusion as support. It is arguing in a circle. This way of trying to prove something says, in effect, "X is true because X is true." Here is a classic example:

The Bible says that God exists.
The Bible is true because God wrote it.
Therefore, God exists.

The conclusion here ("God exists") is supported by premises that assume that very conclusion.

Here's another one:

All citizens have the right to a fair trial because those whom the state is obliged to protect and give consideration are automatically due judicial criminal proceedings that are equitable by any reasonable standard.

This passage may at first seem like a good argument, but it isn't. It reduces to this unimpressive assertion: "All citizens have the right to a fair trial because all citizens have the right to a fair trial." The conclusion is "All citizens have the right to a fair trial," but that is more or less what the premise says. The premise—"those whom the state is obliged to protect and give consideration are automatically due judicial criminal proceedings that are equitable by any reasonable standard"— is equivalent to "All citizens have the right to a fair trial."

Slippery Slope

The metaphor behind this fallacy suggests the danger of stepping on a dicey incline, losing your footing, and sliding to disaster. The fallacy of slippery slope, then, is arguing erroneously that a particular action should not be taken because it will lead inevitably to other actions resulting in some dire outcome. The key word here is *erroneously*. A slippery slope scenario becomes fallacious when there is no reason to believe that the chain of events predicted will ever happen. For example:

> *If dying patients are permitted to refuse treatment, then soon doctors will be refusing the treatment on their behalf. Then physician-assisted suicide will become rampant, and soon killing patients for almost any reason will become the norm.*

This argument is fallacious because there are no reasons for believing that the first step will ultimately result in the chain of events described. If good reasons could be given, the argument might be salvaged.

Moral Theories

Very often when we assess moral arguments and in other ways think critically about morality, we are trying to come to a moral judgment about a particular issue or kind of action. We deliberate because we want to understand what's right or wrong, good or bad. Our moral judgments may appear as premises or conclusions in our arguments or as sturdy pillars of our moral common sense. They may be justified by appeals to general moral principles, which in turn may gain credibility from the most reliable of our moral judgments. But what of moral theories? In the previous section we saw how a moral theory can strengthen or weaken a moral premise. Yet that's only part of the story.

Theories of morality are attempts to explain what makes an action right or what makes a person or motive good. They try to specify what all right actions and all good things have in common. As such, they can give support, guidance, or validation to our moral decision-making, shaping our moral principles, judgments, and arguments. Traditional utilitarianism is a well-known example of a moral theory. Another is the divine command theory. Ethical egoism asserts that right actions are those that promote one's own best interests.

Interestingly enough, we all have a moral theory. Whether we articulate it or not, we all have some kind of view of what makes actions right or persons good. Even the notion that there is no such thing as right or wrong is a moral theory. Even the idea that all moral theories are worthless or that all moral judgments are subjective, objective, relative, or meaningless is a moral theory. The critical question, then, is not whether you have a moral theory but whether the theory you have is a good one.

Moral theorizing is a fact of the moral life. We do moral theorizing when we ponder what rightness or goodness means, or try to furnish basic justification for a moral standard, or resolve a conflict between principles, or gauge the credibility of moral intuitions, or explain why an action is right or wrong. To theorize is to step back from the specifics of a case and try to see the larger pattern that can help us make sense of it all.

Despite the importance of moral theories, they are not the ultimate authority or sole referee in moral reasoning. A theory gives us very general norms, but morality is about more than just generalities—it's also about the particulars of individual moral judgments. How do the general and the particular fit together? Here is one way. Suppose you must decide whether an action is morally permissible. From a plausible moral theory, you draw general guidance in the form of moral principles that apply to the case. If the principles appear to sanction conflicting decisions, you turn again to the theory for understanding in how to resolve the inconsistency. At the same time you consult your considered moral judgments. If your theory and your considered judgments lead you to the same conclusion, you have good reason to believe that the conclusion is correct. If your theory and considered judgments diverge, you must decide which is more credible. If the implications of your theory seem more plausible, you may decide to revise your considered judgments to cohere better with the theory. If your judgments seem more plausible, you may decide to alter your theory accordingly. If your credible judgments conflict drastically with your theory, you may be justified in giving up the theory altogether.

Evaluating Moral Theories

As you can see, as explanations of what makes actions right or character good, moral theories can differ dramatically in both content and quality. In their own fashion, they try to identify the true determinants of rightness or goodness, and they vary in how close they seem to get to the mark. Most moral philosophers would readily agree: Some moral theories are better than others, and a vital task in ethics is to try to tell which is which. Moral theories can be useful and valuable to us only if there are criteria for judging their worth—and fortunately there are such standards.

In several ways, moral theories are analogous to scientific theories. Scientists devise theories to explain the causes of events. The germ theory is offered to explain the cause and spread of infectious diseases. The Big Bang theory is used to explain the structure and expansion of the universe. The "greenhouse effect" is put forth to explain climate change. For each phenomenon to be explained, scientists usually have several possible theories to consider, and the challenge is to determine which one is best (and is therefore most likely to be correct). The superior theory is the one that fares best when judged by generally accepted yardsticks known as the *scientific criteria of adequacy*. One criterion often invoked is *fruitfulness*—whether the theory makes successful predictions of previously unknown phenomena. All things being equal, a theory that makes successful predictions of novel phenomena is more likely to be true than one that does not. Another important criterion is *conservatism*—how well a theory fits with established facts, with what scientists already know. All things being equal, a theory that conflicts with what scientists already have good reasons to believe is less likely to be true than a theory that has no such conflicts. Of course, an unconservative theory can turn out to be correct, and a conservative theory wrong, but the odds are against this outcome. Analogously, moral theories are meant to explain what makes an action right or a person good, and to try to determine which moral theory is most likely correct, we apply conceptual yardsticks—the *moral criteria of adequacy*. Any plausible moral theory must measure up to these critical standards.

An important criterion of adequacy for moral theories is *consistency with our considered moral judgments.* Any plausible scientific theory must be consistent with the data that the theory is supposed to explain; there should be no conflicts between the theory and the relevant facts. A theory put forth to explain planetary motion, for example, must account for the relevant data— scientific observations of the movements of the planets and related objects. Likewise, a moral theory must also be consistent with the data it is supposed to explain: our considered moral judgments, what some call our moral common sense. We arrive at these judgments after careful deliberation that is as free of bias, self-interest, and other distorting influences as possible. Moral philosophers grant these judgments considerable respect and try to take them into account in their moral theorizing. These judgments are fallible, and they are often revised under pressure from trustworthy principles or theories. But we are entitled to trust them unless we have good reason to doubt them. Therefore, any moral theory that is seriously inconsistent with our considered judgments must be regarded as badly flawed, perhaps fatally so, and in need of radical revision. Our considered judgments, for example, tell us that slavery, murder, rape, and genocide are wrong. A moral theory that implies otherwise fails this criterion and is a candidate for rejection.

In applying this standard, we must keep in mind that in both science and ethics, there is tension between theory and data. A good theory explains the data, which in turn influence the shape of the theory. Particularly strong data can compel scientists to alter a theory to account for the information, but a good theory can also give scientists reasons to question or reject particular data. In the same way, there is a kind of give and take between a moral theory and the relevant data. Our considered moral judgments may give us good reasons for altering or even rejecting our moral theory. But if our moral theory is coherent and well supported, it may oblige us to rethink or reject our considered judgments. In both science and ethics, the goal is to ensure that the fit between theory and data is as tight as possible. The fit is acceptably close when no further changes in the theory or the data are necessary—when there is a kind of balance between the two that moral philosophers call "reflective equilibrium."

Another test of adequacy is *consistency with the facts of the moral life*. In science, good theories are consistent with scientific background knowledge, with what scientists already have good reasons to believe. They are, as mentioned earlier, conservative. This background knowledge includes other well-founded theories, highly reliable findings, and scientific (natural) laws. Moral theories should also be consistent with background knowledge—the *moral* background knowledge, the basic, inescapable experiences of the moral life. These experiences include making moral judgments, disagreeing with others on moral issues, being mistaken in our moral beliefs, and giving reasons for accepting moral beliefs. That we do in fact experience these things from time to time is a matter of moral common sense—seemingly obvious facts of the moral life. Thus, any moral theory that is inconsistent with these aspects of the moral life is deeply problematic. It is possible that we are deluded about the moral life—that we, for example, merely think we are disagreeing with others on moral issues but are actually just venting our feelings. But our experience gives us good grounds for taking the commonsense view until we are given good reasons to believe otherwise.

Finally, we have this criterion: *resourcefulness in moral problem-solving, or workability*. If a scientific theory helps scientists answer questions, solve problems, and control facets of the natural world, it demonstrates both its plausibility and usefulness. All things being equal, such a resourceful theory is better than one that has none of these advantages. Much the same is true for moral theories. A resourceful moral theory helps us solve moral problems. It can help us identify morally relevant aspects of conduct, judge the rightness of actions, resolve conflicts among moral principles and judgments, test and correct our moral intuitions, and understand the underlying point of morality itself. Any moral theory that lacks problem-solving resourcefulness is neither useful nor credible.

Two Important Theories

Now let's see how we can use these criteria to take the measure of two fundamentally different (and very influential) theories: traditional utilitarianism and Kantian ethics.

Traditional utilitarianiism. This theory was founded by Jeremy Bentham (1748–1832) and later refined by John Stuart Mill (1806–1873). Bentham's idea was that right actions are those that achieve the greatest happiness for the greatest number. He declared that by this simple standard all actions could be judged.

Many people embraced the theory, for it seemed so much more rational than moral theories of the time, which often rested on dubious assumptions. In the nineteenth century, traditional utilitarianism inspired reformers who worked to abolish slavery, eliminate child labor, and increase recognition of women's rights.

To be more precise, traditional utilitarianism says that what makes an action right is that it maximizes overall happiness, everyone considered. Acting morally in any given situation, then, involves calculating how much happiness can be produced by several possible actions, identifying the persons who will be affected by those actions, and opting for the one action that produces the greatest amount of happiness in the world. Notice that what matters in utilitarianism is the *consequences* of an action—not whether the action breaks a rule or violates some abstract principle. If happiness is maximized by a particular action, then the action is morally right, regardless of any other considerations. By the lights of utilitarianism, the end justifies the means.

How does traditional utilitarianism fare when judged by the moral criteria of adequacy? For starters, the theory does seem to be consistent with key aspects of our experience of the moral life. The theory assumes that we can and do make moral judgments, have moral disagreements, and act immorally.

Many moral philosophers, however, think the theory's main problem is that it seems to conflict with many of our considered moral judgments. For instance, the theory seems inconsistent with our considered moral judgments involving rights. We tend to think that certain things should not be done to people even if doing them would produce the greatest amount of happiness in the world. We would not think it right to falsely accuse and punish an innocent person just because doing so would make a whole town of people happy. We would not think it right to torture one person just because the action would make a dozen other people extremely happy. Our considered moral judgments say that such actions are wrong, but traditional utilitarianism says they may be right.

Suppose two possible actions will produce exactly the same amount of overall happiness. But one of the actions involves the violation of someone's rights or causes a serious injustice. According to utilitarianism, the two actions are equally right. But to many, this evaluation of the situation seems to conflict with our considered moral judgments.

The same kind of conflict arises in regard to moral duties. Most of us believe that we have certain duties to other people that often seem weightier than considerations of happiness. For example, we believe that in general we have a duty to keep our promises to people. But traditional utilitarianism does not recognize any such duties. It says that our only goal should be to maximize happiness—regardless of whether we have to break a promise to do it.

So for these reasons (and a few others), many critics have accused the theory of being acutely inconsistent with relevant moral data. They believe that any theory that runs afoul of the criterion of consistency in this way cannot be correct.

But take note: Even the fiercest critics of utilitarianism have admitted that the theory does seem to capture something essential to moral theories—the notion that the consequences of actions are indeed relevant to moral judgments. Probably very few people would want to say that in moral decision-making the consequences of their actions never matter.

For the record, the sketch of traditional utilitarianism given here has been oversimplified so we can focus on the process of theory assessment. Over the years, utilitarians have modified the theory to make it more plausible. Detractors, however, still claim that the theory is flawed . . . but that's another story.

Kantian ethics. From the great German philosopher Immanuel Kant (1724–1804) comes what is widely regarded as probably the most sophisticated and influential deontological (duty- or rights-based) theory ever devised. It is the very antithesis of utilitarianism, holding that right actions do not depend in the least on consequences, the maximization of utility, the production of happiness, or the desires and needs of human beings. For Kant, the core of morality consists of following a rational and universally applicable moral rule and doing so solely out of a sense of duty. An action is right only if it conforms to such a rule, and we are morally praiseworthy only if we perform it for duty's sake alone.

In Kant's system, all our moral duties are expressed in the form of *categorical imperatives.* An imperative is a command to do something; it is categorical if it applies without exception and without regard for particular needs or purposes. A categorical imperative says, "Do this—regardless." In contrast, a *hypothetical imperative* is a command to do something if we want to achieve particular aims, as in "If you want good pay, work hard." The moral law, then, rests on absolute directives that do not depend on the contingencies of desire or utility.

Kant says that through reason and reflection we can derive our duties from a single moral principle, what he calls *the* categorical imperative. He formulates it in different ways, the first one being "Act only on that maxim through which you can at the same time will that it should become a universal law."[10] For Kant, our actions have logical implications—they imply general rules, or maxims, of conduct. If you tell a lie for financial gain, you are in effect acting according to a maxim like "It's okay to lie to someone when doing so benefits you financially." The question is whether the maxim corresponding to an action is a legitimate moral law. To find out, we must ask if we could consistently will that the maxim become a universal law applicable to everyone— that is, if everyone could consistently act on the maxim and we would be willing to have them do so. If we could do this, then the action described by the maxim is morally permissible; if not, it is prohibited. Thus, moral laws embody two characteristics thought to be essential to morality itself: universality and impartiality.

To show us how to apply this formulation of the categorical imperative to a specific situation, Kant uses the example of a lying promise. Suppose you need to borrow money from a friend, but you know you could never pay her back.

So to get the loan, you decide to lie, falsely promising to repay the money. To find out if such a lying promise is morally permissible, Kant would have you ask if you could consistently will the maxim of your action to become a universal law, to ask, in effect, "What would happen if everyone did this?" The maxim is "Whenever you need to borrow money you cannot pay back, make a lying promise to repay." So what *would* happen if everyone in need of a loan acted in accordance with this maxim? People would make lying promises to obtain loans, but everyone would also know that such promises were worthless, and the custom of loaning money on promises would disappear. So willing the maxim to be a universal law involves a contradiction: If everyone made lying promises, promise-making itself would be no more; you cannot consistently will the maxim to become a universal law. Therefore, your duty is clear: Making a lying promise to borrow money is morally wrong.

Kant's first formulation of the categorical imperative yields several other duties. Notably he argues that there is an absolute moral prohibition against killing the innocent, lying, committing suicide, and failing to help others when feasible.

Perhaps the most renowned formulation of the categorical imperative is the principle of respect for persons (a formulation distinct from the first one, though Kant thought them equivalent). As he puts it, "Act in such a way that you always treat humanity, whether in your own person or in the person of any other, never simply as a means, but always at the same time as an end."[11] People must never be treated as if they were mere instruments for achieving some further end, for people are ends in themselves, possessors of ultimate inherent worth. People have ultimate value because they are the ultimate source of value for other things. They bestow value; they do not have it bestowed upon them. So we should treat both ourselves and other persons with the respect that all inherently valuable beings deserve.

According to Kant, the inherent worth of persons derives from their nature as free, rational beings capable of directing their own lives, determining their own ends, and decreeing their own rules by which to live. Thus, the inherent value of persons does not depend in any way on their social status, wealth, talent, race, or culture. Moreover, inherent value is something that all persons possess equally. Each person deserves the same measure of respect as any other.

Kant explains that we treat people merely as a means instead of an end in themselves if we disregard these characteristics of personhood—if we thwart people's freely chosen actions by coercing them, undermine their rational decision-making by lying to them, or discount their equality by discriminating against them.

Notice that this formulation of the categorical imperative does not actually prohibit treating a person as a means but forbids treating a person *simply*, or *merely*, as a means—as *nothing but* a means. Kant recognizes that in daily life we often must use people to achieve our various ends. To buy milk, we use the cashier; to find books, we use the librarian; to get well, we use the doctor. But because their actions are freely chosen and we do not undermine their status as persons, we do not use them solely as instruments of our will. Medical researchers use their human subjects as a means to an end—but not merely as a means to an end if the subjects give their informed consent to participate in the research.

Like utilitarianism, Kant's theory seems generally consistent with the basic facts of the moral life, but many philosophers argue that it is not consistent with moral common sense. A major cause of the problem, they say, is Kant's insistence that we have absolute (or "perfect") duties—obligations that must be honored without exception. Thus, in Kantian ethics, we have an absolute duty not to lie or to break a promise or to kill the innocent, come what may. Imagine that a band of killers wants to murder an innocent man who has taken refuge in your house, and the killers come to your door and ask you point blank if he is in your house. To say no is to lie; to answer truthfully is to guarantee the man's death. What should you do? In a case like this, says Kant, you must *do your duty*—you must tell the truth, even though murder is the result and a lie would save a life. But in this case such devotion to moral absolutes seems completely askew, for saving an innocent life seems far more important morally than blindly obeying a rule. Our considered judgments suggest that sometimes the consequences of our actions do matter more than adherence to the letter of the law, even if the law is generally worthy of our respect and obedience.

Some have thought that Kant's theory can yield implausible results for another reason. Recall that the first formulation of the categorical imperative says that an action is permissible if persons could consistently act on the relevant maxim, and we would be willing to have them do so. This requirement seems to make sense if the maxim in question is something like "Do not kill the innocent" or "Treat equals equally." But what if the maxim is "Enslave all Christians" or "Kill all Ethiopians"? We could—without contradiction—will either one of these precepts to become a universal law. And if we were so inclined, we could be willing for everyone to act accordingly, even if we ourselves were Christians or Ethiopians. So by Kantian lights, these actions could very well be morally permissible, and their permissibility would depend on whether someone was willing to have them apply universally. Critics conclude that because the first formulation of the categorical imperative seems to sanction such obviously immoral acts, the theory is deeply flawed. Defenders of Kant's theory, however, view the problems as repairable and have proposed revisions.

This apparent arbitrariness in the first formulation can significantly lessen the theory's usefulness. The categorical imperative is supposed to help us discern moral directives that are rational, universal, and objective. But if it is subjective in the way just described, its helpfulness as a guide for living morally is dubious. Defenders of Kant's theory, however, believe there are remedies for this difficulty.

Some argue, for example, that the problem disappears if the second formulation is viewed as a supplement to the first, rather than as two independent principles.

Between utilitarianism and Kantian ethics, which theory is better and why? An adequate answer to that question would be anything but brief. Comparing the virtues and vices of these two theories, and then deciding which one is preferable, would require a great deal of careful analysis and critical thinking. But however the task proceeds, it is sure to involve applying to both theories some telling criteria of adequacy (either the three criteria discussed here, or variations on them, and perhaps others). Such an investigation would show that neither theory is perfect (no theory is) and would likely yield an edifying conclusion such as (1) one theory is more plausible than the other, or (2) both theories are seriously defective, or (3) the best elements of both can be blended into a new theory, or (4) one of the theories is an especially good candidate for modification to eliminate shortcomings.

Applying the criteria is not like solving a mathematical equation or following a set of instructions to build a gasoline engine. There is no rigid rubric for using or weighting the criteria to sort good theories from bad. But like the scientific criteria of adequacy, these standards do give us guidance in making reasonable judgments about the objective strengths and weaknesses of theories.

BEWARE OF MOTIVATED REASONING

Suppose before beginning your investigation into a crime, before knowing anything about it, you decide what conclusion you will reach: Alex murdered Alice with an ax. So you glom onto evidence that Alex knew Alice, that they attended the same college, that they disliked each other, and that Alex owned an ax. And you disregard evidence that points in the opposite direction—evidence like phone records showing Alex and Alice two thousand miles apart at the time of the crime, and testimony of her friends that her boyfriend, not Alex, threatened to kill her. How likely is it that your investigation will uncover the truth?

Not very. Yet research shows that this is the kind of thinking we all engage in far more often than we would like to admit, especially when we want to protect or promote our cherished political or personal beliefs. It's called **motivated reasoning**—reasoning for the purpose of supporting a predetermined conclusion, not to uncover the truth. It's confirmation bias in overdrive. It's a way of piling up evidence that agrees with our preferred conclusion and of downplaying, ignoring, or devaluing evidence that supports the contrary view. We set out to prove our point, not to determine whether the point is justified.

Online, motivated reasoning has been the modus operandi of those who want to prove to themselves and others that the Apollo moon landing never happened, that climate change is a hoax, that evolution is a fraud, that Barack Obama was not born in the United States, and that the Holocaust didn't happen. Through motivated reasoning, even very smart people can build, without realizing it, a very complex and impressive case for a claim that is complete rubbish. And the Internet, with its vast stores of information easily accessible to anyone, is all the motivated reasoner needs to make the case overwhelming and irresistible—and dead wrong.

On social media, many people spend hours expounding on their one-sided arguments without once examining opposing views (except perhaps to try to trash them), or trying to understand the larger picture that could put issues and evidence in context, or examining contrary evidence impartially without indulging in knee-jerk rejection.

Defeating motivated reasoning is hard (and harder still to debate someone arguing in this way). But experts have offered some advice on how to avoid the trap:

- Be reasonably skeptical of *all* sources—but especially of those that support your beliefs.
- Be wary of your assessments of the credibility of sources that contradict your beliefs. Ask: Is this source *really* irrelevant, weak, or suspect—or is that my bias talking?
- Give opposing views a chance. Examine them carefully before deciding their worth. Do not dismiss them out of hand.
- Break out of the filter bubble. Seek out alternative views, read sources that you often disagree with, don't surround yourself with people who always agree with you.

Moral Principles

Both in everyday life and in ethics, moral principles are widely thought to be indispensable to moral decision-making. As we've seen, moral principles are often drawn from a moral theory, which is a moral standard on the most general level. The principles are derived from or supported by the theory. Many times we simply appeal directly to a plausible moral principle without thinking much about its theoretical underpinnings. We do this because the principle seems consistent with our moral common sense, our considered moral judgments.

These facts have led some philosophers to formulate a different kind of moral theory, one that consists of not one but several plausible moral principles. As we've seen, utilitarianism and Kantian ethics are each based on a single, absolute moral standard: utility and the categorical imperative. In the former, utility is the only moral measure of rightness, and it allows no exceptions; in the latter, every action must be judged against the categorical imperative, and it, too, permits no exceptions. Some theorists, however, think these relatively simple approaches to ethics are *too* simple, leaving too much out of account and failing to capture other important elements of the moral life—in particular, the other moral principles that are essential to moral deliberation. They argue that besides the moral principles of utility and respect embodied in utilitarianism and Kantian ethics, there are others that our moral experience reveals—for example, the principles of justice, nonmaleficence, and beneficence. They infer that there must be more than just one basic moral rule because we obviously have several distinct moral duties, and we cannot derive them from one another or from an all-encompassing one-principle theory.

But a major problem arises if we assume that our moral principles are absolute, as they are in utilitarianism and Kantianism. Since an absolute principle can allow no exceptions, conflicts between two or more such principles cannot be resolved. Honoring one rule will entail the violation of another. Say a moral theory consists of just two absolutist rules: "Do not lie" and "Do not harm persons." And suppose that telling a mentally unstable person the truth about her terminal cancer will cause her immense psychological harm and probably hasten her death. If her doctor tells her the truth, she will be harmed; if her doctor lies and gives her only good news, she will not be harmed. The doctor cannot both tell her the truth and avoid harming her.

A theory with two or more main principles can get around this problem if the principles are *prima facie*—that is, if they apply in all cases unless there is a conflict between principles that requires deciding which principle is weightier. If the two duties in the dying-patient example are prima facie, then we would need to decide which duty was more important in the situation. The two principles would represent our *apparent* duties, but when we determine which duty is weightier, we would discover which is our *actual* duty. This way of thinking about conflicting principles fits well with our moral experience. We know that sometimes our duties do conflict, that some duties are more momentous than others, that occasionally doing the right thing means violating a principle, and that even after breaking or overriding the rules, they are still essential to the moral life.

Such a theory or approach is known as **principlism**. The philosopher W. D. Ross, who articulated the idea of prima facie principles in 1930, advocated a form of principlism that included several strong duties: tell the truth, keep promises, distribute benefits and burdens fairly, benefit others, refrain from harming others, make amends for causing injuries, and repay services done. Other thinkers have argued for a principlism that consists of just three, four, or five prima facie principles, which are thought to subsume all our most important moral duties.[12] These include utilitarianism's and Kant's principles plus a few others:

- *Respect for persons.* Persons are possessors of ultimate inherent worth and must be treated as such. As Kant says, the inherent worth of persons derives from their nature as free, rational beings capable of directing their own lives and determining their own ends This inherent value is possessed equally by all persons and does not depend on any external characteristic such as ethnicity, gender, race, sexual orientation, or social standing. This principle means that persons have rights—specifically, what philosophers call *negative rights*, obligations not to interfere with their legitimately obtaining something. Persons have a right not to have their free and self-directed actions or choices impeded or frustrated. The principle of respect for persons entails the rights of free speech, expression, and privacy, and the right not be discriminated against, coerced, cheated, or falsely accused or imprisoned.
- *Justice.* In its broadest sense, *justice* refers to people getting what is fair or what is their due. In practice, most of us seem to have a rough idea of what justice entails in many situations, even if we cannot articulate exactly what it is. We know, for example, that it is unjust for a bus driver to make a woman sit in the back of the bus because of her religious beliefs, or for a judicial system to arbitrarily treat one group of citizens more harshly than others, or for a doctor to care for some patients but refuse to treat others just because he dislikes them.

Questions of justice arise in different spheres of human endeavor. *Retributive justice*, for example, concerns the fair meting out of punishment for wrongdoing. On this matter, some argue that justice is served only when people are punished for past wrongs, when they get their just deserts. Others insist that justice demands that people be punished not because they deserve punishment, but because the punishment will deter further unacceptable behavior. *Distributive justice* concerns the fair distribution of society's advantages and disadvantages— for example, jobs, income, welfare aid, health care, rights, taxes, and public service.

A basic precept of most theories of justice is what may plausibly be regarded as the core of the principle of justice: *Equals should be treated equally.* (Recall that this is one of the defining elements of ethics itself, impartiality.) The idea is that people should be treated the same unless there is a morally relevant reason for treating them differently. We would think it unjust for a police officer to treat a white motorist more respectfully than she does a black motorist—and to do so for no legitimate reason. We would consider it unfair to award the only available kidney to a transplant candidate only because she belongs to the "right" political party or has the best personal relationship with hospital administrators. We would think it wrong to expel an LGBTQ person from college but not a straight person for the same conduct in virtually identical circumstances.

- *Utility.* The principle of *utility* says that *we should produce the most favorable balance of good over bad (or benefit over harm) for all concerned.* The principle acknowledges that in the real world, we cannot always *just* benefit others or *just* avoid harming them. Often we cannot do good for people without also bringing them some harm, or we cannot help everyone who needs to be helped, or we cannot help some without also hurting or neglecting others. In such situations, the principle says, we should do what yields the best overall outcome—the maximum good and minimum evil, everyone considered.

- *Nonmaleficence.* The principle of *nonmaleficence* asks us not to intentionally or unintentionally inflict harm on others. Its aphoristic expression has been embraced by practitioners of medicine for centuries: "Above all, do no harm." Nonmaleficence is the bedrock precept of countless codes of professional conduct, institutional regulations, and governmental rules and laws designed to protect the welfare of others. And it is the fundamental moral requirement of decent behavior among people everywhere.

- *Beneficence.* The principle of *beneficence* has seemed to many to constitute the very soul of morality—or very close to it. In its most general form, it says that *we should do good to others.* (Benevolence is different, referring more to an attitude of goodwill toward others than to a principle of right action.) Beneficence enjoins us to advance the welfare of others and prevent or remove harm to them. Beneficence demands that we do more than just avoid inflicting pain and suffering. It says that we should actively promote the well-being of others and prevent or remove harm to them.

But not everyone thinks that we all have a duty of active beneficence. Some argue that though there is a general (applicable to all) duty not to harm others, there is no general duty to help others. They say we are not obligated to aid the poor, feed the hungry, or tend to the sick. Such acts are not required, but are supererogatory, beyond the call of duty. Others contend that though we do not have a general duty of active beneficence, we are at least sometimes obligated to look to the welfare of people we care about most—such as our parents, children, spouses, and friends.

Critics of principlism are quick to point out its most serious weakness: the lack of a stable formula or procedure for assigning weights to principles to see which is strongest. Principles don't have preassigned weights. Sometimes respect for persons carries the greatest moral weight; sometimes utility does; sometimes it's unclear (at least initially) which principle is foremost. The challenge is to examine the facts of the case and make a considered moral judgment using the principles as general guides. Advocates of principlism insist that this weighting process is rational, generally reliable, and not excessively subjective.

Nevertheless, deciding which duty is more important is often not easy. Consider these two cases:

> You have witnessed a man rob a bank, but then, he did something completely unusual and unexpected with the money. He donated it to an orphanage that was poor, run-down and lacking in proper food, care, water and amenities. The sum of money would be a great benefit to the orphanage, and the children's lives would turn from poor to prosperous. Would you: A: Call the police and report the robber, even though they would likely take the money away from the orphanage, or B: Do nothing and leave the robber and the orphans alone?
>
> Your best friend is about to get married. The ceremony will be performed in one hour, but you have seen, just before coming to the wedding, that your friend's fiancée has been having an affair. If your friend marries this woman, she is unlikely to be faithful; however, if you tell your friend about the affair, you will ruin his wedding. Would you, or would you not, tell your friend of the affair?[13]

Such cases demand careful moral deliberation, which involves at least these four steps:

1. Learn as much as you can about the *nonmoral* facts of the case. Sometimes the really important facts are hidden below the surface.
2. Minimize bias, self-interest, prejudice, or strong emotions (especially fear, anger, and hatred).
3. Identify the relevant moral principles. Think: What duties apply in this situation?
4. Determine the relative importance of the principles and act accordingly.

There is no formula, algorithm, or standard ranking of duties to help you in weighing the importance of the relevant principles. You must rely on your considered moral judgments, a plausible moral theory, and your own experience. Deciding on your final duty is similar to the way a physician diagnoses an illness: based on the facts of the case, a theory about the cause and treatment of disease, and her medical experience, the physician must make an informed, rational decision.

KEY TERMS

analogical induction	ethics	moral objectivism
availability error	evidence	moral relativism
confirmation bias	inductive argument	moral statement
cultural relativism	inference to the best explanation	motivated reasoning
deductive argument		principlism
divine command theory	morality	subjective relativism
enumerative induction	moral absolutism	

EXERCISES

Exercises marked with * have answers in "Answers to Exercises" (Appendix B).

Exercise 1.1

1. What is a moral theory?
2. According to the text, what is a worldview?
3. What is a moral statement?
4. What is the basic structure of a standard moral argument?
*5. Why can't we infer a moral statement from nonmoral statements alone?
6. Why is it important to spell out implicit premises in a moral argument?
7. What technique can we use to determine whether a general moral principle is true?
8. What is a moral judgment?
*9. According to the text, what precisely does a moral theory try to explain?
10. According to the text, what are the criteria of adequacy for appraising moral theories?
11. According to the text, how are moral theories like scientific theories?
12. Who founded the moral theory known as traditional utilitarianism?
*13. What is principlism?
14. What is legal moralism?
15. What is motivated reasoning?
16. What are considered moral judgments? Are they infallible? How are they used in moral deliberations?
17. What is Kant's theory of ethics?

Exercise 1.2

Specify whether the following statements are moral or nonmoral.
*1. Joan worries whether she's doing the right thing.
2. When the government restricts freedom of the press, it harms every citizen.
3. The government should not restrict freedom of the press.
4. Paul was sure that he saw Gregory steal the book from the library.
5. Because of the terrible results of the bombing, it's clear that the entire war effort was immoral.
*6. The Church should never have allowed pedophile priests to stay in the priesthood.
7. The officer was justified in using deadly force because his life was threatened.
8. The officer used deadly force because his life was threatened.

*9. Lying is wrong unless the lie involves trivial matters.

10. The officials should never have allowed the abuse to continue.

Exercise 1.3

In each of the following passages, add a moral premise to turn it into a valid moral argument.

1. Noah promised to drive Thelma to Los Angeles, so he should stop belly-aching and do it.

2. The refugees were shot at and lied to, and the authorities did nothing to stop any of this. The authorities should have intervened.

3. There was never any imminent threat from the Iraqi government, so the United States should not have invaded Iraq.

*4. The Indian government posed an imminent threat to Pakistan and the world, so the Pakistanis were justified in attacking Indian troops.

5. Burton used a gun in the commission of a crime; therefore, he should get a long prison term.

6. Ellen knew that a murder was going to take place. It was her duty to try to stop it.

7. Ahmed should never have allowed his daughter to receive in vitro fertilization. Such a procedure is unnatural.

8. The doctors performed the experiment on twenty patients without their consent. Obviously, that was wrong.

*9. What you did was immoral. You hacked into a database containing personal information on thousands of people and invaded their privacy.

10. Ling spent all day weeding Mrs. Black's garden for no pay. The least Mrs. Black should do is let Ling borrow some gardening tools.

Exercise 1.4

Use counterexamples to test each of the following general moral principles.

1. Anything that is unnatural is immoral.

2. It is always and everywhere wrong to tell a lie.

*3. In all circumstances the killing of a human being is wrong.

4. In all situations in which our actions can contribute to the welfare, safety, or happiness of others, we should treat all persons equally.

5. Any action that serves one's own best interests is morally permissible.

6. Any action that is approved of by one's society is moral.

*7. Assisted suicide is never morally justified.

8. Whatever action a person approves of is morally right.

9. Making a promise to someone incurs a moral obligation to keep the promise in all circumstances.

10. Any action done for religious reasons is morally acceptable because religious reasons carry more weight than secular ones.

Exercise 1.5

Identify the moral argument in each of the following passages. Specify the premises and the conclusion, adding implicit premises where needed.

1. The movie *Lorenzo's Oil* is about a family's struggle to find a cure for their young son's fatal genetic disease, an illness that usually kills boys before they reach their eleventh birthday. The script is based on the true story of a family's attempt to save Lorenzo, their son, from this fatal genetic disease through the use of a medicinal oil. The movie is a tear-jerker, but it ends on a hopeful note that suggests that the oil will eventually cure Lorenzo and that the oil is an effective treatment for the genetic disease. The problem is, there is no cure for the disease and no good scientific evidence showing that the oil works. But the movie touts the oil anyway—and gives false hope to every family whose son suffers from this terrible illness. Worse, the movie overplays the worth of the oil, seriously misleading people about the medical facts. The movie, therefore, is immoral. It violates the ageless moral dictum to, above all else, "Do no harm." *Lorenzo's Oil* may be just a movie, but it has done harm nonetheless.

2. "I, like many of my fellow Muslims, was appalled by the latest bombings in Saudi Arabia ('Among the Saudis, Attack Has Soured Qaeda Supporters,' front page, Nov. 11). Yet I was disturbed to get the sense that Saudis were angered by this latest act of barbarity because the targets were mainly Arab and Muslim.

   "You quote one person as saying of the bombing in Riyadh in May, 'At that time it was seen as justifiable because there was an invasion of a foreign country, there was frustration.' Another says, 'Jihad is not against your own people.'

   "Regardless of whether the victims are Muslim or not, the vicious murder of innocent human beings is reprehensible and repugnant, an affront to everything Islam stands for. Any sympathy for Al Qaeda among the minority of Saudis should have evaporated after the May bombings in Riyadh, and it should have surprised no one in Saudi Arabia that Al Qaeda would attack a housing complex full of Arabs and Muslims.

   "That is what Al Qaeda is: a band of bloodthirsty murderers." [Letter to the editor, *New York Times*]

3. John and Nancy Jones had a two-year-old son who suffered from a serious but very curable bowel obstruction. For religious reasons, the Joneses decided to treat their son with prayer instead of modern medicine. They refused medical treatment, even though they were told by several doctors that the child would die unless medically treated. As it turned out, the boy did die. The Joneses were arrested and charged with involuntary manslaughter. Were the Joneses wrong to refuse treatment for their son? The answer is yes. Regardless of what faith or religious dogma would have the Joneses do, they allowed their child to die. According to just about any

moral outlook, the care of a child by the parents is a fundamental obligation. Above all other concerns, parents have a duty to ensure the health and safety of their children and to use whatever means are most likely to secure those benefits. The Joneses ignored this basic moral principle. They were wrong—and deserve whatever punishment the state deems appropriate.

Notes

1. Robert Mark Simpson and Amia Srinivasan, "No Platforming," in *Academic Freedom*, ed. Jennifer Lackey (New York: Oxford University Press, 2018), 187.
2. Michele Moody-Adams, "A 'Safe Space' for Academic Freedom?," in *Academic Freedom*, ed. Jennifer Lackey (New York: Oxford University Press, 2018), 56.
3. Manny Fernandez and Richard Perez-Pena, "As Two Oklahoma Students Are Expelled for Racist Chant, Sigma Alpha Epsilon Vows Wider Inquiry," *New York Times*, March 10, 2015, https://www.nytimes.com/2015/03/11/us/university-of-oklahoma-sigma-alpha-epsilon-racist-fraternity-video.html.
4. Laura Kipnis, "My Title IX Inquisition," *The Chronicle of Higher Education*, May 29, 2015, https://www.chronicle.com/article/My-Title-IX-Inquisition/230489; Laura Kipnis, "Sexual Paranoia Strikes Academe," *The Chronicle of Higher Education*, February 27, 2015, https://www.chronicle.com/article/sexual-paranoia-strikes/190351.
5. Mariel Padilla and Jaclyn Peiser, "2 UConn Students Arrested After Shouting Racist Slur, Officials Say," *New York Times*, October 21, 2019.
6. Liam Stack, "Yale's Halloween Advice Stokes a Racially Charged Debate," *New York Times*, November 8, 2015, https://www.nytimes.com/2015/11/09/nyregion/yale-culturally-insensitive-halloween-costumes-free-speech.html?action=click&module=RelatedCoverage&pgtype=Article&region=Footer.
7. Amanda Taub, "The Real Story about Fact News Is Partisanship," *New York Times*, January 11, 2017.
8. Walter Sinnott-Armstrong, "How to Win Every Argument," *Time*, July 2, 2018, Ideas and Society section.
9. James Rachels, *The Elements of Moral Philosophy*, 4th ed. (New York: McGraw-Hill, 2003), 14.
10. Immanuel Kant, *Groundwork of the Metaphysics of Morals*, trans. H. J. Paton (New York: Harper & Row, 1964), 88.
11. Kant, *Groundwork of the Metaphysics of Morals*, 96.
12. Tom L. Beauchamp and James F. Childress, *Principles of Biomedical Ethics*, 5th ed. (New York: Oxford University Press, 2001); Lewis Vaughn, *Beginning Ethics: An Introduction to Moral Philosophy* (New York: W.W. Norton, 2015); Robert Audi, *Business Ethics and Ethical Business* (New York: Oxford University Press, 2009).
13. David Hopkins, "10 More Moral Dilemmas," *Listverse*, April 18, 2011, http://listverse.com/2011/04/18/10-more-moral-dilemmas.

Free Speech, Equality, and Harm 2

We have had good reason to be concerned about the state of free speech on America's college campuses. In recent years, the political and moral tensions that have poisoned public discourse nationally have spread to the academy. The symptoms are disconcerting: extreme political polarization, increased racial tensions, profound intolerance of opposing views, the weaponization of Internet speech, social media–stoked outrage, and hate-inspired words and intimidation. The hate comes through in political tirades, racist invective, racist and anti-Semitic symbols, hate crimes, white-supremacist rants, anti-LGBTQ diatribes, and a profusion of other less subtle forms of loathing.

Here's a small slice of some of the discord, as reported by PEN America, a human rights association of writers and editors:

> The struggles at the University of Minnesota [over political slogans painted on a campus bridge] reflect both campus politics and national mood. In recent years, there has been a new wave of provocative speakers stirring up massive student protests, a constant stream of news stories about professors making controversial comments, and a rise in political scrutiny leading to new efforts to reform campuses through both legislative, judicial, and executive channels. The controversy over one bridge is instructive because it highlights how campuses have become a proxy for national political and social conflicts writ large in which speech has taken on great significance, and in which neither side is willing to cede an inch—or a mural—to the other.
>
> Similar incidents have been reported at universities nationwide. At Sonoma State University in June 2017, anger erupted when a student read a poem at commencement that referenced police violence against African Americans and

contained expletives and some derogatory references to Trump. At the University of California at Riverside in September 2017, a student allegedly removed a "Make America Great Again" hat from a classmate's head and accused him of "promoting 'genocide.'" In April 2018, there were calls to remove a new mural at the University of Southern California that read, "Dismantle Whiteness and Misogyny on This Campus," with some calling the statement racist. At the University of Maine in December 2018, a group of Republican students faced public criticism for a "Deck the Wall" party that some considered insensitive.[1]

In such disputes, the flashpoints vary, but the heart of the matter is often a clash between two essential values: (1) the need to make campuses equally inclusive and welcoming for all students and (2) the importance of safeguarding freedom of expression, without which free inquiry and open-ended learning is impaired. In the name of the former value, students insist that free speech be curbed to shield marginalized groups from harm; moved by the latter, students claim the right to express and hear offensive views.

Properly balancing these two values is a moral challenge, requiring a careful examination of moral arguments and values but also a review of many nonmoral factors that can shed light on today's debates. These factors include the recent history of campus free speech, the role of free speech in modern democracies, the importance of free speech in securing rights for minorities and dissidents, Supreme Court rulings on what is and is not protected speech, and realistic assessments of the harms that speech may or may not inflict.

Fig. 2.1 Demonstrators protest before a speech by Donald Trump, Jr. and his girlfriend, Kimberly Guilfoyle, who appeared at the University of Florida campus and spoke to a capacity crowd of about 850 students in what was billed as a keynote presentation.

Perceptions of Campus Speech

Unfortunately, much of what is said in the media by commentators and politicians about campus speech controversies is mistaken or distorted. The stereotypical view of campus speech—reinforced by sensationalistic news stories and critics of higher education—is something like this: free speech on campuses is dying, choked by left-wing faculty and radical students who want to quash politically incorrect ideas and banish views that unsettle their delicate, snowflake sensibilities.

The truth is more complicated. A survey of full-time students by the Knight Foundation showed that 58 percent do not favor restrictions on free speech, believing that hate speech should continue to be protected under the First Amendment, while 41 percent disagree. Seventy-four percent of college men think hate speech should be protected, while 53 percent of college women say it should not. Although 62 percent of white students favor protection for hate speech, only 48 percent of black students and 52 percent of Hispanic students think so. Most gay and lesbian students and students who identify as gender nonbinary believe hate speech should not have First Amendment protection.[2]

According to the PEN America report,

> Attempts to depict progressive students as universally dismissive of free speech principles is an over-simplification: many students are thoughtfully working to reconcile support for free speech with on-campus concerns over solidarity, inclusion, and their own values. Meanwhile, conservative students have expressed feelings of isolation and stigmatization because of their political beliefs, but here too, there are differing views. While some conservative students find themselves defensively supporting provocative speakers as a form of protest against campus climates they perceive as dismissing their viewpoints or beliefs, others remain highly skeptical of these confrontational tactics.[3]

Student attitudes toward protests against campus speakers are also diverse. According to the Knight survey,

> Roughly one-third (32 percent) of students say that it is always acceptable to engage in protests against speakers who are invited to campus, while six in 10 (60 percent) say this type of activity is sometimes acceptable. Only 8 percent say it is never acceptable. There is little variation in student views by race and ethnicity, gender, religious affiliation or political identity. . . .
>
> College students are generally unlikely to believe that shouting down speakers is acceptable. Only 6 percent of college students report that this type of behavior is always acceptable, while close to half (45 percent) say it is sometimes acceptable. About half (48 percent) of college students say this type of activity is never acceptable. . . .
>
> Substantially fewer college students say it is acceptable to employ violence to stop a speech or rally from taking place. Only 2 percent of students say this is always acceptable, and 14 percent say it is sometimes acceptable. The overwhelming majority (83 percent) say this type of behavior is never acceptable.[4]

Despite the small number of headline-grabbing incidents (occurring mostly at a few elite schools), student protests against speakers have not been nearly as prevalent as some might assume. Lee C. Bollinger, president of Columbia University, explains:

> At Columbia and at thousands of other schools across the United States, controversial ideas are routinely expressed by speakers on both the left *and* the right, and have been for decades. . . .
>
> It's true that, in recent years, there have been more than a few sensational reports— at places such as Middlebury, William & Mary, and UC Berkeley—of misguided demands for censorship on campus, providing a ready, if false, narrative about liberal colleges and universities retreating from the open debate they claim to champion.
>
> Still, the surest evidence of censorship or the suppression of ideas on college campuses is the disinvitation of controversial speakers. There are more than 4,500 colleges and universities in the United States, and each year they host thousands of speakers of all political stripes. According to FIRE, a watchdog group that focuses on civil liberties in academia, only 11 speakers were disinvited from addressing college audiences in 2018. This is a minuscule fraction of the universe of speakers who express their views annually on American campuses.[5]

The notion that today's college students are overwhelmingly liberal is also more myth than reality. A report on the subject published by *The Chronicle of Higher Education* concludes:

> College students are regularly caricatured as left-wing radicals, whether they're thought to have arrived on campus that way or been indoctrinated by professors. It's true that among students, liberals do outnumber conservatives. But a large share are moderates, and different types of institutions see different proportions of students claiming one of five political identities.[6]

The report reveals that at four-year colleges and universities, 32 percent of students are liberal, while 20 percent are conservatives. But there are far more students who are moderates—41 percent. Only 4 percent of students identify as far left, and only 2 percent as far right.

For many people, including most conservatives, the biggest threat to campus free speech is the social and political liberalism of the faculty. Surveys have revealed what is surprising to no one: professors are overwhelmingly liberal and very likely to vote Democratic. This fact has led an army of critics to suppose that colleges suppress conservative ideas and discriminate against conservative students. But research on the subject tells a different story. *The Chronicle of Higher Education* sums up the findings:

> Most students, including conservatives, feel that their colleges support free speech and open debate, and that they can speak freely in class. Hostile interactions are relatively rare.

Still, conservative students do feel more under fire than liberal ones, and there is wide variation in the ways in which all kinds of students feel comfortable to speak, when they do speak, and how they do it. . . .

While many students and faculty members worry about the perception of political bias, other studies have found little evidence that it affects how professors grade or treat students. . . .

FIRE [Foundation for Individual Rights in Education], which surveyed 1,250 students in 2017, found that almost 90 percent were comfortable sharing ideas and opinions in class.

Still, most students said they've kept themselves from doing so at least once. When they do, it's most often because they feared they would be mistaken. Generally, they were more worried about what their classmates might think, rather than their professors.

Those data points changed for the most conservative students. Very conservative students were 14 percentage points less likely than very liberal ones to say they were comfortable speaking up in class. They were also more likely to report self-censoring, and more likely to do so because of how their professor might respond.[7]

American colleges and universities have often been accused of being left-wing indoctrination mills. But this characterization is doubtful. Jonathan Zimmerman, author of *Campus Politics*, explains why:

If our universities aim to "indoctrinate" young America into hard-core leftism, they're doing a pretty lousy job of it. American professors are overwhelmingly liberal, but their students aren't; instead, students have hewed closely to larger political trends in American society. And that's been true for a very long time. . . . Self-described moderates are still the largest category on American campuses; liberals are second and conservatives are third, but both have grown steadily as the moderates wane.[8]

Many of the misrepresentations and exaggerations involving free speech controversies come not from outside critics but from students themselves, who often mischaracterize the views and motives of those in opposing camps. According to the PEN America report,

Conservatives and progressives put out dueling narratives that increasingly promote caricatures of their "opponents": the snowflake-liberals who do not understand the value of free speech, versus callous and complicit conservatives who hide behind free speech to promote noxious and hateful views. In order to craft thoughtful solutions to these campus controversies, all stakeholders— students, faculty, administrators, journalists, policymakers, and others—must move past these simplistic narratives and accept that no group has a monopoly on the truth. There is danger in accepting only a single story about the current state of affairs.[9]

Why Free Speech Matters

Freedom of speech or expression is the right to express, either verbally or nonverbally, opinions or ideas without onerous limitations imposed by government or society. "Speech" or "expression" refers not just to spoken words, but to writing, shouting, creating works of art, acting on stage, singing, carrying signs, waving or burning flags, and much more. Free speech is a cherished value essential to freedom of thought, democratic self-government, pursuit of knowledge, and moral deliberation. It is recognized as a bedrock principle in liberal democracies throughout the world, codified as a human right by international bodies, and inscribed in the US Constitution's First Amendment as a guard against government attempts to constrain what people say. According to Nadine Strossen, free speech scholar and professor of constitutional law,

> Freedom of speech has been a long and widely cherished right for multiple reasons, venerated under international human rights law and in most national legal systems. For individuals, it is essential for forming and communicating thoughts, as well as for expressing emotions. It is a prerequisite for democratic self-government in the United States, allowing "We the People" to exchange information and opinions with each other, and with our elected officials, in order to influence policy and to hold officials accountable. Additionally, freedom of speech is the prerequisite for exercising all other rights and freedoms, enabling us to advocate and organize in support of such rights, and to petition the government for redress of rights violations. Free speech also facilitates the search for truth and promotes tolerance. Speaking from his prison cell in 2010, upon having been awarded the Nobel Peace Prize, Chinese human rights activist Liu Xiaobo eloquently described his precious freedom, for which he had sacrificed his physical liberty: "Free expression is the foundation of human rights, the source of humanity, and the mother of truth."[10]

The right of free speech, though extremely important, is not absolute. Like any other right, speech can be legitimately restricted when it conflicts with other important values in society. The US Supreme Court, for example, has consistently ruled that the government may punish certain kinds of speech that it deems harmful. The narrowly defined types of speech considered worthy of punishment include true threats, punishable incitement, harassment, fighting words, and expression that facilitates criminal conduct.

The First Amendment was devised as a shield against *government* restraints on our basic rights. With few exceptions, it does not restrict the actions of *private* persons or organizations. As far as the Constitution is concerned, employees do not have a right to free speech in the workplace. In general, a private company is free to fire employees who espouse views at work that the company doesn't like. State colleges and universities are legal extensions of the government and are thus bound by the First Amendment. Nonstate schools are not constrained in the

Fig. 2.2 Black and white participants marching in the five-day, fifty-four-mile civil rights march from Selma to Montgomery, Alabama, in March 1965.

same way but may still try to align themselves with First Amendment require-ments. In any case, free speech is widely regarded as a *moral* right, whatever its legal or political status.

Historically, the right of free speech has been the supreme ally of citizens who demand justice while governments try to silence them—marginalized, vulner-able minority groups, dissenters, nonconformists, the unpopular, the disdained. Over the last half century, the Supreme Court has affirmed again and again that speech may not be censored or punished just because it is disfavored, disturb-ing, or feared. As free speech scholars Erwin Chemerinsky and Howard Gillman point out, this interpretation of free speech rights has had profound effects in American history:

> In the 1950s and 1960s, the most important beneficiaries of [the Supreme Court's] newly expanded free speech protections were participants in the civil rights movement. The messages of civil rights protestors were considered deeply offensive, harmful, and dangerous to many southern government officials, and citizens considered the ideas of civil rights protestors "subversive" to southern life in the same way that communist and anarchist ideas were considered subversive to the country as a whole. . . . Under any standard that allowed the government to censor or punish speech that was offensive or had a tendency to cause harm or danger, the civil rights movement could not have gotten off the ground. . . .

The Supreme Court was also remarkably protective of speech during the Vietnam War. Although the justices did not extend free speech protection to the act of burning a draft card, there was no repeat of the prosecutions of anti-war speech that occurred during World War I. . . .

[In 1971], California prosecuted nineteen-year-old Paul Robert Cohen for disturbing the peace in the corridor of a courthouse by wearing a jacket bearing the words "Fuck the Draft." In *Cohen v. California* (1971) the justices overturned his conviction, asserting that it was not within the power of government to "remove this offensive word from the public vocabulary." Justice John Marshall Harlan acknowledged that this ruling would create a marketplace of ideas that included "verbal tumult, discord, and even offensive utterance," but these were "necessary side effects of the broader enduring values which the process of open debate permits us to achieve." He added, "one man's vulgarity is another's lyric." . . .

The Court's embrace of free speech had other beneficiaries. Historically, people who spoke out against religion could be convicted of "blasphemy," but in 1952 the justices in *Joseph Burstyn, Inc. v. Wilson* ruled that it is not the business of government in our nation to suppress real or imagined attacks upon a particular religious doctrine." . . .

If today we take for granted that the government cannot put people in jail for asserting "countercultural" attitudes or identities—including forms of expression that challenge traditional religion, prevailing social mores, familiar lifestyle choices, inherited views about sexuality, or historic gender roles—then it is good to keep in mind that this was made possible by the twentieth-century revolution in free speech rights.[11]

Many of today's students would nod approvingly at this history while taking up very different attitudes toward the right of free speech. On one side are students who want to restrict speech to protect vulnerable groups who may be harmed by expressions of hate or intolerance. The scholar Sigal R. Ben-Porath describes this attitude:

> For students and others—mostly on the left—who espouse this view, "free speech" is another one of the master's tools, a lofty idea that helps people in power preserve their position while dismissing women as fitted mostly for domestic work, gay people as mentally ill, and racial minorities as intellectually inferior.[12]

> On the other side of the issue are the free speech advocates who think this view is nothing but a politically correct effort to prevent anyone from voicing views that do not fall in line with a narrow "social justice" ideology. It is seen as a mark of weakness on the part of students who purportedly prefer support and protection over the intellectual courage that is required to explore new and different ideas.[13]

Some claim that the gap between these two positions is unbridgeable, while many others say there are ways to accommodate both values. This bridging work

Fig. 2.3 Antiwar protestors on the US Capitol grounds and the Mall during massive demonstrations against the Vietnam War on April 23, 1971.

can only arise from a better understanding of what the right of free expression does and does not entail.

Protected and Unprotected Speech

The US Constitution as interpreted by the Supreme Court asserts unequivocally that most speech is immune from censorship or punishment—that is, it is *constitutionally protected* (unregulated). People are free to say, write, depict, or circulate all sorts of opinions, ideas, feelings, and expressions in almost any type of media. But some forms of speech, a very short list, can be censored or punished—they are *constitutionally unprotected*.

The Supreme Court has time and again declared that speech does not fall into the unprotected category merely because governments or citizens disfavor it, find it disturbing, or fear it. The Court has argued that censoring speech because it is disfavored or disturbing would violate the "viewpoint neutrality rule," the foundation of the nation's right of free speech. As the Court sees it, to punish speech because of these features is to punish the speech's message, and that's poison to democratic government. Strossen explains:

> Viewpoint-based restrictions pose the greatest danger to the core value underlying the First Amendment: our right as individuals to make our own choices about

what ideas we choose to express, receive, and believe. Because they distort public debate, viewpoint-based regulations are also antithetical to our democratic political system. Additionally, they violate equality principles because, reflecting majoritarian political pressures, they generally target unpopular, minority, and dissenting views and speakers.[14]

In addition, the Court has consistently ruled that speech cannot be deemed unprotected just because it provokes a fear of possible harmful behavior. As Justice Louis Brandeis asserted in his opinion in *Whitney v. California* (1927), "Fear of serious injury cannot alone justify suppression of free speech. . . . Men feared witches and burnt women." Banning fear-provoking speech would violate the "emergency test," which says fearful speech can only be punished when it poses a danger of directly causing certain specific, imminent, serious harms. According to the Court, such punishable speech includes the following:

True threats—statements through which the speaker "means to communicate a serious intent to commit an act of unlawful violence to a particular individual or group of individuals. The speaker need not actually intend to carry out the threat." The point, the Court says, is to protect persons from *fear of bodily harm*, not from emotional hurt or stress. In the eyes of the Court, campus speech that causes a reasonable person to fear for his or her safety is punishable. By this standard, an email message sent to a particular person seriously threatening violence against him or her could be taken as a punishable true threat. A burning cross (a symbol of racial terrorism linked to the Ku Klux Klan) deliberately placed in an African American's front yard could be judged a punishable true threat. So could tacking a noose on the dorm door of an African American with a note saying, "This is for YOU, Smith!" The Court has held, however, that threatening language uttered in a public forum could be construed as overblown rhetoric unlikely to arouse reasonable fear of a physical attack.

Harassment—unwelcome speech directed at a person or group of persons that repeatedly undermines or interferes with their freedom or privacy. Someone who sends a particular student unwanted, disturbing, sexually explicit emails every day is guilty of harassment. Following a student around campus while shouting degrading or derisive insults at her is an act of punishable harassment. Posting an anti-LGBTQ rant on Twitter is not punishable harassment, but repeatedly sending harassing emails to LGBTQ students is.

The Supreme Court has also recognized what is called "hostile environment" harassment, which can happen in the workplace as well as in educational settings. Hostile environment harassment in schools has been described by the American Civil Liberties Union (ACLU) as

conduct, including verbal conduct, (1) that creates (or will certainly create) a hostile environment by substantially interfering with a student's educational benefits, opportunities, or performance, or with a student's physical or psychological well-being; or (2) that is threatening or seriously intimidating.

Sexual harassment is a form of harassment that also violates school policy. Punishable sexual harassment is an unwelcome sexual advance or sexual conduct, including verbal conduct, (1) that is tied to a student's educational benefits, opportunities, or performance, or to a student's physical or psychological well-being; (2) that creates (or will certainly create) a hostile environment by substantially interfering with a student's educational benefits, opportunities, or performance, or with a student's physical or psychological well-being; or (3) that is threatening or seriously intimidating.[15]

Punishable incitement—speech in which the speaker intentionally incites an immediate and specific act of violence or other illegal conduct. Punishable incitement refers not to theoretical future violence but to an *immediate risk of real harm to actual persons.*

Using this conception of incitement, the Court has ruled in favor of hate speech that emanates from both white bigots and black activists. In the case of *Brandenburg v. Ohio* (1969), the Court ruled that Charles Brandenburg was not guilty of incitement to violence when at an Ohio Ku Klux Klan rally he spewed abhorrent racist, genocidal invective against black people and Jews. Brandenburg declared "that there might have to be some revengeance [sic] taken" for the "continued suppression of the white, Caucasian race." The Court deemed his words protected by the First Amendment because they did not constitute an immediate risk of real violence but merely expressed fantasies about violence in an unspecified future. In *Claiborne Hardware v. NAACP* (1982), the Court ruled that the NAACP leader and civil rights activist Charles Evers could not be prosecuted for delivering a fiery, threatening speech supporting a boycott of white-owned, racially discriminatory businesses. Evers railed against those who would violate the boycott: "If we catch any of you going in any of them racist stores, we're gonna break your damn neck." Evers speech did not constitute punishable incitement, the Court held, because the risk of violence was not immediate and real but theoretical and not yet occurring.

The Court has based these and similar rulings on two basic principles, says the ACLU:

> The First Amendment's robust protections in this context reflect two fundamentally important values. First, political advocacy—rhetoric meant to inspire action against unjust laws or policies—is essential to democracy. Second, people should be held accountable for their own conduct, regardless of what someone else may have said. To protect these values, the First Amendment allows lots of breathing room for the messy, chaotic, ad hominem, passionate, and even bigoted speech that is part and parcel of American politics. It's the price we pay to keep bullhorns in the hands of political activists.[16]

Fighting words—intimidating face-to-face speech aimed directly at a specific person and likely to cause an immediate violent reaction against the speaker. The Court has gradually refined the fighting words doctrine so that fewer and fewer cases meet the criteria. Since 1942, when the fighting words doctrine was first upheld, the Court has overturned every fighting words conviction brought before it. It's still possible, however, for a particular kind of hateful speech to meet the strict criteria and therefore be deemed punishable. Imagine this campus scene: a white supremacist student screams racist slurs in the face of a black student activist, or the black student activist does the same to a white supremacist student. These instances, in the view of the Court, would likely constitute punishable speech.

The Court insists, however, that the fighting words principle applies only to provocative speech aimed at a specific person in face-to-face encounters.

> The "fighting words" doctrine does not apply to speakers addressing a large crowd on campus, no matter how much discomfort, offense, or emotional pain their speech may cause.
>
> In fact, the Supreme Court has made clear that the government cannot prevent speech on the ground that it is likely to provoke a hostile response—this is called the rule against a "heckler's veto." Without this vital protection, government officials could use safety concerns as a smokescreen to justify shutting down speech they don't like, including speech that challenges the status quo. Instead, the First Amendment requires the government to provide protection to all speakers, no matter how provocative their speech might be. This includes taking reasonable measures to ensure that speakers are able to safely and effectively address their audience, free from violence or censorship. It's how our society ensures that the free exchange of ideas is uninhibited, robust, and wide-open.[17]

The Court's distinctions between constitutionally protected and unprotected speech directly pertain to the volatile issue of hate speech, a topic covered here and in the next chapter. **Hate speech** has no precise legal definition but generally refers to hateful, abusive, or discriminatory speech directed against a person or group because of their race, religion, sexual orientation, gender identity, ethnicity, or national origin. The Court's decisions make it clear that under the Constitution, it is not the case that all hate speech is fully protected, nor is it the case that all hate speech is unprotected. As we have seen, the government may punish speech, including hate speech, when it constitutes true threats, punishable incitement, harassment, and fighting words. But the government is barred from punishing speech just because it is hateful, fear-provoking, offensive, or disturbing.

Confusion on these points has led some to demand that laws be passed to allow punishment of hate speech that is already prohibited by law and thus already subject to punishment (because, for example, the speech is a true threat or punishable incitement). Others believe that all forms of hate speech are protected, and so they oppose restrictions on any hate speech, including threats, harassment, and incitement.

Although the First Amendment grants the broadest possible space for the exercise of free speech, it permits the imposition of some limits on speech that

Fig. 2.4 Protestors shout down white nationalist Richard Spencer during a speech October 19, 2017, at the University of Florida in Gainesville.

is otherwise protected. Specifically, it allows viewpoint-neutral regulations. Chemerinsky and Gillman explain:

> It has been a long-standing aspect of First-Amendment law that communities can impose reasonable "time, place, and manner" restrictions on expression. This phrase refers to government's ability to regulate speech in a public forum— government property that it is required to make available for speech—in a manner that minimizes disruption of a public place while still protecting free speech. You have a right to protest, but not to block the freeway. You can use a bullhorn in a public park, but not in a library. In some locations, what you are allowed to say in public at noon perhaps may not be said at midnight. You can hold up placards or signs, unless your doing so would block the views of the people behind you. As a rule, the Court has approved reasonable time, place, and manner restrictions "provided that they are justified without reference to the content of the regulated speech, that they serve a significant governmental interest, and that in doing so they leave open ample alternative channels for communication of the information."[18]

Speech and Harm

So according to First Amendment law, speech that is merely disfavored, disturbing, or fear-inducing cannot be punished. It is constitutionally protected. But any speech, including hate speech, that constitutes true threats, harassment, punishable incitement, or fighting words can be punished, because it directly causes specific, verifiable, serious harms. It is unprotected. By virtue of these serious harms, the speech would also be judged by almost any moral theory to be morally wrong.

But what about hate speech that is protected? Can't it also cause harms? And if it causes harms, shouldn't it also be censored or punished? These questions get to the heart of debates about hate speech on campus and in the larger society. They call for a thoughtful examination of the possible harms of hate speech and what should or should not be done about them.

First, we should acknowledge that speech can indeed affect people in profound ways. Words are not physical things, but neither are they inert. Sticks and stones can hurt us, but words can wound just as well. Words can lead to laughter or tears, spread fear or comfort, promote peace or discord, humiliate or elevate, and engender love or hate. More to the point, hate speech, both protected and unprotected, can inflict harm on its targeted victims.

The scholars Richard Delgado and Jean Stefancic contend that hate speech can harm its intended victims both psychologically and physiologically:

> Hate speech is not merely unpleasant or offensive. It may leave physical impacts on those it visits, particularly when uttered in one-on-one situations accompanied by at least an implicit threat. . . .
>
> The immediate, short-term harms of hate speech include rapid breathing, headaches, raised blood pressure, dizziness, rapid pulse rate, drug-taking, risk-taking behavior, and even suicide. The stresses of repeated racial abuse may have long-term consequences, including damaged self-esteem, lower aspiration level, and depression. . . .
>
> In addition to the immediate physical harms . . . hate speech can cause mental and psychological effects. These include fear, nightmares, and withdrawal from society. . . .
>
> The harms of hate speech go beyond damage to the psyches and bodies of its victims. It can also affect their pecuniary prospects and life chances.[19]

It is unclear, however, whether hateful, ugly words *always* cause psychic or emotional harms. There is no doubt that hate speech can cause stress and that chronic stress—long-term, continuing stress like the kind caused by nonstop bullying—can be physically and psychologically damaging. But stress caused by hate speech is not always chronic in this sense but is often sporadic and brief. More importantly, research shows that the stressful impact of disturbing messages can be altered, lessened, and even negated by many factors. Whether speech is harmful depends on where the speech happens, the speech's apparent purpose, the reactions of bystanders, the body language and tone of the speaker, the speaker's and listener's relationship, the traits and past experiences of the listener, and more. When confronted with disparaging, subordinating speech, listeners have reacted with anger and hurt but also with quiet defiance, calm retorts, contemptuous disregard, and empowering determination to work against hate and bigotry.

Psychologists have pointed out that when we are exposed to hate speech, much depends on how we choose to perceive the situation. According to psychologist Pamela B. Paresky,

> Two people can interact with the same circumstances and perceive the stress of that experience differently. If one person tells herself that listening to a speaker is going to be intolerable and harmful, it stands to reason that the experience will be more stressful for her than it will be for the person who tells herself it will be illuminating, or an opportunity to defeat a bad idea. (Or a chance to take a nap . . .)
>
> It has long been understood that how we think about things can influence their physiological impact. The perception of physical pain, the effectiveness of medications, hormonal reactions, how food tastes, and perhaps even longevity are mediated by our thoughts. . . .
>
> Similarly, telling people they will suffer can make it more likely that they will. Students who believe that hearing certain words or listening to certain speakers can harm them may, in fact, succumb to a self-fulfilling prophecy. . . .
>
> Changing our interpretations changes both our emotional reactions and our physiological responses. Encouraging students to shift their disempowering and derisive interpretations of speakers whose ideas they loathe could counteract both the purportedly malignant ideas, and whatever harm might otherwise result from the potential stress of listening to them.[20]

Jeremy Waldron has argued that hate speech causes an even more serious harm than psychological or physical distress—the harm done to a person's dignity. He maintains that dignity is the assurance that a person has that he or she is a fully accepted, equal member of society:

> For the members of vulnerable minorities, minorities who in the recent past have been hated or despised by others within the society, the assurance offers a confirmation of their memberships: they, too, are members of society in good standing; they have what it takes to interact on a straightforward basis with others around here, in public, on the streets, in the shops, in business, and to be treated— along with everyone else—as proper objects of society's protection and concern . . . A person's dignity is not just some Kantian aura. It is their social standing, the fundamentals of basic reputation that entitle them to be treated as equals in the ordinary operations of society. Their dignity is something they can rely on—in the best case implicitly and without fuss, as they live their lives, go about their business, and raise their families.
>
> The publication of hate speech is calculated to undermine this. Its aim is to compromise the dignity of those at whom it is targeted, both in their own eyes and in the eyes of other members of society.[21]

FREE SPEECH AND CIVILITY

Hoping to facilitate free speech and respectful dialogue and to squelch uncivil exchanges on campus, schools have put out calls for civility. But many academic observers think this emphasis on civility—that is, on courtesy, decorum, respectability, and the avoidance of offense—is decidedly unhelpful. Jonathan Zimmerman, for example, insists that

> The goal of civility has created an often uncivil environment, where people either censor their own opinions—for fear of causing offense—or muzzle others. The best route to real civility turns out to be free speech, which teaches us how to disagree across our differences instead of keeping silent about them.[25]

Ben-Porath agrees that adherence to conventions of civility can often impede free speech and open debate generally, but he cautions that they can also severely restrain the speech of minorities and marginalized groups:

> Campus communities should not aspire to institute civility rules or aspire for a civil discussion on tough issues, especially not in the broader campus community. . . . Civility requires both too little and too much: it requires too little in that it is based on norms of respectability and reasonableness rather than on substance (which could make it acceptable, for instance, to express racist views as long as it is done in a civil manner); it requires too much in that it further marginalizes those whose anger, frustration, and other emotions are deemed uncivil and thus unacceptable. . . .
>
> [Civility] leans too strongly to the side of order, reasonableness, and avoidance of challenge. To protect inclusive free speech, much more room should be made for messy, inappropriate, challenging, and sometimes uncivil expression. . . .
>
> Civility, which can be seen as a foundational dimension of a democratic open marketplace of ideas, can be used and has been used to limit speech based on viewpoint; it also can too easily be translated into a set of requirements for proper expression that chills the free (and sometimes emotional or rowdy) exchange of ideas that characterizes an open campus environment. . . .
>
> Calls for civility in the exercise of free speech can too easily be used to suppress and exclude others by posing requirements of decorum and politeness and demands about content of speech, focusing on what can permissibly be discussed "in polite company." Instead, inclusive freedom should be satisfied with what Teresa Bejan calls "mere civility," or the minimal, even begrudging norms of respectful behavior needed to keep the conversation going.[26]

If speech should not be restrained by rules of civility, does that mean anything goes? Virtually no critic of civility believes that. A report by the University of Chicago's Committee on Freedom of Expression explains the limits this way:

The freedom to debate and discuss the merits of competing ideas does not, of course, mean that individuals may say whatever they wish, wherever they wish. The University may restrict expression that violates the law, that falsely defames a specific individual, that constitutes a genuine threat or harassment, that unjustifiably invades substantial privacy or confidentiality interests, or that is otherwise directly incompatible with the functioning of the University. In addition, the University may reasonably regulate the time, place, and manner of expression to ensure that it does not disrupt the ordinary activities of the University.[27]

Within these limits, there is still much we can do for the sake of civility. Writing for the Association of American Colleges and Universities, former president of Brandeis University Frederick M. Lawrence says, "We must search for respectful ways to disagree, whether we debate and discuss in person or virtually."

Waldron argues that when constitutionally protected speech amounts to an attack on human dignity, it should be restricted. Many who have studied the possible harms of free speech agree with Waldron that dignitary harms are a serious concern both in society and on campus, but they disagree with his regulatory solution. Ben-Porath is one of them:

When some members of the campus community are effectively barred from speaking, when they avoid speaking their minds for fear of humiliation or ridicule, or when they do not feel they belong or that they are appreciated, free speech is limited just as much as it can be limited by censorship. Defenders of free speech should be worried about both types of limits. . . .

The claims that students make about harm, their demands for safety, and the counterclaims made in defense of free speech often fail to distinguish between *dignitary safety* and *intellectual safety*. Dignitary safety is the sense of being an equal member of the community and of being invited to contribute to a discussion as a valued participant. Dignitary safety and the avoidance of dignitary harms are necessary for the creation and maintenance of a democratic campus community. On the other hand, intellectual safety—the refusal to listen to challenges to one's views or to consider opposing viewpoints—is harmful to the open-minded inquiry that defines any university worth the name.[22]

Protected hate speech could rightfully be considered a very serious harm if it were literally an act of violence. But is hate speech violence? Some have asserted that it is. The late novelist and Nobel laureate Toni Morrison declared that "Oppressive language does more than represent violence; it is violence." In 2017, in reaction to the invited campus speaker Milo Yiannopoulos, a right-wing provocateur, students at UC Berkeley staged violent protests. One student said,

"His words are violent, or a form of violence," which seemed to capture the sentiments of many who have regarded offensive, noxious speech as equivalent to violent acts. Some of the protestors at Berkeley argued that a violent assault was justified to silence a speaker whose ideas were inherently violent. Students have spoken of being "assaulted" when they hear speech that they find insulting.

The psychologist Lisa Feldman Barrett has argued that there is a scientific basis for equating some kinds of speech with violence. She points to the large body of research showing that chronic stress can cause physiological harm and that speech can cause stress. She reasons that "If words can cause stress, and if prolonged stress can cause physical harm, then it seems that speech—at least certain types of speech—can be a form of violence."[23]

Feldman Barrett's critics say her argument fails because she doesn't adequately distinguish between chronic and transitory stress and because she unjustifiably equates stress with violence. Paresky, along with many others, is concerned that equating speech with violence actually promotes violence:

> When is speech violence? The answer is *never*. Speech may be upsetting, but that doesn't make it violence. Speech may be ugly or hateful, but that doesn't make it violence. Speech may be associated with deleterious physiological effects or even harm, but that still doesn't make it violence. Speech may even intimidate or threaten violence. That makes it illegal, but it doesn't make it violence. Equating speech with violence not only robs us of our understanding of ourselves as competent and civil human beings capable of defeating bad ideas with better ones, it gives us license to use physical violence in response to speech—or even in advance, as "self-defense." For psychologists to assert that speech is violence is not merely incorrect, it's harmful.
> But it's not violence.[24]

Free Speech and Inclusion

In the campus controversies involving free speech, three positions have dominated. The first takes free speech to be the overriding value at stake. It's the view (sometimes called "free speech absolutism") that the right of free speech must be preserved above all else and that any perceived harms, offense, or emotional distress caused by protected speech are irrelevant. For many proponents of this view, protecting students from contrary, challenging views (through speech codes, for example) undermines democracy, promotes emotional immaturity, and leads to intellectual weakness (or, as some have alleged, "snowflake" fragility). According to outspoken advocates Greg Lukianoff and Jonathan Haidt,

> Attempts to shield students from words, ideas, and people that might cause them emotional discomfort are bad for students. They are bad for the workplace, which will be mired in unending litigation if student expectations of safety are carried forward. And they are bad for American democracy, which is already paralyzed by worsening partisanship. When the ideas, values, and speech of the other side are seen not just as wrong but as willfully aggressive toward innocent victims, it is hard to imagine the kind of mutual respect, negotiation, and compromise that are needed to make politics a positive-sum game.

Rather than trying to protect students from words and ideas that they will inevitably encounter, colleges should do all they can to equip students to thrive in a world full of words and ideas that they cannot control.[28]

A second position, directly opposed to the first, says speech that deliberately demeans or offends vulnerable groups should be banned to protect those groups from harm. Those who take this view favor speech codes that forbid certain kinds of offensive language, especially hate speech. (Speech codes and hate speech will be covered in the next chapter.) They take the possible harms of speech very seriously and are less impressed by arguments about the benefits of unfettered speech. According to Ulrich Baer, author of *What Snowflakes Get Right: Free Speech, Truth, and Equality on Campus*:

It has become evident that hate speech cannot be simply defeated with more speech. It has also become more evident that defending an absolute principle of free speech only works for everyone when the principle of equality is defended vigorously at the same time. Defending free speech as an absolute right, without also rejecting the content of virulent racist and misogynist speech, creates a moral vacuum. It turns free speech into a weapon for a partisan agenda, rather than a neutral principle that serves all equally well.[29]

A third position represents a middle way. It recognizes the need to protect free speech to preserve democracy and to advance knowledge while ensuring that all voices, all races, and all genders have an equal opportunity to be heard. It says that free speech is too important to be restricted and yet we can't ignore the harm that it can do. It calls for conscientious efforts to make campuses safe for *both* the free and uninhibited exchange of ideas as well as the full and equal participation of all students in the expression and debate of those ideas. From this perspective, both the free speech absolutists and those who want to protect minorities from harmful speech have missed the point—which is to try to accommodate both these important demands. Ben-Porath calls this accommodation "inclusive freedom":

An inclusive freedom framework for speech on campus takes seriously the importance of a free and open exchange as a necessary condition to the development of civic and democratic capacities. It lends similar weight to the related demand that all members of the campus community be able to participate in this free and open exchange if it is to accomplish the goals of free inquiry, open-minded research, and equal access to learning and to civic development. . . .

There seems to be an agreement—even if thin, even if only as lip service—that free speech and inquiry are central tenets of university or college life and its mission, and that diversity, equity, and inclusion need to be respected. Not often enough is it acknowledged that equity and inclusion do not have to stand in the way of free speech and open-minded inquiry and that the two can go hand in hand in promoting the key mission of higher education institutions.

Moreover, both sides fail to take into account how their views can readily become self-defeating. When social justice advocates call for the curtailment of free speech through censoring speakers and canceling events, they neglect to recognize the historical reality that curtailing free speech might harm vulnerable groups. Once censorship based on content is possible, what is to stop people in power—administrators, religious majority groups, or other established centers of power—from limiting speech by dissenters, opponents, or anyone who threatens the status quo?

On the other hand, free speech advocates who insist that unfettered free speech is a necessary condition for the open-minded free inquiry that makes a university worth its name sidestep the fact that when many on campus are effectively silenced, inquiry is in effect neither free nor open-minded. . . . Many women, racial and sexual minorities, first-generation students, and other individuals who may not see themselves (or be seen by others) as belonging or possess the tools required to hit the ground running remain outside the conversation, impoverishing the conversation and hindering the search for truth and knowledge.[30]

Chemerinsky and Gillman argue that we must simultaneously value the benefits of free speech, take into account its potential harms to the vulnerable, and appreciate why students are so concerned about those harms:

> We are deeply troubled by the efforts to suppress and punish the expression of unpopular ideas. Those who call for punishment of speech that makes students feel uncomfortable fail to recognize the importance of speech and the danger in giving the government the power to regulate it.
>
> But at the same time, much of the criticism of current students and their sensibilities fails to reflect the laudable compassion that motivates them. . . .
>
> But mocking these students or treating their concerns as pathological misses the point. It is hardly a constructive approach to the tensions over offensive speech on college campuses. Nor is the response that students should "suck it up" and deal with it, which harkens back to a thankfully bygone age when racial and ethnic slurs were more common, disrespect of women was more acceptable, LGBTQ people were ridiculed and tormented, and teachers and coaches routinely used shaming to discourage poor performance.
>
> Society is better now, and students are right to expect empathy for victims of hate and intolerance. Telling them to "toughen up" does not address their laudable desire to create a campus that is inclusive and conducive for learning by all students. Campuses have the duty to act—sometimes legally, always morally—to protect their students from injury. The challenge is to develop an approach to free speech on campus that both protects expression and respects the need to make sure that a campus is a conducive learning environment for all students.[31]

But what exactly can campuses do to promote tolerance, dignitary safety, and inclusion while protecting free expression? The ACLU recommends the following actions that administrators can take:

- Speak out loudly and clearly against expressions of racist, sexist, homophobic, and transphobic speech, as well as other instances of discrimination against marginalized individuals or groups.
- React promptly and firmly to counter acts of discriminatory harassment, intimidation, or invasion of privacy.
- Create forums and workshops to raise awareness and promote dialogue on issues of race, sex, sexual orientation, and gender identity.
- Intensify their efforts to ensure broad diversity among the student body, throughout the faculty, and within the college administration.
- Vigilantly defend the equal rights of all speakers and all ideas to be heard, and promote a climate of robust and uninhibited dialogue and debate open to all views, no matter how controversial.

To this list, Chemerinsky and Gillman add these steps:

- Protect the rights of all students to engage in meaningful protest and to distribute materials that get their message out.
- Punish speech that constitutes "true threats" or that meets the definition of harassment under federal anti-discrimination law.
- Prevent discrimination by official campus organizations.
- Ensure that learning environments are safe for the civil expression of ideas.
- Require institution-wide training on the obligation to create inclusive workplace and educational environments.
- Establish clear reporting requirements so that incidents of discriminatory practices can be quickly investigated and addressed.
- Encourage faculty and students to research and learn about the harms associated with intolerance and structural discrimination, including through the creation of appropriate academic departments, the establishment of educational requirements on diversity and structural inequality, the publication of research, and the sponsoring of academic symposia.
- Organize co-curricular activities that celebrate cultural diversity and provide victims of hateful and bullying acts the opportunity to be heard.
- Speak out to condemn egregious acts of intolerance as a way of demonstrating the power of "more speech" rather than enforced silence.

Cancel Culture

While conflicts over free speech and equality have simmered on college campuses, analogous clashes have been occurring across the country, mostly on social media, over what has been called "cancel culture." The term generally refers to backlash against someone for something they said or did that's deemed offensive, shameful, or disqualifying by critics who threaten the person's reputation or employment. Canceling someone is not just lambasting, vilifying, or insulting them. Those who participate in cancel culture call for the offending person to be fired from their job, kicked off an online platform, removed from their position, or have their work environment rendered intolerable.

Cancel culture is not a violation of constitutional free speech rights, which bar only the government from interfering with free expression. Being fired from a job or being de-platformed is not a constitutional issue. But in a liberal, democratic society, free speech is also a moral right; we want and expect a great deal of freedom to express ideas and debate issues. For many, cancel culture runs counter to this ethos of free expression.

Cancel culture has been condemned—and practiced—on both the political Left and Right. Many on the Right have complained for years about "politically

correct" detractors who try to cancel or silence conservative writers and speakers. Yet conservatives have also called for the cancellation of left-leaning people
with whom they disagree. The most notable example is former President Donald
Trump, who has had a long history of condemning "political correctness" while
demanding cancellations and firings of people and organizations who merely
said something he didn't like.

Among liberals and progressives, cancel culture has become the subject of
contentious debate, as evidenced by an open letter on free speech signed by
153 prominent writers and academics published in *Harper's Magazine* in July
2020 and then promptly and harshly criticized by other writers and academics.
The signers included Thomas Chatterton Williams (who headed up the effort),
John McWhorter, Francis Fukuyama, Katha Pollitt, Margaret Atwood, Nadine
Strossen, Salman Rushdie, Noam Chomsky, Randal Kennedy, and Wendy
Kaminer. Titled "A Letter on Justice and Open Debate," it began by acknowledging that "Powerful protests for racial and social justice are leading to overdue
demands for police reform, along with wider calls for greater equality and inclu-
sion across our society." It then warned that

> This needed reckoning has also intensified a new set of moral attitudes and
> political commitments that tend to weaken our norms of open debate and
> toleration of differences in favor of ideological conformity. As we applaud the first
> development, we also raise our voices against the second. . . .
>
> The free exchange of information and ideas, the lifeblood of a liberal society, is
> daily becoming more constricted. While we have come to expect this on the radical
> right, censoriousness is also spreading more widely in our culture: an intolerance
> of opposing views, a vogue for public shaming and ostracism, and the tendency to
> dissolve complex policy issues in a blinding moral certainty. We uphold the value
> of robust and even caustic counter-speech from all quarters. But it is now all too
> common to hear calls for swift and severe retribution in response to perceived
> transgressions of speech and thought. More troubling still, institutional leaders,
> in a spirit of panicked damage control, are delivering hasty and disproportionate
> punishments instead of considered reforms.[32]

The letter was vague about the victims of this punishment, but critics of
cancel culture have pointed to several examples, the most notorious being that
of David Shor. In the wake of street protests over George Floyd's killing, Shor,
a data analyst, was fired from the progressive firm Civis Analytics after tweeting about research linking violent protests and the 1968 election of Richard
Nixon. Citing the research, Shor seemed to suggest that violent protests were
counterproductive. But other examples have also been mentioned: Alexis
Jones, a black reporter at the *Pittsburgh Post-Gazette*; Bari Weiss, former senior
New York Times opinion editor; William Peris, lecturer in political science at

UCLA; Steven Pinker, Harvard psychologist; and half the board members of the National Book Critics Circle. To this list some would also add the campus speakers who have been disinvited or blocked from speaking in recent years and faculty members who have resigned or been investigated because of their views.

The signatories insist that a few specific examples are doubly worrisome because of the chill they can spread over free expression generally:

> Whatever the arguments around each particular incident, the result has been to steadily narrow the boundaries of what can be said without the threat of reprisal. We are already paying the price in greater risk aversion among writers, artists, and journalists who fear for their livelihoods if they depart from the consensus, or even lack sufficient zeal in agreement.

Michelle Goldberg, a columnist and one of the signatories, says,

> Still, there's no question that many people feel intimidated. John McWhorter, an associate professor of English and comparative literature at Columbia who signed the *Harper's* Letter, told me that in recent days he's heard from over 100 graduate students and professors, most of them left of center, who fear for their professional prospects if they get on the wrong side of left-wing opinion.[33]

The letter caused a furious outcry among many progressives who ridiculed the signatories as privileged authors and intellectuals who are concerned not with free speech rights but with an erosion of their influence and power. They saw the letter—and the charge of cancel culture—as a reaction against marginalized people who, thanks largely to new media, can now talk back to the powerful and call out injustice. An open letter in response to the original letter declares:

> In truth, Black, brown, and LGBTQ+ people—particularly Black and trans people—can now critique elites publicly and hold them accountable socially; this seems to be the letter's greatest concern. What's perhaps even more grating to many of the signatories is that a critique of their long held views is persuasive. . . .
>
> It is impossible to see how these signatories are contributing to "the most vital causes of our time" during this moment of widespread reckoning with oppressive social systems. Their letter seeks to uphold a "stifling atmosphere" and prioritizes signal-blasting their discomfort in the face of valid criticism. The intellectual freedom of cis white intellectuals has never been under threat en masse, especially when compared to how writers from marginalized groups have been treated for generations. In fact, they have never faced serious consequences—only momentary discomfort.[34]

Reacting to this kind of criticism, Williams, a *Harper's* columnist and the author of the memoir *Self-Portrait in Black and White*, said the letter was meant to support all voices, not just prominent ones. In an interview for the *New York Times*, he asserted,

> We're not just a bunch of old white guys sitting around writing this letter. [Williams is African American.] It includes plenty of Black thinkers, Muslim thinkers, Jewish thinkers, people who are trans and gay, old and young, right wing and left wing. We believe these are values that are widespread and shared, and we wanted the list [of signatories] to reflect that.

Criticisms of the *Harper's* letter raised a host of questions about whether cases of cancellations are numerous enough or serious enough to be concerned about, whether the actual intent of the (privileged) signatories was to preserve their power, and whether such a letter should even have been written while so many marginalized people are struggling to have their voices heard. But whatever the answers to these questions—whatever the extent of cancel culture, whatever the motivations of the signers, and regardless of the urgency of the vital struggle for social justice—it's still legitimate to ask: is

Fig. 2.5 Thomas Chatterton Williams, journalist and author of the memoir *Self-Portrait in Black and White*.

it ever morally permissible to cancel (fire, de-platform, punish) someone for speech that others find offensive or disturbing or otherwise objectionable? If so, why? If not, why not?

Counterspeech

You can see now that the main free speech debate on campus is whether restrictions on hate speech are the best way to defeat the harms that it can cause. Many argue that they are not—that they are either ineffective or counterproductive or both and do not serve the interests of those targeted by the speech. Others say banning hateful speech is a powerful weapon against hate and can protect vulnerable groups from messages that cause dignitary harms. We'll examine this dispute in more depth in Chapter 3, but for now we need to examine a related issue—whether the harms of hate speech can be blocked or limited through counterspeech.

Counterspeech refers to any speech that tries to counter or undermine hateful or discriminatory messages. It includes peaceful counterspeech efforts by individuals (face to face, in print, or on social media), online counterspeech groups, educational organizations, and media platforms like Facebook and Twitter. The goal is to change the mind or the behavior of the speaker or to affect the views of a wider audience.

Counterspeech is a firmly established First Amendment doctrine, articulated by Justice Louis D. Brandeis in *Whitney v. California* (1927) as the wisest alternative to censorship:

> The fitting remedy for evil counsels is good ones. . . . If there be time to expose through discussion, the falsehoods and fallacies, to avert the evil by the processes of education, the remedy to be applied is more speech, not enforced silence.

For strong supporters of free speech like the ACLU, this "more speech" approach is a far better response to hate speech than speech codes:

> Bigoted speech is symptomatic of a huge problem in our country. Our schools, colleges, and universities must prepare students to combat this problem. That means being an advocate: speaking out and convincing others. Confronting, hearing, and countering offensive speech is an important skill, and it should be considered a core requirement at any school worth its salt.
>
> When schools shut down speakers who espouse bigoted views, they deprive their students of the opportunity to confront those views themselves. Such incidents do not shut down a single bad idea, nor do they protect students from the harsh realities of an often unjust world. Silencing a bigot accomplishes nothing except turning them into a martyr for the principle of free expression. The better approach, and the one more consistent with our constitutional tradition, is to respond to ideas we hate with the ideals we cherish.[35]

But critics argue that counterspeech is not an option for many vulnerable groups who are the targets of hate speech. Many may be silenced by the hateful messages and the dignitary harms inflicted, or they may not know how to respond effectively to aggressive or abusive words, or they may not have access to the means to counter hateful speech.

The critics are right, but these facts don't show that counterspeech doesn't work, only that more needs to be done to widen its use among targeted groups and everyone else. And more *is* being done by a variety of schools and organizations, including many international programs and online associations dedicated to studying harmful speech and training people to counteract it effectively. A few examples: the *Dangerous Speech Project* (https://dangerousspeech.org), the *Berkman Klein Center* (at Harvard University, https://cyber.harvard.edu/), *Southern Poverty Law Center* (https://www.splcenter.org/), *Facebook Counterspeech* (https://counterspeech.fb.com/en/), and *PEN America Webinar: Counter-Speech: Speaking Out to Fight Hate* (https://www.youtube.com/watch?v=lOXR9KWHcKE).

Some observers think counterspeech can be an especially powerful tool for minorities. For example:

> The counterspeech approach can have significant benefits for minority students. One commentator writes that "[o]nly by pointing out the weaknesses and the moral wrongness of an oppressor's speech can an oppressed group realize the strength of advocating a morally just outcome." As is the case whenever one participates in campus dialogue and debate, minority students can expect to bolster their arguments and sharpen their views; "[t]hrough the active, engaging, and often relentless debate on issues of social and political concern," they "learn the strengths of their own arguments and the weaknesses of their opponents." With this knowledge, these groups are better able to strike at the heart of a bigoted argument with all of the fervor and force necessary to combat hateful ideas." Therefore, the experience and knowledge gained through the process of debate and discussion will serve minority students well in the long run.[36]

Of course, counterspeech is always an option for those who are not directly targeted by hate speech but who nevertheless seek to blunt its effects on others. If they are committed to social justice and equality, it follows that they have a moral obligation to verbally address hate speech when confronted by it.

But can counterspeech diminish the expression of hate or its harmful effects? The sparse data available (based on online studies and anecdotal evidence) suggest that it can. The success of counterspeech is defined either by its impact on hateful speakers (whether they alter their beliefs or behavior) or by its positive influence on the larger audience (whether, for example, audience members stop speaking hatefully or the counterspeech prompts more counterspeech). Effectiveness is measured in different ways and depends on many factors, including the number of people using counterspeech ("counterspeakers"); the number of hateful speakers involved; characteristics of who is speaking and who is listening (their race, credibility, number of followers); and the content, style, and tone of the counterspeech.[37] Success in influencing hateful speakers has been limited; success in turning others against hate speech or in igniting contagions of counterspeech is more common.

Hate speech is everywhere online, and counterspeech is there, too. Many people try to counteract or condemn hate speech when they come across it, and many are volunteer counterspeakers—aka counterspeech practitioners—acting alone or coordinating with counterspeech groups throughout the world. Counterspeech efforts are international, varied, and inventive. Susan Benesch, executive director of the Dangerous Speech Project and faculty associate at Harvard's Berkman Klein Center for Internet and Society, cites some of her favorite examples:

> One of my favorites is #Jagärhär, a Swedish group that collectively responds to hateful posts in the comment sections of news articles posted on Facebook. They have a very specific method of action. On the #Jagärhär Facebook page, group administrators post links to articles with hateful comments, directing their members to counterspeak there. Members tag their posts with #Jagärhär (which means, "I am here"), so that other members can find their posts and like them. Most of the news outlets have their comments ranked by what Facebook calls "relevance." Relevance is, in part, determined by how much interaction (likes and replies) a comment receives. Liking the counterspeech posts, therefore, drives them up in relevance ranking, moving them to the top and ideally drowning out the hateful comments.
>
> The group is huge—around 74,000 members, and the model has spread to 13 other countries as well. The name of each group is "#iamhere" in the local language (for example, #jesusilà in France and #somtu in Slovakia). I like this example because it demonstrates how powerful counterspeech can be when people work together. In the bigger groups (the groups range in size from 64 in #iamhereIndia to 74,274 in #Jagärhär), their posts regularly have the most interaction, and therefore become the most visible comments. . . .
>
> I'm also very interested in efforts that try to counter hateful messages by sharing those messages more widely. The Instagram account Bye Felipe, for example, is dedicated to "calling out dudes who turn hostile when rejected or ignored." The account allows users to submit screenshots of conversations they have had with men—often on dating sites—where the man has lashed out after being ignored or rejected. I interviewed Alexandra Tweten, who founded and runs the account, and she told me that although she started it mostly to make fun of the men in the interactions, she quickly realized that it could be a tool to spark a larger conversation about online harassment against women. A similar effort is the Twitter account @YesYoureRacist. Logan Smith, who runs the anti-racism account, retweets racist posts that he finds to his nearly 400,000 followers in an effort to make people aware that the racism exists.[38]

COUNTERSPEECH: WHAT WORKS, WHAT DOESN'T

Some counterspeech strategies work better than others. Fortunately, we have some preliminary research (and the experience of counterspeakers) to help guide us in deciding which is which. Here are some recommendations and cautions from the Dangerous Speech Project based on research conducted on Twitter posts.

Recommended Strategies

Warning of Consequences

Counterspeakers often warn of the possible consequences of speaking hatefully on a public platform like Twitter, and in many cases this seems to have been effective at getting the speaker to delete the hateful tweet. Such counterspeakers can:

- Remind the speaker of the harm that hateful or dangerous speech may do to the target group, since words can catalyze action.
- Remind the speaker how many people in his or her offline world (including employers, friends, family, and future employers) can see what is online, and note that offline consequences can include losing one's job and relationships.
- Remind the speaker of the permanence of online communication.
- Remind the speaker of the possible online consequences of hateful or dangerous speech, such as blocking, reporting, and suspended accounts.

Shaming and Labeling

We have observed successful counterspeech which labels tweets as hateful, racist, bigoted, misogynist, and so on. Since these words carry such a shameful stigma for many people in contemporary North America, speakers who do not perceive themselves as racists, for example, are often quick to alter such tweets. With this strategy, counterspeakers can also:

- Denounce the speech as hateful or dangerous. This can help cyberbystanders identify, interpret, and respond to it.
- Explain to the original speaker why their statement is hateful or dangerous. In addition to eliciting the favorable reaction that often comes from labeling, this can also help to educate the speaker so he or she will repeat the mistake.

Empathy and Affiliation

Changing the tone of a hateful conversation is an effective way of ending the exchange. While we have scant evidence that it will change behavior in the long term, it may prevent the escalation of the hateful rhetoric being used in the present moment. Counterspeakers can consider:

- Using a friendly, empathetic, or peaceful tone in responses to messages with a hostile, hateful, or violent tone.
- Affiliating with the original speaker to establish a connection (e.g., I am also a conservative, but . . .).
- Affiliating with the group targeted by the hateful speech to generate empathy (e.g., What you said was hurtful to me as an Asian . . .).

Discouraged Strategies

We have observed that these strategies are often ineffective at favorably influencing the original speaker. In some cases, they may even be counterproductive or harmful.

Hostile or Aggressive Tone, Insults

Many counterspeakers respond to hateful speech with a hostile, aggressive tone, and insults. This includes but is not limited to the use of profanity, slurs, name-calling, and aspersions. We have observed that counterspeech which uses these strategies can:

- Cause a backfire effect (e.g., stronger adherence to original speech).
- Cause an escalation of hateful rhetoric.
- Turn off other potential counterspeakers from joining any intervention.

The distinction between this strategy and shaming is important. While counterspeakers often use profanity and name-calling in their tweets when shaming another user, this counterspeech will likely be more effective without the negative or hostile tone.

Fact-checking

Counterspeakers often react to hateful speech by correcting falsehoods or misperceptions contained in the speech. Unfortunately, this is usually not an effective method of influencing the original speaker. Especially when original speakers are entrenched in their views, they tend to find a way to fit the new facts presented to the conclusion to which they are already committed (social psychologists have named this process "motivated reasoning") or find different evidence to support their position rather than concede. Corrections that insult or threaten an original speaker's worldview can lead him/her/them to dig in their heels.

It is possible that fact checking can have a positive impact on the audience of a counterspeech exchange, especially when the audience is uninformed, but this causal link is difficult to prove.[39]

Argument Analysis

As you can see, arguments about free speech are many and varied, yet they all can be evaluated using the methods discussed in Chapter 1. Let's assess an argument similar to one we encountered earlier about the harms of hate speech.

1. If constitutionally protected speech on campus causes dignitary harms (if it says or implies that certain students are not equal and valued members of the community and that their participation in discussions is not valued), it should be punished.
2. A particular student's criticism of Black Lives Matter causes dignitary harms.
3. Therefore, the student's criticism should be punished.

This argument is valid—that is, the conclusion follows from the premises—and let's assume that premise 2 is true.

The sticking point is premise 1; it can be disputed on several grounds. Ben-Porath contends that although dignitary safety and the avoidance of dignitary harms are necessary to maintain a democratic campus community, censorship of offensive or opposing views is harmful to a university's open-minded pursuit of knowledge. Others argue that censorship of (protected) speech causes more harm than it prevents. They maintain that censorship of disfavored or offensive views can be (and has been) used against the very marginalized people it was designed to protect, that hate speech laws are so inherently overbroad and vague that they can be (and have been) used to punish political views (including calls for social justice and civil rights), that speech laws stifle debate about topics that require vigorous and honest discussion, and that laws banning hate speech have historically been wielded to the disadvantage of people who lack political power. As Chemerinsky and Gilman say, "Protecting hate speech is necessary because the alternative—granting governments the power to punish speakers they don't like—creates even more harm."[40]

In addition, many observers have emphasized that there are useful alternatives to censorship, including counterspeech and what Ben-Porath calls "inclusive freedom."

If these responses to premise 1 can be blunted—that is, if it can be shown to be true after all—then the argument will go through.

This brief evaluation shows that sometimes moral arguments that at first seem simple are not simple at all. In this case, the soundness of the argument hangs on the truth of a single premise, but determining the premise's truth requires a deeper inquiry.

KEY TERMS

counterspeech	harassment	punishable incitement
fighting words	hate speech	true threat

 EXERCISES

Exercises marked with * have answers in "Answers to Exercises" (Appendix B).

Exercise 2.1: Review Questions

*1. What is hate speech?
2. What is a true threat? What is harassment? What is punishable incitement?
3. Do hateful, ugly words always cause psychic or emotional harms? Why or why not?
4. What is constitutionally protected and unprotected speech?
5. What has been the role of free speech rights in American protest movements?

6. What is the viewpoint neutrality rule?

*7. Does the Constitution prohibit all hate speech? Does it allow all hate speech?

8. What is Ben-Porath's "inclusion freedom"?

9. What is cancel culture?

*10. Is the right of free speech absolute? Why or why not?

Exercise 2.2: Moral Arguments

1. What is your opinion of the *Harper's* letter discussed in this chapter? Justify your answers: Were the signers right to be concerned about cancel culture? Do you believe their concerns were overblown, just a complaint about their loss of influence? Is it ever morally permissible to cancel (fire or de-platform) someone for speech thought to be offensive or disturbing?

2. Should speech be limited by civility rules? Why or why not?

3. Should hate speech be banned on campus? Give reasons for your answer.

4. Should campus speech be censored or punished if it offends or upsets members of marginalized groups?

5. Do you think hate speech is violence? Why or why not? If you think it is violence, is violence an appropriate response to it? Explain.

Notes

1. PEN America, "Chasm in the Classroom: Campus Free Speech in a Divided America," April 2, 2019, 6, https://pen.org/wp-content/uploads/2019/04/2019-PEN-Chasm-in-the-Classroom-04.25.pdf.

2. Knight Foundation, "Free Expression on College Campuses," May 2019, file:///C:/Users/LV/Google%20Drive/BOOKS/BOOKS/Campus%20Conflicts/Knight-CP-Report-FINAL.pdf, 2-12.

3. PEN America, "Chasm in the Classroom: Campus Free Speech in a Divided America—Executive Summary," https://pen.org/wp-content/uploads/2019/04/Chasm-in-the-Classroom-Executive-Summary-April-2-2019.pdf.

4. Knight Foundation, Free Expression on College Campuses," 4–6.

5. Lee C. Bollinger, "Free Speech on Campus Is Doing Just Fine, Thank You," *The Atlantic*, June 12, 2019, https://www.theatlantic.com/ideas/archive/2019/06/free-speech-crisis-campus-isnt-real/591394/.

6. Alex Williamson, "Diversity of Thought," *Chronicle of Higher Education*, September 2019, https://www.chronicle.com/interactives/091919-Diversity-of-Thought.

7. Steven Johnson, "Conservatives Say Professors' Politics Ruins College. Students Say It's More Complicated," *Chronicle of Higher Education*, August 2019, https://www.chronicle.com/article/Conservatives-Say/246981.

8. Jonathan Zimmerman, *Campus Politics: What Everyone Needs to Know* (New York: Oxford University Press, 2016), 16–17.

9. PEN America, "Chasm in the Classroom: Campus Free Speech in a Divided America—Executive Summary," https://pen.org/wp-content/uploads/2019/04/Chasm-in-the-Classroom-Executive-Summary-April-2-2019.pdf.

10. Nadine Strossen, *Hate: Why We Should Resist It with Free Speech, Not Censorship* (New York: Oxford University Press, 2018), 21.

11. Erwin Chemerinsky and Howard Gillman, *Free Speech on Campus* (New Haven, CT: Yale University Press, 2017), 43–46.

12. Sigal R. Ben-Porath, *Free Speech on Campus* (Philadelphia: University of Pennsylvania Press, 2017), 11.
13. Ben-Porath, *Free Speech on Campus*, 11.
14. Strossen, *Hate: Why We Should Resist It with Free Speech, Not Censorship*, 4.
15. American Civil Liberties Union, "Model Anti-Harassment and Discrimination Policies for Schools," 2020, https://www.aclu.org/other/model-anti-harassment-and-discrimination-policies-schools.
16. American Civil Liberties Union, https://www.aclu.org/other/speech-campus.
17. American Civil Liberties Union, https://www.aclu.org/other/speech-campus.
18. Chemerinsky and Gillman, *Free Speech on Campus*, 126.
19. Richard Delgado and Jean Stefancic, *Understanding Words That Wound* (New York: Westview Press, 2004).
20. Pamela B. Paresky, "When Is Speech Violence and What's the Real Harm?," *Psychology Today*, August 4, 2017, https://www.psychologytoday.com/us/blog/happiness-and-the-pursuit-leadership/201708/when-is-speech-violence-and-what-s-the-real-harm.
21. Jeremy Waldron, *The Harm in Hate Speech* (Cambridge, MA: Harvard University Press, 2012), 5.
22. Ben-Porath, *Free Speech on Campus*, 62.
23. Lisa Feldman Barrett, "When Is Speech Violence?" *New York Times*, July 14, 2017.
24. Paresky, "When Is Speech Violence and What's the Real Harm?"
25. Zimmerman, *Campus Politics*, 117.
26. Ben-Porath, *Free Speech on Campus*, 69–72, 77.
27. University of Chicago, "Report of the Committee on Freedom of Expression," 2015, https://provost.uchicago.edu/sites/default/files/documents/reports/FOECommitteeReport.pdf (August 9, 2020).
28. Greg Lukianoff and Jonathan Haidt, "The Coddling of the American Mind," *The Atlantic*, September 2015, https://www.theatlantic.com/magazine/archive/2015/09/the-coddling-of-the-american-mind/399356/.
29. Ulrich Baer, *What Snowflakes Get Right: Free Speech, Truth, and Equality on Campus* (New York: Oxford University Press, 2019), xiv.
30. Ben-Porath, *Free Speech on Campus*, 37, 42–43.
31. Chemerinsky and Gillman, *Free Speech on Campus*, 17–19.
32. "A Letter on Justice and Open Debate," *Harper's Magazine*, July 7, 2020, https://harpers.org/a-letter-on-justice-and-open-debate/.
33. Michelle Goldberg, "Do Progressives Have a Free Speech Problem?," *New York Times*, July 17, 2020, https://www.nytimes.com/2020/07/17/opinion/sunday/harpers-letter-free-speech.html.
34. "A More Specific Letter on Justice and Open Debate," *The Objective*, July 10, 2020, https://theobjective.substack.com/p/a-more-specific-letter-on-justice.
35. American Civil Liberties Union, https://www.aclu.org/other/speech-campus.
36. Azhar Majeed, "Defying the Constitution: The Rise, Persistence, and Prevalence of Campus Speech Codes," *Journal of Law & Public Policy*, 7 Geo. J.L. & Pub. Policy 481 (2009).
37. Cathy Buerger, Dangerous Speech Project, "Counterspeech: A Literature Review," February 20, 2020, https://dangerousspeech.org/counterspeech-a-literature-review/.
38. Daniel Jones and Susan Benesch, "Combating Hate Speech through Counterspeech," Berkman Klein Center, August 9, 2019, https://cyber.harvard.edu/story/2019-08/combating-hate-speech-through-counterspeech.
39. Susan Benesch, Derek Ruths, Kelly P. Dillon, Haji Mohammad Saleem, and Lucas Wright, "Considerations for Successful Counterspeech," https://dangerousspeech.org/wp-content/uploads/2016/10/Considerations-for-Successful-Counterspeech.pdf.
40. Chemerinsky and Gillman, *Free Speech on Campus*, 108.

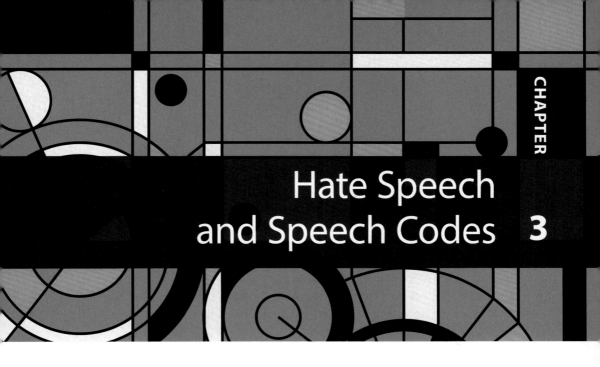

Hate Speech and Speech Codes 3

Let's take stock of what we know about free speech and the conflicts it has engendered on college campuses. First, freedom of speech is the right to express, either verbally or nonverbally, opinions or ideas without onerous limitations imposed by government or society. It is essential to freedom of thought, democratic self-government, pursuit of knowledge, and moral deliberation. Throughout American history, the right of free speech has been an invaluable ally of citizens who demand justice while governments try to silence them. In their struggles for equality and freedom, disempowered people, minority groups, and dissenters have staked much on the right of free expression.

Second, the US Constitution as interpreted by the Supreme Court asserts that most speech is immune from censorship or punishment—that is, it is constitutionally protected. But some forms of speech can be censored or punished—they are constitutionally unprotected. The Court has declared that speech does not fall into the unprotected category merely because people disfavor it, find it disturbing, or are offended by it. In addition, the Court has consistently ruled that speech cannot be deemed unprotected just because it provokes a fear of possible harmful behavior. As Justice Louis Brandeis said, "Fear of serious injury cannot alone justify suppression of free speech. . . . Men feared witches and burnt women." Fearful speech can only be punished when it poses a danger of directly causing certain specific, imminent, serious harms. Punishable speech includes true threats, harassment, punishable incitement, and fighting words.

Third, constitutionally protected hate speech can cause psychological, emotional, physiological, and dignitary harms. (Hate speech is hateful, abusive, or discriminatory speech directed against a person or group because of their race, religion, sexual orientation, gender identity, ethnicity, or national origin.) It can convey to vulnerable groups that they are subordinate, unequal, and unwanted. Research suggests that such harms can be altered, lessened, or negated by many variables, including the circumstances of the speech and how listeners choose to perceive the disturbing messages. Many speech harms can be addressed on campus through conscientious efforts to establish "inclusive freedom," and hate speech can often be countered directly through counterspeech.

But even given all this, we can still ask: to prevent harm to vulnerable people, why shouldn't we ban speech that is hateful or discriminatory? Why shouldn't we enact campus speech regulations to censor or punish speech that distresses or demeans marginalized groups? Aren't speech regulations a more direct and effective way to block the harm of hateful messages than counterspeech and efforts to promote dignitary safety and inclusion? In other words, is it morally permissible to outlaw hate speech?

Punishing Speech

A **speech code** is a campus regulation that restricts, forbids, or punishes what is generally considered protected speech. Speech codes come in many forms, says the Foundation for Individual Rights in Education (FIRE):

> College speech regulations are referred to by many other names. For example, "speech zone" policies like the one maintained by Valdosta State University which limited the free speech activities of 11,000 students to less than 1% of a 168-acre campus; or "student rights and obligations" policies like Pennsylvania State University's "Penn State Principles," which prohibit students from violating others' "rights" by "taunting, ridiculing, [or] insulting" other students. . . . Other examples include computer use policies like the one at the University of Alabama-Huntsville, which prohibits "[a]ny inappropriate e-mail," including "unofficial, unsolicited e-mail," or "diversity" policies like the one at Texas Southern University, which prohibits "intentional mental . . . harm."[1]

A central precept of modern democratic societies is that free speech is so fundamentally important that it cannot be limited without strong justification, and the strongest justification is to prevent harm. The mere existence of the harm, however, is not enough to justify restricting speech. Restricting the speech must be less harmful than allowing the speech. So it is with speech codes. If we must impose them, we want whatever harms they prevent to outweigh any harm they might cause.

As we've seen, the harms of hate speech are real, and hate speech (regardless of its harms) is morally contemptible, and its purveyors are morally blameworthy. Racial slurs, misogynistic invective, anti-LGBTQ insults, anti-Semitic epithets—all these and more stand condemned by any moral theory. In the 1980s and early

Fig. 3.1 Protesters burn a Confederate flag outside California Polytechnic State University's Spanos Theatre ahead of Milo Yiannopoulos's talk on campus in San Luis Obispo, California, January 31, 2017.

1990s, colleges and universities began using speech codes to try to block such harms, most especially the harms of discriminatory harassment. Restrictions on hate speech help promote equality, proponents argued, giving vulnerable minority voices an equal chance to be heard and to participate in an inclusive learning environment. Yet many theorists who would readily condemn hate speech in all forms have inquired whether curbing it through speech codes causes more harms than the speech itself.

Opponents of speech codes have argued that, historically, speech codes have caused significant harms to minorities, political dissenters, and many who simply hold views that are different. Aside from violating the First Amendment's viewpoint neutrality and emergency test rules, they contend, speech laws are inherently vague and overbroad. A speech law is vague if it is unclear what speech is allowed and what is forbidden. It is overbroad if it ends up banning protected speech while regulating unprotected speech. Free speech scholars argue that vague and overbroad speech laws result in enforcement by authorities that is arbitrary, subjective, and inimical to disempowered people and unpopular ideas.

The courts have consistently warned against the vagueness and overbreadth of campus speech laws. In fact, since the early 1990s, hundreds of schools have adopted speech codes, and almost all of the codes reviewed by the courts have been declared unconstitutional.

Scholars cite the speech code enacted by the University of Michigan in 1988 as an instructive example of how good intentions can go awry. The school adopted the regulations after several despicable incidents involving racist hate speech. A flyer appeared on campus declaring "open season" on blacks, who were referred to as "saucer lips, porch monkeys, and jigaboos." A campus radio station broadcast racist jokes. Another flyer used racial slurs to demand that blacks get off campus. At a protest against racism, someone displayed a Ku Klux Klan uniform from a dormitory window. The code prohibited:

> Any behavior, verbal or physical, that stigmatizes or victimizes an individual on the basis of race, ethnicity, religion, sex, sexual orientation, creed, national origin, ancestry, age . . . and that . . . creates an intimidating, hostile, or demeaning environment for educational pursuits, employment or participation in University sponsored extra-curricular activities.[2]

Later the university published an interpretive guide for its regulations that gave examples of sanctionable conduct, which included:

- A flyer containing racist threats distributed in a residence hall.
- Racist graffiti written on the door of an Asian student's study carrel.
- A male student makes remarks in class like "Women just aren't as good in this field as men," thus creating a hostile learning atmosphere for female classmates.
- Students in a residence hall have a floor party and invite everyone on their floor except one person because they think she might be a lesbian.
- A black student is confronted and racially insulted by two white students in a cafeteria.
- Male students leave pornographic pictures and jokes on the desk of a female graduate student.
- Two men demand that their roommate in the residence hall move out and be tested for AIDS.[3]

The code was in effect for a year and a half and was used not against the kinds of hateful expression that had first raised alarms but against the people the code was meant to protect as well as against those who had expressed views that others didn't like. Author and historian Henry Louis Gates, Jr., director of Harvard's Hutchins Center for African and African-American Research, explains:

> During the year in which Michigan's speech code was enforced, more than twenty blacks were charged—by whites—with racist speech. . . . Not a single instance of racist speech by whites was punished. . . . A full disciplinary hearing was conducted only in the case of a black social work student who was charged with saying, in a

Fig. 3.2 Harvard Professor Henry Louis Gates, Jr., literary critic, historian, and filmmaker.

class discussion of research projects, that he believed that homosexuality was an illness, and that he was developing a social work approach to move homosexuals toward heterosexuality. ("These charges will haunt me for the rest of my life," the black student claimed in a court affidavit.)[4]

In other incidents, the code was used to punish a black student who used the words "white trash" while speaking with a white student. Complaints were lodged against a student who said Jewish people used the Holocaust to excuse Israel's treatment of Palestinians. Some students were punished or threatened with punishment because of comments they made in classrooms.

In federal court, the University of Michigan's speech code was struck down and declared to be so vague and overbroad that it was impossible to discern what speech was allowed and what was to be punished. The court noted that "The Supreme Court has consistently held that statutes punishing speech or conduct solely on the grounds that they are unseemly or offensive are unconstitutionally overbroad."[5]

Two years later the University of Wisconsin adopted a speech code that allowed the university to punish students

For racist or discriminatory comments, epithets or other expressive behavior directed at an individual or on separate occasions at different individuals, or for physical conduct, if such comments, epithets or other expressive behavior or physical conduct intentionally:

1. Demean the race, sex, religion, color, creed, disability, sexual orientation, national origin, ancestry, or age of the individual or individuals; and
2. Create an intimidating, hostile, or demeaning environment for education, university-related work, or other university-authorized activity. . . .

A student would be in violation if:

a. He or she intentionally made demeaning remarks to an individual based on that person's ethnicity, such as name calling, racial slurs, or "jokes"; and
b. His or her purpose in uttering the remarks was to make the educational environment hostile for the person to whom the demeaning remark was addressed.[6]

In federal court, this code was declared unconstitutional due to its excessively overbroad language that permitted the punishment of protected speech. In its ruling, the court declared:

This commitment to free expression must be unwavering, because there exist many situations where, in the short run, it appears advantageous to limit speech to solve pressing social problems, such as discriminatory harassment. If a balancing approach is applied, these pressing and tangible short run concerns are likely to outweigh the more amorphous and long run benefits of free speech. However, the suppression of speech, even where the speech's content appears to have little value and great costs, amounts to governmental thought control.[7]

In 2010, a federal appeals court invalidated speech regulations enacted by the University of the Virgin Islands that prohibited the display of "offensive" or "unauthorized" signs. The court (quoting findings in previous cases) declared,

[The use of the word] "offensive" is, "on its face, sufficiently broad and subjective that [it] could conceivably be applied to cover any speech th[at] offends someone. . . . . [T]he mere dissemination of ideas—no matter how offensive to good taste— on a state university campus may not be shut off in the name alone of 'conventions of decency." . . . [T]he ban on "offensive" signs is hopelessly ambiguous and subjective. . . . [T]he ban's prohibitions on "offensive" and "unauthorized" speech have no plainly legitimate sweep and may be used to arbitrarily silence protected speech. . . . As such, we conclude that the paragraph is facially overbroad in violation of the First Amendment.[8]

The court also rejected the code's prohibition of speech that causes "emotional distress," finding that the term is "entirely subjective and provides no shelter for core protected speech." The panel of judges asserted that scenarios in which the code could be violated because a student feels emotional distress are endless—and then listed a few examples:

> a religious student organization inviting an atheist to attend a group prayer meeting on campus could prompt him to seek assistance in dealing with the distress of being invited to the event; minority students may feel emotional distress when other students protest against affirmative action; a pro-life student may feel emotional distress when a pro-choice student distributes Planned Parenthood pamphlets on campus; even simple name-calling could be punished.[9]

The court noted that according to the school's speech law, "Every time a student speaks, she risks causing another student emotional distress and receiving punishment. . . . This is a heavy weight for students to bear."

Scholars point out that speech codes have often been used to punish political views, arguing that such regulations *cannot avoid* being political. For many groups, vague terms like "stigmatizing," "demeaning," and "insulting" are very much about political issues. According to Chemerinsky and Gillman,

> The upshot is that people will inevitably be punished for their political views, with arbitrary and often surprising results. Given the definitional problems, how could it be otherwise? Suppose gay and lesbian students complain that they are demeaned by a Christian student's expressed belief that traditional heterosexual marriage is the only true marriage. Should the university deny that this belief is demeaning, or punish the student? What if the Christian student then complains that the gay students' complaint demeans and stigmatizes her religious beliefs? The door is open to an endless succession of claims and counterclaims. Justice Clarence Thomas believes that affirmative action programs stigmatize minorities on the basis of race and "stamp minorities with a badge of inferiority." Could a student's advocacy of affirmative action be taken as stigmatizing minorities as inferior? What of Laura Kipnis's argument that overly protective approaches to sex on campus stigmatize women? Or the claim that some anti-racism rhetoric demeans whites and is calculated to stir up hatred against them? These challenges are inherent to the entire enterprise. They cannot be solved with better definitions.[10]

For Speech Codes

Advocates of speech codes, however, take a different view. They think the benefits of speech regulations can outweigh the harms that opponents say are inevitable. The distinguished professor of law Mari J. Matsuda, for example, has argued that speech codes are necessary to prevent serious harm to historically disadvantaged students caused by hateful, demeaning speech. She recognizes

TWO VIEWS OF SPEECH LAWS

Richard Stengel, a former editor of *Time* and the State Department's former under-secretary for public diplomacy and public affairs, argues that America needs a hate speech law. Conor Friedersdorf, staff writer at *The Atlantic*, disagrees. Here are brief excerpts from their dueling essays.

Stengel

Yes, the First Amendment protects the "thought that we hate," but it should not protect hateful speech that can cause violence by one group against another. In an age when everyone has a megaphone, that seems like a design flaw.

It is important to remember that our First Amendment doesn't just protect the good guys; our foremost liberty also protects any bad actors who hide behind it to weaken our society . . . .

That's partly because the intellectual underpinning of the First Amendment was engineered for a simpler era. The amendment rests on the notion that the truth will win out in what Supreme Court Justice William O. Douglas called "the marketplace of ideas." This "marketplace" model has a long history going back to 17th-century English intellectual John Milton, but in all that time, no one ever quite explained how good ideas drive out bad ones, how truth triumphs over falsehood. . . .

The presumption has always been that the marketplace would offer a level playing field. But in the age of social media, that landscape is neither level nor fair.

On the Internet, truth is not optimized. On the Web, it's not enough to battle falsehood with truth; the truth doesn't always win. In the age of social media, the marketplace model doesn't work. . . .

Since World War II, many nations have passed laws to curb the incitement of racial and religious hatred. These laws started out as protections against the kinds of anti-Semitic bigotry that gave rise to the Holocaust. . . .

I think it's time to consider these statutes. . . . Domestic terrorists such as Dylann Roof and Omar Mateen and the El Paso shooter were consumers of hate speech. Speech doesn't pull the trigger, but does anyone seriously doubt that such hateful speech creates a climate where such acts are more likely?

Let the debate begin. Hate speech has a less violent, but nearly as damaging, impact in another way: It diminishes tolerance. It enables discrimination. Isn't that, by definition, speech that undermines the values that the First Amendment was designed to protect: fairness, due process, equality before the law? Why shouldn't the states experiment with their own version of hate speech statutes to penalize speech that deliberately insults people based on religion, race, ethnicity and sexual orientation?

All speech is not equal. And where truth cannot drive out lies, we must add new guardrails. I'm all for protecting "thought that we hate," but not speech that incites hate. It undermines the very values of a fair marketplace of ideas that the First Amendment is designed to protect.[11]

Friedersdorf

"Yes, the First Amendment protects the 'thought that we hate,'" Stengel grants in his op-ed, "but it should not protect hateful speech that can cause violence by one group against another." But if the U.S. outlaws speech that causes violence, that will create a perverse incentive—anyone who wants a viewpoint outlawed need only stoke violence to get his way. If Islamist radicals react with violence to feminist speech or Hollywood movies that portray two men kissing, will Stengel advocate for laws that infringe on the ability of Americans to so express themselves? . . .

The First Amendment is as important and as salutary in its effects now as ever, giving the United States an extra bulwark against authoritarians at a moment when their power is ascendant in dozens of countries. . . .

But there is no reason to believe that the truth was simpler to figure out in 1789 than in 2019. The First Amendment was adopted to limit federal power—to protect vigorous self-governance by the people—without any presumption that truth would always win out. . . .

Liberal free-speech regimes are better than any alternative ever tried at subjecting all ideas to scrutiny, and at preventing powerful actors from quashing truth seekers. . . .

There was never a time when truth always won, but let's set that aside. How strange to simultaneously believe that it's more difficult than ever to tell truths from falsehoods, that many citizens do not, in fact, possess the *ability* to do so, *and* to imply that elected officials chosen by those citizens should make determinations about what is true and false and punish people for the latter. . . .

But laws against hate speech don't necessarily create a climate where such acts are less likely, because any law narrow enough to avoid punishing a lot of innocent people is broad enough to permit hateful bigots to convey information that a tiny number of people respond to with violence. . . .

In his conclusion, Stengel poses a question . . . Why shouldn't the states experiment with their own version of hate speech statutes to penalize speech that deliberately insults people based on religion, race, ethnicity and sexual orientation?

Because it is immoral to marshal state violence to punish people for expressing their beliefs. Because laws against speech that insults people based on religion, race, ethnicity, and sexual orientation would have punished essayists like Christopher Hitchens, comedians like Eddie Murphy, hip-hop artists, feminist radicals like Andrea Dworkin, and radical gay activists who dislike "breeders."[12]

the problems of overbreadth and vagueness in speech regulations and proposes to ban only a narrowly defined type of protected hate speech:

> In order to respect first amendment values, a narrow definition of actionable racist speech is required. Racist speech is best treated as a *sui generis* category, presenting

an idea so historically untenable, so dangerous, and so tied to perpetuation of violence and degradation of the very classes of human beings who are least equipped to respond that it is properly treated as outside the realm of protected discourse. . . .

In order to distinguish the worst, paradigm example of racist hate messages from other forms of racist and nonracist speech, three identifying characteristics are suggested here:

1. The message is of racial inferiority;
2. The message is directed against a historically oppressed group; and
3. The message is persecutorial, hateful, and degrading.

Making each element a prerequisite to prosecution prevents opening of the dreaded floodgates of censorship.[13]

Matsuda believes that historically disadvantaged minority groups on campus are especially vulnerable to the harms of hate speech.

Many of the new adults who come to live and study at the major universities are away from home for the first time, and at a vulnerable stage of psychological development. Students are particularly dependent on the university for community, for intellectual development, and for self-definition. Official tolerance of racist speech in this setting is more harmful than generalized tolerance in the community-at-large. It is harmful to student perpetrators in that it is a lesson in getting-away-with-it that will have lifelong repercussions. It is harmful to targets, who perceive the university as taking sides through inaction, and who are left to their own resources in coping with the damage wrought. Finally, it is a harm to the goals of inclusion, education, development of knowledge, and ethics that universities exist and stand for. Lessons of cynicism and hate replace lessons in critical thought and inquiry. . . .

Campus racism targets minority students and faculty. Minority students often come to the university at risk academically, socially, and psychologically. Minority faculty are typically untenured, overburdened, isolated, or even nonexistent, as is the case at several law schools. The marginalized position of minority faculty further marginalizes minority students. . . .

The student, like the private figure, has fewer avenues of retreat. Living on or near campus, studying in the library, and interacting with fellow students are integral parts of university life. When racist propaganda appears on campus, target-group students experience debilitated access to the full university experience. This is so even when hate propaganda is directed at groups rather than individuals.[14]

Most critics of speech codes would probably concur with this assessment of harms to minority groups, but they would balk at Matsuda's regulatory remedy. One criticism is that her proposal might help reduce the overbreadth problem in speech codes but not their vagueness. Nadine Strossen, for example, says that at least some of Matsuda's defining characteristics of racist hate messages are "irreducibly vague":

> Consider the following illustration Matsuda provides of the distinction she attempts to draw between protected and punishable "hate speech": an expression of "[a] belief in intellectual differences between the races . . . is not subject to sanctions unless it is coupled with an element of hatred or persecution." Now consider whether Professor Charles Murray's controversial writings on this topic [in which he argues that black people are less successful than whites because of differences in intelligence] would satisfy Matsuda's standard. As recent campus protests against him have shown, many critics of his writings assert that they do reflect "hatred or persecution," but other critics of his views would reject that characterization. Indeed, Matsuda recognizes the vagueness problems with her standard and discusses multiple examples of speech that, she acknowledges, arguably could either satisfy or not satisfy her definition. In short, people "of ordinary intelligence must guess at [the] meaning" of her proposed law, rendering it unacceptably vague.[15]

Those who reject speech codes think there's a more fundamental flaw in Matsuda's attempt to address hate speech that is injurious to minority groups. They believe her speech code isn't necessary because the First Amendment and

Fig. 3.3 Nadine Strossen, professor of law and former president of the American Civil Liberties Union.

HOW HATE SPEECH LAWS ARE USED IN EUROPE

The United States grants stronger free speech rights than almost any other country in the world. Hate speech laws elsewhere are often far stricter, and enforcement much harsher, even in liberal democracies, and some Americans are calling for European-style restrictions on hate speech to be adopted here. But many observers, including journalists familiar with European hate speech regulations, point out that such laws are routinely used to punish not just right-wing hate speech but left-leaning political views as well. Consider this report from investigative journalist Glenn Greenwald:

> Many Americans who long for Europe's hate speech restrictions assume that those laws are used to outlaw and punish expression of the bigoted ideas they most hate: racism, homophobia, Islamophobia, misogyny. Often, such laws are used that way. . . .
>
> But hate speech restrictions are used in those countries to suppress, outlaw, and punish more than far-right bigotry. Those laws have frequently been used to constrain and sanction a wide range of political views that many left-wing censorship advocates would never dream could be deemed "hateful," and even against opinions which many of them likely share.
>
> France is probably the most extreme case of hate speech laws being abused in this manner. In 2015, France's highest court upheld the criminal conviction of 12 pro-Palestinian activists for violating restrictions against hate speech. Their crime? Wearing T-shirts that advocated a boycott of Israel—"Long live Palestine, boycott Israel," the shirts read—which, the court ruled, violated French law that "prescribes imprisonment or a fine of up to $50,000 for parties that 'provoke discrimination, hatred or violence toward a person or group of people on grounds of their origin, their belonging or their not belonging to an ethnic group, a nation, a race or a certain religion.'"
>
> As we reported at the time, France's use of hate speech laws to outlaw activism against Israeli policy—on the grounds that it constitutes "anti-Semitism" and hatred against people for their national origin—is part of a worldwide trend. . . .
>
> Does anyone doubt that high on the list of "hate speech" for many US officials, judges, and functionaries would be groups, such as Black Lives Matter and antifa, far-left groups that fight against white supremacists? . . .
>
> In the UK, "hate speech" has come to include anyone expressing virulent criticism of UK soldiers fighting in war. In 2012, a British Muslim teenager, Azhar Ahmed, was arrested for committing a "racially aggravated public order offence." His crime? After British soldiers were killed in Afghanistan, he cited on his Facebook page the countless innocent Afghans killed by British soldiers and wrote: "All soldiers should DIE & go to HELL! THE LOWLIFE F*****N SCUM! gotta problem go cry at your soldiers grave & wish him hell because that where he is going." . . .
>
> In 2010, a militant atheist was given a six-month suspended sentence for leaving anti-Christian and anti-Islam fliers in a religious room of the Liverpool airport; according to the BBC, "jurors found him guilty of causing religiously aggravated

> intentional harassment." . . . Cases in Turkey are common where citizens have
> been prosecuted under hate speech laws for criticizing government officials or the
> military. Radical imams are prosecuted in Europe if they are too strident in their
> support for sharia law or their defense of violence against western aggression.[16]

harassment laws already forbid speech that is seriously injurious to targeted people. Azhar Majeed explains:

> Of the exceptions to the First Amendment, "incitement to imminent lawless action" and "true threats and intimidation" are most relevant here, in terms of the harm created by prejudicial and hateful messages. Incitement to imminent lawless action encompasses advocacy of the use of force or of law violation "where such advocacy is directed to inciting or producing imminent lawless action and is likely to incite or produce such action." True threats consist of "statements where the speaker means to communicate a serious expression of an intent to commit an act of unlawful violence to a particular individual or group of individuals." Within this last exception, intimidation is "a type of true threat, where a speaker directs a threat to a person or group of persons with the intent of placing the victim in fear of bodily harm or death."
>
> Put together, these exceptions encompass much of the verbal conduct which truly can be considered injurious to the intended targets under the First Amendment, as injured sensibilities and hurt feelings are simply insufficient justifications for censorship under the law. The exception for incitement to imminent lawless action would apply to the type of situation where a speaker urges a crowd of listeners to immediately disperse across campus and commit acts of violence against students of a particular race, ethnicity, or religion. Therefore, universities, in their efforts to protect minority groups on campus, do not need to draft and enforce speech codes proscribing any and all provocative, uncivil, or antagonistic speech, even where the speech takes a favorable position toward the use of violence. Not only are such regulations superfluous, they invite trivialization and administrative abuse. Meanwhile, the exception for true threats and intimidation would apply to those circumstances where an individual attempts to use a threat of violence or bodily harm to coerce a minority student into withdrawing from an academic program, relinquishing a position within a student organization, or taking some other action which he or she does not wish to take. Consequently, there is no need for universities to maintain speech codes which construe clearly protected forms of speech as threatening or intimidating in the constitutionally proscribable sense.
>
> Additionally, true harassment codes address the types of verbal conduct which prevent another student from obtaining the benefits of a university education.[17]

Advocates of speech codes can readily admit that attempts to restrict hate speech are not perfect, that overbreadth and vagueness are a risk, and that sometimes code enforcement can have unintended and unfortunate consequences. But they may still argue that the possible benefits of speech codes—the lessening of psychological harms, discrimination, and violence—outweigh whatever negative effects they might have.

But there is little direct evidence that hate speech laws promote tolerance or significantly curtail hateful speech or its expected harmful effects. In many countries that enacted strong hate speech laws in recent years, there seems to have been very little if any decrease in hateful speech, racism, discrimination, inequality, or right-wing extremist violence. In European Union countries, hate speech and bias crimes even increased.[18]

Argument Analysis

Let's consider a moral argument similar to one you are likely to hear on campus and that incorporates many of the points discussed in this chapter:

1. Protected speech that demeans, stigmatizes, or insults an individual because of their race, sex, religion, or sexual orientation always causes psychological and dignitary harms to that individual.
2. A proposed speech code that censors or punishes such speech can decrease the psychological and dignitary harms of the speech.
3. The psychological and dignitary harms prevented by this speech code outweigh any harms that might be caused by the code's overbreadth or vagueness—that is, the code causes an overall decrease in harms.
4. If the code causes an overall decrease in harms, it should be adopted and enforced.
5. Therefore, the code should be adopted and enforced.

This argument is valid: the conclusion follows logically from the premises. But whether this argument is sound depends on the truth of the premises. Premise 1 is false. As we've seen, hate speech can indeed cause psychological or dignitary harms, but not always, and its impact can be altered, lessened, and even negated by many factors, including the attitudes and characteristics of the listener. In First Amendment law, speech that is merely disturbing, upsetting, or feared does not cause harms deemed serious enough to censor.

Premise 2 is dubious. Evidence that speech laws promote tolerance or significantly curtail hateful speech or its expected harmful effects is scant, and the European experience with speech laws conflicts with the idea that they diminish hate or discrimination.

If premise 2 is dubious, then premise 3 is dubious as well. Evidence that could help us determine the truth of this premise is suggestive but limited. In any case, it is not obvious that speech codes prevent more harm than they cause.

Premise 4 states a moral principle, which at first glance seems difficult to deny. But for many free speech advocates, even if protected speech causes harms, it should not be punished unless those harms are very serious (as in the case of threats and punishable incitement).

The verdict on this argument is that it fails.

KEY TERM

speech code

 EXERCISES

Exercises marked with * have answers in "Answers to Exercises" (Appendix B).

Exercise 3.1: Review Questions

*1. What is a speech code?
2. What was the court's verdict in the case of the University of Michigan's speech code?
3. What do the terms "overbreadth" and "vagueness" refer to in speech code cases?
4. What was the verdict in the 2010 federal appeals court case involving speech regulations at the University of the Virgin Islands? Why did the court reject the code's prohibition of speech that causes "emotional distress"?
5. Why do Chemerinsky and Gillman say that speech codes will inevitably be used to punish political views?
*6. What is hate speech?
7. Why do some critics of Matsuda's view say her speech code isn't necessary?
8. What is Conor Friedersdorf's view of hate speech laws?
9. How are hate speech laws misused in Europe, according to Glenn Greenwood?
10. What is Matsuda's proposed remedy for campus hate speech?

Exercise 3.2: Moral Arguments

1. What is Richard Stengel's argument for hate speech laws? Do you agree with him? Why or why not?
2. How does Conor Friedersdorf argue against Stengel's view on hate speech laws? Do you agree with Friedersdorf? Why or why not?
3. Do you believe that hate speech codes do more harm than good? Explain.

4. Do you think that Matsuda's hate speech law is a good idea? Why or why not?

5. Do you agree with Strossen that Matsuda's proposed speech law has a vagueness problem? Explain.

Notes

1. FIRE, "State of the Law: Speech Codes," https://www.thefire.org/legal/state-of-the-law-speech-codes/.
2. *Doe v. University of Michigan*, 721 F. Supp. 852 (E.D. Mich. 1989).
3. Found in *Doe v. University of Michigan*, 721 F. Supp. 852 (E.D. Mich. 1989).
4. Henry Louis Gates, Jr., "War of Words: Critical Race Theory and the First Amendment," in Henry Louis Gates, Jr., et al, *Speaking of Race, Speaking of Sex: Hate Speech, Civil Rights, and Civil Liberties* (New York: New York University Press, 1994), 45.
5. *Doe v. University of Michigan*, 721 F. Supp. 852 (E.D. Mich. 1989).
6. *UWM Post v. Board of Regents of U. of Wis.*, 774 F. Supp. 1163 (E.D. Wis. 1991).
7. *UWM Post v. Board of Regents of U. of Wis.*, 774 F. Supp. 1163 (E.D. Wis. 1991).
8. *McCauley v. University of the Virgin Islands*, 618 F.3d 232 (3rd Cir. 2010).
9 *McCauley v. University of the Virgin Islands*, 618 F.3d 232 (3rd Cir. 2010).
10. Erwin Chemerinsky and Howard Gillman, *Free Speech on Campus* (New Haven, CT: Yale University Press, 2017), 105–106.
11. Richard Stengel, "Why America Needs a Hate Speech Law," *Washington Post*, October 29, 2019, https://www.washingtonpost.com/opinions/2019/10/29/why-america-needs-hate-speech-law/.
12. Conor Friedersdorf, "Bad Arguments for Limiting Speech," *The Atlantic*, October 31, 2019, https://www.theatlantic.com/ideas/archive/2019/10/arguments-limiting-speech/601066/.
13. Mari J. Matsuda, "Public Response to Racist Speech: Considering the Victim's Story," *Michigan Law Review* 87, no. 8, Legal Storytelling (Aug., 1989): 2320–2381.
14. Matsuda, "Public Response to Racist Speech."
15. Matsuda, "Public Response to Racist Speech."
16. Azhar Majeed, "Defying the Constitution: The Rise, Persistence, and Prevalence of Campus Speech Codes," *Journal of Law & Public Policy*, 7 Geo. J.L. & Pub. Policy 481 (2009).
17. Glenn Greenwald, "In Europe, Hate Speech Laws Are Often Used to Suppress and Punish Left-Wing Viewpoints," *The Intercept*, August 29, 2017, https://theintercept.com/2017/08/29/in-europe-hate-speech-laws-are-often-used-to-suppress-and-punish-left-wing-viewpoints/.
18. Reports issued from the EU Fundamental Rights Agency, the Anti-Defamation League, Human Rights Watch, the European Parliament, and the UN High Commissioner for Human Rights.

Academic Freedom 4

For much of their history, American colleges and universities were not citadels of free inquiry and the open-ended search for knowledge. They were sectarian institutions where the main emphasis was on Christian piety and received wisdom, not on harnessing facts and reason to explore new ideas and discover truth. Academic freedom—roughly, the idea that professors should have maximum freedom to research, teach, and express new ideas—came slowly to American higher education, and after much struggle. Yet the idea is essential to the entire educational enterprise of modern colleges and universities. The role of professors is to create knowledge, notes Jonathan Zimmerman, "which requires continuous testing, discussion, and analysis":

> The process is both idiosyncratic and collective: professors need maximal personal freedom to try out new ideas, but they can't know if they've come up with anything truly new (or useful, or valuable, or visionary) until they have subjected it to a full and free examination by their peers. Hence any threat to their academic freedom threatens the core purpose of the academy itself. "No person of intelligence believes that all our political problems have been solved, or that the final stage of social evolution has been reached," the American Association of University of Professors (AAUP) resolved in 1915, in its first official statement on academic freedom. So the modern university "should be an intellectual experiment station," the AAUP continued, "where new ideas may germinate and where their fruit, though still distasteful to the community as a whole, may be allowed to ripen until finally, perchance, it may become part of the accepted intellectual food of the nation or of the world."[1]

According to the Association of Governing Boards of Universities and Colleges,

> American higher education relies on the fundamental value of academic freedom. Academic freedom protects college and university faculty members from unreasonable constraints on their professional activities. It is a broad doctrine giving faculty great leeway in addressing their academic subjects, allowing them even to challenge conventional wisdom. Under principles of academic freedom, a faculty member may research any topic. He or she may raise difficult subjects in a classroom discussion or may publish a controversial research paper. The excellence of America's higher education system rests on academic freedom.[2]

Yet in the last hundred years, the principle and practice of academic freedom have been resisted or thwarted again and again by university trustees, administrators, faculty members, the government, politicians, and the public (which often seemed not to be entirely comfortable with the idea of universities promoting free inquiry). In the early twentieth century, professors were fired for holding or expressing ideas deemed unacceptable or wrongheaded—for favoring union rights, for example, or for opposing the entry of the United States into World War I. In the 1950s, fear of communism and its influence seeped through society and the academy, giving rise to the McCarthy era when scores of professors were fired or refused tenure because of their real or imagined communist sympathies.

McCarthyism is long dead, and its threat to academic freedom is now widely recognized as extremist and antithetical to the core aims of higher education. But more recent events have raised questions not about the importance of academic freedom but about exactly what activities it does and does not protect. Consider a few cases cited in the *National Law Review*:

> At the University of Connecticut, a student group invited a right-wing blogger to deliver a lecture titled, "It's OK to be White." Before the speech even began, the audience began chanting, "Go home Nazi." Things spiraled out of control when a student snatched the blogger's speech and a scuffle ensued. Sonoma State University faced a similar controversy when a student read a politically charged poem during commencement. The poem promoted Black Lives Matter, disparaged Donald Trump, attacked Fox News, and used several expletives. The president of the university sparked backlash from students, alumni, and faculty when she apologized for the "mistake.". . .
>
> [In] *Bonnell v. Lorenzo*, a community college suspended a professor after a student filed a complaint about frequent profanity. The professor circulated the complaint to 200 faculty members, redacting the student's identifying information, and attached a satirical response titled *"An Apology: Yes, Virginia, There is a Sanity Clause."* The court held that free speech protected his distribution of the complaint and the "apology." But it did not protect the use of profanity that has no relation to the professor's coursework and that violated the college's sexual harassment policy.

More recently, a public university terminated a tenured professor for inappropriate and offensive classroom comments and behavior. The professor used profanity and discussed her sex life in the classroom. The Fifth Circuit recognized that while "classroom discussion is a protected activity" under academic freedom, even these protections have their limits. The court explained, "students, teachers, and professors are not permitted to say anything and everything simply because the words are uttered in the classroom context." The court emphasized that the use of profanity and the offensive discussion at issue was unrelated to her duties as a faculty member.[3]

Academic freedom is about both the liberty to learn and to teach. It applies to what professors and students say, believe, and do in and out of the classroom, to demands for trigger warnings and safe spaces, to the inviting or disinviting of visiting speakers, to defunding campus newspapers, and more. Controversies arise when the conventions of academic freedom conflict—or seem to conflict—with other important values such as equality, justice, dignity, and safety. Sorting out the conflicts requires a grasp of the nonmoral facts, knowledge of what academic freedom entails, and moral reasoning that's as clear-headed and unbiased as possible.

Faculty Freedom

Many in higher education—professors and students alike—aren't sure exactly what protections academic freedom provides, even though there is general agreement about their main elements. Here's an outline of some of the basic requirements, adapted from reports and policy statements from the American Association of University Professors (AAUP), the body that helped articulate the fundamentals of academic freedom a hundred years ago and has been refining and defending them ever since:

What Academic Freedom Does

1. Academic freedom means that both faculty members and students can engage in intellectual debate without fear of censorship or retaliation.
2. Academic freedom establishes a faculty member's right to remain true to his or her pedagogical philosophy and intellectual commitments. It preserves the intellectual integrity of our educational system and thus serves the public good.
3. Academic freedom in teaching means that both faculty members and students can make comparisons and contrasts between subjects taught in a course and any field of human knowledge or period of history.
4. Academic freedom gives both students and faculty the right to express their views—in speech, writing, and through electronic communication, both on and off campus—without fear of sanction, unless the manner

of expression substantially impairs the rights of others or, in the case of faculty members, those views demonstrate that they are professionally ignorant, incompetent, or dishonest with regard to their discipline or fields of expertise.

5. Academic freedom gives both students and faculty the right to study and do research on the topics they choose and to draw what conclusions they find consistent with their research, though it does not prevent others from judging whether their work is valuable and their conclusions sound. To protect academic freedom, universities should oppose efforts by corporate or government sponsors to block dissemination of any research findings.

6. Academic freedom means that the political, religious, or philosophical beliefs of politicians, administrators, and members of the public cannot be imposed on students or faculty.

What Academic Freedom Doesn't Do

1. Academic freedom does not mean a faculty member can harass, threaten, intimidate, ridicule, or impose his or her views on students.

2. Student academic freedom does not deny faculty members the right to require students to master course material and the fundamentals of the disciplines that faculty teach.

3. Neither academic freedom nor tenure protects an incompetent teacher from losing his or her job. Academic freedom thus does not grant an unqualified guarantee of lifetime employment.

4. Academic freedom does not protect faculty members from colleague or student challenges to or disagreement with their educational philosophy and practices.

5. Academic freedom does not protect faculty members from non–university penalties if they break the law.

6. Academic freedom does not give students or faculty the right to ignore college or university regulations, though it does give faculty and students the right to criticize regulations they believe are unfair.

7. Academic freedom does not protect students or faculty from disciplinary action, but it does require that they receive fair treatment and due process.

8. Academic freedom does not protect faculty members from sanctions for professional misconduct, though sanctions require clear proof established through due process.[4]

These conditions suggest that the core value in higher education is not free speech but academic freedom, which demands adherence to standards of intellectual honesty and professional conduct that can actually constrain free speech. As Sigal Ben-Porath says,

> [As] part of their commitment to teaching—developing and disseminating knowledge—instructors are bound by intellectual honesty in ways that can in fact limit their expression. For example, they must not lie in class, even as free speech permits them to lie; they must focus on the relevant and important subject matter, even as free speech allows them to read their favorite poems rather than teach. In other words, academic freedom is more demanding and more limiting than free speech rules, and it is academic freedom, rather than the more general contours of free speech, that should guide classroom (and lab clinic) work.[5]

Plenty of campus conflicts have tested just how much freedom professors really have—or should have—to express controversial ideas outside the educational setting (what academics call extramural speech). One of the more publicized cases is that of Steven Salaita, whose offer of tenure was revoked by the University of Illinois because of some contentious tweets:

> Professor Steven G. Salaita had tweeted, "If you're defending Israel right now, you're an awful human being" and used obscenities and vitriolic language in denouncing Israel's military actions in Gaza. At one point, he said, "At this point, if Netanyahu appeared on TV with a necklace made from the teeth of Palestinian children, would anybody be surprised?"
>
> Supporting the revocation, the former president of the AAUP said, "Academic freedom does not require you to hire someone whose views you consider despicable." He continued, "It's not a violation of academic freedom to decide you don't approve of someone's publications or their public use of social media. It's not a violation of academic freedom to decide not to hire someone with a deplorable role as a public intellectual." But the Illinois division of the AAUP disagreed, calling the decision "a clear violation of Professor Salaita's academic freedom and an affront to free speech that we enjoy in this country." The Illinois division argued that nothing in the statements raised questions about Salaita's fitness to teach and the statements were on social media outside the presence of students. Ultimately, Professor Salaita sued, and the case settled for $875,000. However, the University did not give him the job, and both sides claim it as a win.[6]

So the question is, should academic freedom protect the right of professors to express ideas outside the university setting that are inflammatory and vicious?

What if the ideas are not just controversial but demonstrably false? Consider the case of Joy Karega, who in 2016 was an assistant professor of rhetoric and composition at Oberlin College and an impassioned supporter of the Israel boycott movement. Her social media posts shocked the school's trustees, who considered them "anti-Semitic and abhorrent." As reported in *Inside Higher Ed*,

Fig. 4.1 Protesters stand in the back with signs during the University of Illinois Faculty Senate meeting in Urbana, Illinois, where university Chancellor Phyllis Wise spoke about the decision not to hire professor Steven Salaita over his profane, anti-Israel Twitter messages.

she also posted a series of "declarations that most educated people, let alone people with doctorates and regardless of their positions on Israel, would reject as unsupported by fact. All were posted while she was on the faculty at Oberlin."

> In November 2015, for example, she wrote that ISIS is really part of Mossad, an Israeli intelligence unit, and the U.S. Central Intelligence Agency. "It's troubling that in this day and age, where there is all this access to information, most of the general public doesn't know who and what ISIS really is. I promise you, ISIS is not a jihadist, Islamic terrorist organization. It's a CIA and Mossad operation and there's too much information out there for the general public not to know this."
>
> Quoting a blog that reports on many conspiracy theories and describes itself as a "weekly whack at the global oligarchy," Karega also last year posted that Israel was responsible for the downing of Malaysian Airlines Flight No. 17, which has widely been attributed to Russian-backed separatists in Ukraine. In another post, she wrote that Netanyahu visited Paris after the Charlie Hebdo massacre "just in case the message wasn't received via Mossad and the 'attacks' they orchestrated on Paris." (Netanyahu was in Paris after the attacks, but to visit Jewish people in France who were attacked.) Karega shared a video from Nation of Islam leader Louis Farrakhan suggesting that Zionists and Israeli Jews were behind 9/11, and wrote that he was "truth-telling," as well, according to The Tower.[7]

At first the college, while not condoning Karega's statements, affirmed that academic freedom gave her the right to express them. But after an investigation, the board of trustees voted to dismiss her for "failing to meet the academic standards that Oberlin requires of its faculty and failing to demonstrate intellectual honesty."

So while tweeting about a serious issue, does a professor have the right to make outrageous extramural assertions that are unsupported by the facts, as Karega did? What if a professor says online that the QAnon conspiracy theory is true and that Democrats are Satanic pedophiles? Or that the 2012 Sandy Hook Elementary School massacre was a hoax? Or that the moon landings were faked?

The AAUP position on faculty asserting such dubious ideas is straightforward: professors have the right to make all sorts of extramural claims, even baseless ones, unless their views demonstrate professional incompetence or dishonesty in their field of expertise. As one AAUP associate says,

> If, for example, a physics professor declared on Twitter that the Sept. 11 attacks were a hoax, AAUP would advocate for the professor's right to free speech in extramural utterances (it doesn't distinguish between free speech in person or online). But if the physics professor declared that the world is flat, denying all scientific evidence to the contrary, that could call into question his or her professional fitness.[8]

Some scholars would go further than the AAUP and insist that academic freedom protects *all* extramural speech, even if it is demonstrably false and would be, if asserted as part of professional duties, reason to question a professor's competence. What matters is the professor's work and words in his or her profession. They say professional standards cannot and should not be applied to Twitter posts and random comments made in a health club or bar.

But what if a professor's extramural pronouncements are not just false or ridiculous but alleged to be bigoted or racist? Karega's behavior was thought to fall into this category, but here's an even more provocative and sensational case, that of Charles Negy, an associate professor of psychology. According to the *Tampa Bay Times*:

> A spate of Twitter posts by a controversial University of Central Florida professor has prompted calls for his firing and denunciations from university officials who said his remarks were racist.
>
> The school also said it will investigate the teaching practices of the faculty member, Charles Negy, a long-time psychology professor with tenure.
>
> In remarks posted this week, Negy said leaders who encourage diversity are promoting divisiveness and tribalism, and he described African Americans as a privileged group "shielded from legitimate criticism."
>
> An online petition with more than 16,000 signatures calls for Negy to be fired for his "abhorrent racist comments" and "perverse transphobia and sexism."

Fig. 4.2 Charles Negy, associate professor of psychology at the University of Central Florida.

[Negy had posted:]

> Sincere question: If Afr. Americans as a group, had the same behavioral profile as Asian Americans (on average, performing the best academically, having the highest income, committing the lowest crime, etc.), would we still be proclaiming "systematic racism" exists?
>
> This article is spot on (will infuriate folks). Black privilege is real: Besides affirm. action, special scholarships and other set asides, being shielded from legitimate criticism is a privilege. But as a group, they're missing out on much needed feedback.
>
> Hilarious. Okay Whiteys. Get on your knees and start atoning for being white. While you're at it, start sharing your paycheck with random POC and donate your house to a POC. LMAO.

The university tweeted that Negy's posts are "completely counter" to UCF's values and that officials were "reviewing the matter while being mindful of the First Amendment."

On Thursday night, the university also sent out a note signed by the UCF president Alexander Cartwright and other top administrators condemning Negy's posts and thanking students who have spoken up.

"At a time when so many of our community members are hurting, we are disgusted by the racist posts one of our faculty members has shared on his personal Twitter account," the note said. "At all times, we uphold the principles of academic freedom, but we have a responsibility to denounce intolerance. Racism is an undeniable reality across our society, and people of color frequently experience overt and covert racism. That is why Negy's words are not only wrong, but particularly painful." . . .

In an email interview with the *New York Times*, Negy defended his comments and said he was not a white supremacist or racist and was critical of all ethnic and cultural groups. "Despite what so many 'haters' are saying about me on Twitter, I've never said ANYTHING critical of George Floyd," Nagy told the *Times*, referring to the Minnesota man who died May 25 at the hands of police. "The man was murdered in cold blood by a man who was a total sadist. So cruel."[9]

UCF said it was investigating both Negy's Twitter posts and accusations of bias in his classroom. The university's response seemed in line with the AAUP's principles on academic freedom: bias or discrimination against students in the classroom is unacceptable and punishable, but extramural speech is protected. According to the *New York Times*,

Michael Johnson, the interim provost [at UCF], said that tenured faculty members at the public university can generally be removed only for incompetence or misconduct, which would have to be proved through a careful investigation.

"We can act when people's conduct is in the course of their job, when it's in their classroom, when it's with their colleagues," he said during an online meeting with students angered by Dr. Negy's comments. "People's behavior is something we can act upon. But we can't act on people's speech outside the university."[10]

Many students accused Negy of discriminatory conduct in class, and some saw his online comments as evidence of that. In any case, they wanted him fired. As one student said, "As a black woman, if it's not safe for me in a classroom, then where is it safe? . . . I'm paying a lot of money to come here. And I'm funding someone who makes other people, other students, feel small."[11]

But even assuming Negy's classroom behavior was above reproach, his Twitter posts still pose some critical questions. First, did his extramural speech cause harm, as many students believed—specifically, did it cause the kind of harm to marginalized students that Jeremy Waldron calls dignitary harm, and if so what response to that is morally justified? This issue of harm can be sorted out using the analysis proposed in Chapter 2.

Second, were Negy's online comments indeed racist? If they were, then the question becomes whether his racist attitude rendered him professionally incompetent. Should having racist beliefs alone disqualify someone from holding a professorship? This question is not as easy to answer as some might think: scholars point out that many people don't understand what racism is and often misidentify who or what is racist. We will interrogate the concepts of race and racism in the next chapter.

Classroom Freedom

In recent years, classroom instruction has become a political issue, with numerous critics contending that it is politically biased, doctrinaire, offensive, or discriminatory. As in most campus conflicts, there is truth in some of these charges but also misunderstandings and flawed reasoning.

Indoctrination versus Education

Many Americans believe that higher education is not really education but *indoctrination*—often meaning indoctrination in the dogmas of liberal politics. As we've seen, early American higher education was indeed more about indoctrination than critical thinking and open-minded learning. The evidence cited in Chapter 2, however, suggests that the contemporary charge of rampant indoctrination is an exaggeration. But we still need to ask: what is the difference between education and indoctrination? The AAUP agrees that indoctrination should be avoided and distinguishes it from education:

> It is not indoctrination for professors to expect students to comprehend ideas and apply knowledge that is accepted within a relevant discipline. For example, it is not indoctrination for professors of biology to require students to understand principles of evolution; indeed, it would be a dereliction of professional responsibility to fail to do so. Students must remain free to question generally accepted beliefs if they can do so, in the words of the 1915 *Declaration of Principles on Academic Freedom and Academic Tenure*, using "a scholar's method and . . . in a scholar's spirit." But professors of logic may insist that students accept the logical validity of the syllogism, and professors of astronomy may insist that students accept the proposition that the earth orbits around the sun, unless in either case students have good logical or astronomical grounds to differ.
>
> This process is instruction, not indoctrination. As John Dewey pointed out a century ago, the methods by which these particular conclusions have been drawn have become largely uncontested. Dewey believed that it was an abuse of "freedom in the classroom" for an instructor to "promulgate *as truth* ideas or opinions which have *not* been tested," that is, which have not been accepted as true within a discipline.
>
> Dewey's point suggests that indoctrination occurs whenever an instructor insists that students accept *as truth* propositions that are in fact professionally contestable. If an instructor advances such propositions dogmatically, without allowing students to challenge their validity or advance alternative understandings, the instructor stands guilty of indoctrination.[12]

Merely exposing students to particular beliefs—whether unorthodox, unpopular, liberal, or conservative—is not in itself indoctrination. Nor is it indoctrination for instructors to tell students that, based on their research and study, they think a particular view is true, even if the view does not represent the consensus of opinion in the field. As the AAUP notes,

> It is not indoctrination for an economist to say to his students that in his view the creation of markets is the most effective means for promoting growth in underdeveloped nations, or for a biologist to assert her belief that evolution occurs through punctuated equilibriums rather than through continuous processes.[13]

Nor is it indoctrination for an instructor to assign a particular book for study, even a controversial, provocative, or partisan book. Assigning teaching materials does not constitute their endorsement or indicate how they will be used in the course. From their assignment, we can conclude only that the instructor believes they are worth discussing.

"Indoctrination occurs," says the AAUP, "when instructors dogmatically insist on the truth of . . . propositions by refusing to accord their students the opportunity to contest them."[14] Instructors indoctrinate not when they assert particular propositions but when they assert them and will permit no disagreement from students.

Indoctrination is bad because the central role of higher education is not the transmission of dogma but the fostering of an independence of mind and critical thinking. Education is not indoctrination just because it is challenging, uncomfortable, and contrary to our preferred beliefs.

Trigger Warnings

Trigger, or content, warnings are statements from teachers alerting students to course material that might be traumatizing, stigmatizing, offensive, or disturbing. Students have demanded trigger warnings to counter expression they believe could harm those who have been traumatized (by sexual assault or war, for example) or who are members of vulnerable groups that have been discriminated against or oppressed. Trigger warnings have been applied to course material about rape, racism, homophobia, transphobia, bullying, pregnancy, suicide, and literary classics like Ovid's *Metamorphoses* and F. Scott Fitzgerald's *The Great Gatsby*. Oberlin College considered (but did not implement) a policy that would have required trigger warnings on any course content that discussed racism, classism, sexism, heterosexism, cissexism, and ableism. Many teachers use trigger warnings to prepare students who might be disturbed by particular course content or class discussions, and they have been doing so for years. But most faculty members object to being required to use them, regarding them as

Fig. 4.3 Michele Moody-Adams, professor of political philosophy and legal theory at Columbia University. She says that trigger warnings designed to shield students against offense raise a serious question: do students have a right *not to be offended*? She argues that they do not.

threats to their academic freedom and as restraints on their ability to teach a subject properly. Many teachers have also charged that trigger warnings are bad because they treat adult students like children who need to be shielded from harsh realities.

Trigger warnings are thought to counteract two different negative effects of course content: *offense* and *harm*. Offense happens, as Michele Moody-Adams explains, when students "find material offensive to their sensibilities, their moral and religious, or their sense of their own identities."[15] Trigger warnings designed to shield students against offense raise a serious question: do students have a right *not to be offended*? Moody-Adams thinks not:

> In agreement with (current) American constitutional law, I have argued that they do not have such a right, although instructors (and other campus officials) have a morally and professionally weighty duty to be as respectful as possible of earnest disagreement.[16]

The AAUP agrees and argues that shielding students from uncomfortable content directly conflicts with the central aim of higher education:

> The presumption that students need to be protected rather than challenged in a classroom is at once infantilizing and anti-intellectual. It makes comfort a higher priority than intellectual engagement and—as the Oberlin list demonstrates—it

singles out politically controversial topics like sex, race, class, capitalism, and colonialism for attention. Indeed, if such topics are associated with triggers, correctly or not, they are likely to be marginalized if not avoided altogether by faculty who fear complaints for offending or discomforting some of their students. Although all faculty are affected by potential charges of this kind, non-tenured and contingent faculty are particularly at risk. In this way the demand for trigger warnings creates a repressive, "chilly climate" for critical thinking in the classroom. . . .

Some discomfort is inevitable in classrooms if the goal is to expose students to new ideas, have them question beliefs they have taken for granted, grapple with ethical problems they have never considered, and, more generally, expand their horizons so as to become informed and responsible democratic citizens. Trigger warnings suggest that classrooms should offer protection and comfort rather than an intellectually challenging education. They reduce students to vulnerable victims rather than full participants in the intellectual process of education. The effect is to stifle thought on the part of both teachers and students who fear to raise questions that might make others "uncomfortable."[17]

Moody-Adams says that the strong desire not to be offended can be found on both the political Left (when, for example, students are offended by a Western classic) and political Right (when discussions turn to cultural and religious diversity). She contends that these aversions

often reflect a widespread tendency toward intolerance, and that this intolerance is usually rooted in anti-intellectual resistance to the possibility that serious disagreement can be discussed in a civil and respectful fashion.

This anti-intellectualism means that contemporary students . . . are skeptical of the transformative power of ideas, and fundamentally resistant to the defining purposes of a university education—especially the aims of education in the liberal arts.[18]

Preventing harm (rather than offense) to vulnerable students is probably the most common justification given for using trigger warnings. The warnings first used on campus covered sexual assault and rape out of concern that the words and images might provoke traumatic memories, panic, or anxiety in victims. Soon trigger warnings were requested for students who had endured any significant trauma, including veterans suffering from posttraumatic stress disorder (PTSD), as well as for those who claimed much less disturbing experiences or phobias.

Health experts maintain that serious trauma, like the kind caused by extreme violence or abuse, requires medical treatment. Trigger warnings for these conditions, then, would be an inadequate response, especially since reactions to triggers are variable and unpredictable, with some individuals triggered by sensory stimuli, some by words, some dramatically affected, some hardly at all.

Many teachers are nevertheless willing to use trigger warnings in some cases as long as their use can be reconciled with intellectual honesty—that is, with covering material essential to understanding the course's subject. Sigal Ben-Porath is one of those teachers:

> An instructor will be smart to let her students know what is coming ahead in a course so that they can decide how to prepare and even whether participating is in their best interest. Intellectual candor does not demand springing surprises on students to see how they respond or how resilient they are. Preparing for class requires reading the material, thinking ahead, and planning. Trigger warnings—or whatever else one might call the courteous forewarning by a professor ("tough topic ahead!")—should be seen as a matter of good pedagogy and academic practice rather than a surrender to weakness and laziness of thought. In most cases, there is no need or strong justification to permit students to avoid a class because of its "triggering"—painful, traumatic, harmful—content, but sometimes that allowance is acceptable. It's a small price for a criminal law class to pay if a student who suffered trauma avoids class discussion on rape laws. She would still need to pass the same requirements and do the same (or equivalent) work as decided in consultation with her professor. Deriding her for her difficulty does nothing to improve the discussion or strengthen her knowledge and educational experience. On the other hand, expanding the demand for trigger warnings to include exemptions from classes or assignments for trivial reasons undermines the overall justified cause of this pedagogic mechanism.[19]

Some scholars and students have called for trigger warnings to counter a more generalized kind of trauma—the kind thought to occur when marginalized students are exposed to material (literary, historical, etc.) that is stigmatizing, discriminatory, or demeaning. An assumption often underlying this view is that the trauma or harm of past oppression or discrimination is intrinsically injurious—that is, there is nothing you can do about it except avoid being triggered. Many experts, however, have called this assumption into question. As noted in Chapter 2, psychologists point out that whether words or images are harmful depends on a host of factors, not the least of which is how they are received. When confronted with disparaging, subordinating speech, some people react with anger and hurt while others respond with defiance, courage, or counterspeech. Moreover, the idea that those who suffer psychological pain due to oppression and discrimination are helpless to overcome it is belied by history and human experience. The list of counterexamples to this helplessness narrative is long, running from African American abolitionists like Frederick Douglass and Harriet Tubman to the heroes of the American civil rights movement to many champions of social justice today.

Many educators go further and insist that one of the central functions of liberal education is to help students confront expressive harm and channel their own experiences of harm into something constructive. Moody-Adams cites the famous African American writer James Baldwin as an exemplar of this attitude:

> Baldwin gestures toward a powerful defense of a liberal education with this fundamentally hopeful view that sustained engagement with the suffering of others can enable both a deeper understanding of one's own suffering, and a sense of how one's own capacity to suffer *really* (and constructively) connects one to other human beings. . . . Developing such an understanding sometimes depends on the willingness to try to divest troubling and disturbing expression of its power to wound. This process of divesting expression of the power to wound draws, in turn, on our capacity to temporarily inure ourselves against expressive harm so that we can ask what we might be able to learn *even* from texts, or traditions of thought, with the power to produce that harm. It seems likely that inuring himself against expressive harm was precisely what allowed Baldwin to produce essays like *The Fire Next Time* which not only challenged the cruelties and injustices of discrimination and oppression even as they continued, but unsparingly demanded that both the oppressed and the oppressors learn how to see the world, and themselves, in new ways.[20]

Safe Spaces

In the most general sense, a **safe space** is an environment or atmosphere on campus thought to be a refuge or haven for students. The term immediately raises the questions, Safe *from* what? and Safe *for* what? Answers vary, some of them more defensible than others. One answer that has been relentlessly ridiculed in the media is that students need spaces where they can be shielded from words or ideas that make them feel offended, uncomfortable, or unsafe. Critics of higher education have enjoyed mocking this attitude, calling students overprotected "crybullies" who can't handle encounters with contrary views. But whatever the merits of this criticism, it misses some larger truths implicit in the notion of safe spaces.

First, a foundational premise of modern higher education is that students should feel free to *express* the widest range of views while being recognized as equal members of the campus community in good standing. In this sense, *every* space should be a safe space for student expression. But simply declaring that students have a right of free speech is not enough because, as noted previously, free speech can be constrained by more than censorship. If students decline to express their opinions out of fear of being ridiculed or demeaned, or when their dignity, humanity, or worthiness is called into question, they certainly don't inhabit a safe space. They may have a right to speak, but they may be effectively silenced nonetheless. For many students, a call for safe spaces is a call not for protection from contrary ideas but a plea that free speech be made available to all in practice as well as in theory. Erwin Chemerinsky and Howard Gillman make the point:

> It is appropriate—and even necessary—for campuses and professors to do all they can to make sure that the classroom is a safe space for scholarly exploration, civil debate, reasoned discussion, and making mistakes. The best educational environments remove fears that students may have about asking certain questions or challenging prevailing explanations; the worst environments are those where students feel that they can be punished for expressing views that the professor or other classmates consider heretical. A classroom should be a place where antiracism advocates can ask about the role of race in the choice of course materials, conservatives can question the wisdom or constitutionality of affirmative action, and socialists can criticize the dominant position of the concept of efficiency in economic models. It is a good thing when the idea of a "safe space" refers to a place where one feels safe to *express* an opinion, without punishment, harassing judgment, or bullying condemnation.[21]

Michael S. Roth, president of Wesleyan University, agrees and calls this sense of safety on campus "safe enough":

> To be sure, there are plenty of examples of sanctimonious "safetyism"— counterproductive coddling of students who feel fragile. Instead of teaching young people to find resources in themselves to deal with chagrin and anxiety, some school officials offer hand-holding, beanbags and puppies. . . .
>
> On the other hand, the outright dismissal of safe spaces can amount to a harmful disregard for the well-being of students; it can perpetuate environments where the entitled continue to dominate those around them and students never learn how to build a more equitable, inclusive community. With mental health and suicide crises emerging on some campuses, the idea of universities taking conscious steps to protect and nurture students emotionally as well as physically should be welcome.
>
> So what's a university to do?
>
> The first answer is obvious: We should begin by destigmatizing the notion of safe spaces and stop talking about them as if they were part of a zero-sum ideological war.
>
> As a college president for almost 20 years, I am a strong proponent of creating spaces that are "safe enough" on college campuses. . . . Like families, campus cultures are different, but each should promote a basic sense of inclusion and respect that enables students to learn and grow—to be open to ideas and perspectives so that the differences they encounter are educative. That basic sense is feeling "safe enough."[22]

Of course, the prerequisite for this or any other kind of protected discourse on campus is *physical* safety. Roth explains:

> For different people at different times, safety can mean different things, but the baseline is certainly physical security. For most of the past 100 years,

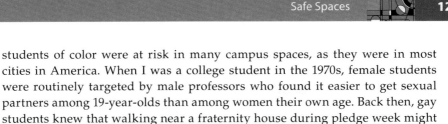
students of color were at risk in many campus spaces, as they were in most cities in America. When I was a college student in the 1970s, female students were routinely targeted by male professors who found it easier to get sexual partners among 19-year-olds than among women their own age. Back then, gay students knew that walking near a fraternity house during pledge week might result in getting beaten up as part of a pledging ritual. There were plenty of campus spaces that weren't safe for different segments of the student body. Today, campuses are safer, and it would be hard to find anyone arguing that this isn't a good thing.[23]

The concept of safe spaces has also been applied to places on campus where students related by race, ethnicity, politics, religion, sexual orientation, or life experiences can gather for mutual support in a welcoming environment. Students have a right of association, and dorms, fraternities, sororities, societies, and clubs are ways to exercise that right. These gatherings of like-minded groups function best not as isolation chambers but as places to draw comfort and strength for meeting the challenges posed by unfamiliar people and ideas that make up college life.

The most controversial conception of safe spaces is the one mentioned earlier, which refers not to freedom to express views but freedom *from* expressed views (meaning views that are protected speech, not threats or harassment, for example). Students have said things like "His words make me feel unsafe, and I don't deserve to feel afraid at my school"—and they believe the words should be restricted accordingly. The arguments just cited about offense and expressive harm related to trigger warnings could apply here, and so could arguments cited in Chapters 2 and 3 about hate speech and speech codes. Thus, it is at least not obvious that banning protected speech that threatens a person's sense of safety is morally justified.

Some commentators have asked, in effect, if censorship of offending viewpoints is used to carve out a safe space for those who feel unsafe when exposed to those viewpoints, where will the censorship end? If censorship of particular views is mandated, then how can censorship of opposing views be justifiably denied? If LGBTQ students feel offended by religious students who condemn homosexuality as depraved, what should be done about LGBTQ speech that makes religious students feel unsafe? Campus debates about Israel have involved dueling claims of safe spaces. Jewish students have declared that the campus Boycott, Diversity, and Sanctions (BDS) movement against Israel makes them feel unsafe, and BDS members with Middle Eastern backgrounds have reportedly also felt unsafe.

One of the claims often heard in safe space debates is that the university should not be just a place of learning but also a home for its students. This expectation is understandable. It also fits with the modern conception of colleges as businesses designed to keep its customers (students) happy and comfortable.

Critics, however, say the emphasis on home does not, in the long run, serve the interests of students. Moody-Adams explains:

> Maya Angelou once observed that "the ache for home lives in all of us," and that, at the very least, home is "the safe place where we can go as we are and not be questioned." But the university should not try to be a "home" in this sense. The intellectual ferment of the 1960s and 1970s helped to make the university less "safe" for exclusion because the university contained "spaces" in which its constituents could not avoid challenges to its own homogeneity. The ideals of diversity and inclusion that arose as part of these challenges are now being called into question by the "new tribalism" of the twenty-first century. The university can provide contexts for substantive debate about a constructive response only if we protect academic freedom *in* the classroom, and reasonable freedom of expression in campus spaces *outside of it*. Of course, the confrontation and contestation that are essential to vigorous debate must be balanced by civility and respect. But we must strike that balance in a way that enhances the transformative projects of a liberal education and restores confidence that these projects are critical to democratic flourishing. . . .
>
> [W]e should support well thought-out efforts to make all students feel welcome in, and valued by, the institutions they attend. But being welcome in college or university is not the same thing as being "at home." When the university is purged of every form of expression that may cause discomfort, the only thing it will be "safe" for is the worst excesses of the "new tribalism."[24]

It should not be surprising that many, perhaps most, college professors consider ideological comfort and safety to be impediments to education and intellectual maturity. Ruth Simmons, former Brown University president and the first African American president of an Ivy League school, has asserted this attitude bluntly:

> You know something that I hate? When people say, "That doesn't make me feel good about myself." I say, "That's not what you're here for." . . . I believe that learning at its best is the antithesis of comfort. If you come to the [campus] for comfort, I would urge you to walk [through] yon iron gate. . . . But if you seek betterment for yourself, for your community and posterity, stay and fight.[25]

No Platforming

No platforming (deplatforming) raises many of the same moral issues that relate to trigger warnings and safe spaces, but it deserves separate treatment here. **No platforming** is the policy or practice of barring someone from speaking on campus because of their expressed opinions. It is not just a form of protest, but a way to deny speakers a venue for expressing their views, and it encompasses both banning and disinviting. No platforming was implemented in the United

Kingdom in the 1970s by the National Union of Students (NUS) to prohibit student organizations from inviting fascists from the National Front Party to speak on British campuses. Eventually the NUS expanded its blacklist to include a variety of speakers whose opinions were deemed anti-Semitic, Islamophobic, racist, misogynistic, or otherwise offensive or discriminatory. No platforming is still practiced in the United Kingdom, welcomed by some, condemned by others, and controversial everywhere.

In the United States, no platforming has been used for years, although the number of occurrences has been declining recently. There have been calls from activists on both the political Left and Right to no-platform speakers. The list of those no-platformed is long and includes feminist and social critic Camille Paglia; conservative columnist Ann Coulter; Palestinian feminist and militant Leila Khaled; former US Secretary of State Madeleine Albright; feminist, human rights activist, and critic of Islam Ayaan Hirsi Ali; former US Secretary of Homeland Security Jeh Johnson; literary theorist, author, and public intellectual Stanley Fish; founder of the private military company Blackwater Erik Prince; cognitive psychologist Elizabeth Loftus; conservative political commentator

Fig. 4.4 Protesters shout before a speaking engagement by Ben Shapiro on the campus of the University of California Berkeley, September 14, 2017. Several streets around the University were closed off with concrete and plastic barriers ahead of an evening appearance by the conservative commentator.

Ben Shapiro; philosopher and social critic Cornel West; and daughter of President Trump and businesswoman Ivanka Trump.

Probably the most well-known argument for no platforming is one that appeals to the principle of equality. Ulrich Baer lays out the case in his 2019 book *What Snowflakes Get Right: Free Speech, Truth, and Equality on Campus.* ("Snowflakes" is the derisive term critics have used to refer to students who protest speakers.) He maintains that speakers who demean or marginalize minorities or other vulnerable groups are not just being offensive. They are calling into question people's moral worth and humanity and therefore undermining their freedom of speech and their right of equal participation. Hate speech—racist, homophobic, transphobic, misogynistic, Islamophobic—sends the message that certain people are not qualified to take part in debate or dialogue. Here is Baer making the argument:

> For the concept of free speech to be meaningful, the participation of some speakers must not be restricted on the basis of inalienable qualities. You may be refuted in a debate because your arguments are weak, wrong or badly phrased, but you must not be excluded a priori based on whether or not you count as fully human. To invite a speaker who categorically excludes some human beings from the consideration of rights, which is what some of the most contentious campus debates are about, severs the idea of speech rights from its goal of protecting individual liberty. A campus speaker who argues that some students are inherently inferior, materially undermines the conditions that make speech free. . . .
>
> Racism . . . serves to place additional burdens and requirements on some people, but not others. It alters the conditions of participation not incidentally but by design, and in this way materially undermines the workings of an equality-based society. . . .
>
> The recent student demonstrations at Auburn against [Richard] Spencer's visit— as well as protests on other campuses against Charles Murray, Milo Yiannopoulos, and others—should be understood as an attempt to ensure the conditions of free speech for a greater group of people, rather than censorship.[26]

As Baer sees it, the central value to be defended in no-platforming controversies is not free speech absolutism but equality, and curtailing the speech of invited speakers may be necessary to protect the equal rights of students. He believes, along with most other theorists, that speech is never just a vehicle for content. It can be an exercise of power, a way to elevate the rights and status of some and to devalue the status and rights of others.

As we've seen, many observers recognize the harms that hate speech can provoke but also reject censorship on several grounds. They argue that censorship is a risky response that, once used, can be directed against almost anyone, including those who call for censoring. Free speech advocate Samantha Harris, for example, says that those who demand censorship for what they believe to be hate speech "fail to grasp that when an individual's or group's subjective reaction to speech is allowed to determine what can or can't be said, no one's expressive rights are secure."[27] Chemerinsky and Gillman remind us that historically "the power to punish speech has been used primarily against social outcasts, vulnerable minorities, and those protesting for positive change—the very people toward whom our students are most sympathetic."[28] Critics of censorship have also noted with alarm that speech bans designed to counter hate speech often end up being used to punish people simply for voicing ideas that others don't like. This is the slippery slope problem of censorship.

We also know that scholars dispute the idea that the harms of hate speech (both dignitary and psychological harms) are unavoidable or unalterable. They reject the view that students are helpless and vulnerable victims of expressive harm, arguing that students have the ability to divest such expression of its power to wound and to resist and counter it. They assert that available evidence suggests censorship of hate speech does not effectively promote equality and does not reduce the amount of hate speech, discriminatory conduct, or racial or ethnic violence.

Many contend that students are right to demand protection of their equal status and rights (what Ben-Porath calls "dignitary safety") but that dignitary safety should not amount to "intellectual safety." She maintains that "intellectual safety—the refusal to listen to challenges to one's views or to consider opposing viewpoints—is harmful to the open-minded inquiry that defines any university worth the name."[29]

Censorship, several commentators argue, short-circuits the essential task of understanding, debunking, and defanging hateful, racist, bigoted messages. Harris declares:

> Such a view [that we must protect adult college students from hateful, offensive expression] is also wholly counterproductive to the goal of producing informed citizens who can effectively counter views they find dangerous. Shielding students from controversial or offensive viewpoints deprives them of the opportunity to develop the argumentation and critical thinking skills necessary to lead the country in a different direction. Bad ideas cannot simply be wished away; they must be defeated in the marketplace of ideas. And to be defeated, they must first be fully understood.[30]

In a statement to Rutgers graduates—a statement that students have both praised and criticized—former president Barack Obama explained why he was opposed to no platforming:

> I know a couple years ago, folks on this campus got upset that Condoleezza Rice was supposed to speak at a commencement. Now, I don't think it's a secret that I disagree with many of the foreign policies of Dr. Rice and the previous

administration. But the notion that this community or the country would be better served by not hearing from a former Secretary of State, or shutting out what she had to say—I believe that's misguided. I don't think that's how democracy works best, when we're not even willing to listen to each other. I believe that's misguided.

If you disagree with somebody, bring them in and ask them tough questions. Hold their feet to the fire. Make them defend their positions. If somebody has got a bad or offensive idea, prove it wrong. Engage it. Debate it. Stand up for what you believe in. Don't be scared to take somebody on. Don't feel like you got to shut your ears off because you're too fragile and somebody might offend your sensibilities. Go at them if they're not making any sense.

Use your logic and reason and words. And by doing so, you'll strengthen your own position, and you'll hone your arguments. And maybe you'll learn something and realize you don't know everything. And you may have a new understanding not only about what your opponents believe but maybe what you believe. Either way, you win. And more importantly, our democracy wins.[31]

The prevention of expressive harm versus free speech, however, is not the only way to frame the controversy over no platforming. Robert Mark Simpson and Amia Srinivasan argue that no platforming can be justified not by appealing to prevention of speech harms but by defending the norms of academic freedom. They say the case for barring speakers on grounds that their words may harm listeners is weak, and it is based on the dubious assumption that the academy is an extension of the public square, where the content of protected speech is governed by principles of free speech. They argue that principles of academic freedom, unlike principles of free speech, can justify no platforming of speakers based on the content of their viewpoints. According to the norms of academic freedom, the no platforming of some speakers is necessary to allow teachers and researchers to uphold the academic standards of their disciplines and do their work free from external interference. By these lights, speakers espousing views that conflict with the well-established findings of academic disciplines should be no-platformed. Those who deny climate change, declare there are racial differences in intelligence, deny the historical reality of the Holocaust, reject the theory of biological evolution, or argue women cannot understand mathematics as well as men can would be—and should be—excluded from speaking. According to Simpson and Srinivasan,

> The civil libertarians who condemn no platforming routinely characterize the university as an institution that should be defined by a commitment to free speech. And this seems credible at face value. . . .
>
> The problem, however, is that this view treats the university as if it were just an outlet in the marketplace of ideas or an extension of the public square. This is a mischaracterization. Universities are specialized technical institutions that exist for purposes of teaching and research. Communicative norms and practices in universities reflect these purposes. . . .

In addition, the communicative norms and practices of universities also give recognized disciplinary experts—that is, academic faculty—various kinds of control over the speech of others, as is needed to uphold the intellectual rigors of, and thus promote the epistemic aims of, their disciplines. In the public square we tolerate the speech of flat-earth cranks, shills paid to undermine climate science, and revisionist historians who espouse conspiratorial misreadings of the evidence. As long as they don't harass anyone we let them say their piece. But such people aren't owed an opportunity to teach History 101 or publish in scientific journals, any more than they are owed a platform to address parliament or a corporate board meeting. It is permissible for disciplinary gatekeepers to exclude cranks and shills from valuable communicative platforms in academic contexts, because effective teaching and research requires that communicative privileges be given to some and not to others, based on people's disciplinary competence. . . .

When universities restrict speakers and viewpoints this should not be, and indeed is not, based solely or even primarily on purely procedural standards aimed at harm-prevention. Given that no platforming is a practice that takes place in universities, our questions should be whether it is compatible with norms of *academic* freedom in particular, where these norms are understood as distinct from general liberal principles of free speech.[32]

Simpson and Srinivasan's argument is premised on a particular understanding of the proper role of higher education, a view that other educators reject. "[Universities] are not arenas reserved for high-minded and approved ways of thinking," say Chemerinsky and Gillman. "They are spaces where all ideas can be expressed and challenged. The platform that campuses provide is designed to be an open platform, not one reserved for those who are thinking correct thoughts."[33]

Argument Analysis

Here's a question that many students think is easy to answer: Should a scholar whose controversial views are widely thought to be racist be allowed to speak on campus? The inspiration for this question comes from the case of Charles Murray, whose appearance at Middlebury College was disrupted by student protesters. Here's a report about the incident from *Inside Higher Ed*:

Hundreds of students at Middlebury College on Thursday chanted and shouted at Charles Murray, the controversial writer whom many accuse of espousing racist ideas, preventing him from giving a public lecture at the college.

Murray had been invited by Middlebury's student group affiliated with the American Enterprise Institute, a think tank at which Murray is a scholar. Many of his writings are controversial, but perhaps none more than *The Bell Curve*, a book that linked intelligence and race and that has been widely condemned by many social scientists (even as Murray has been supported by others).[34]

According to an account in *The Chronicle of Higher Education*:

> On Wednesday, a day before the event, the student newspaper published a letter from a group of nearly 500 alumni and students who condemned Mr. Murray's visit, calling it "a decision that directly endangers members of the community and stains Middlebury's reputation by jeopardizing the institution's claims to intellectual rigor and compassionate inclusivity." . . .
>
> Amid the fiery off-campus response, Middlebury students and faculty took stock. Some expressed dismay at the disruption of Mr. Murray's speech and the chaos that ensued.
>
> "It is understandable why some students may find Murray's research findings offensive," wrote Matthew Dickinson, a professor of political science at Middlebury. "It is less clear, however, why so many believe that the appropriate response was not to simply skip his talk, but instead to prevent others from hearing him and, in so doing, inadvertently give him the platform and national exposure they purportedly opposed."
>
> But the view that student protesters erred in shouting down Mr. Murray is far from unanimous. "I am angry that free speech is conflated with civil discourse," wrote Linus Owens, an associate professor of sociology. Mr. Owens argued that Middlebury legitimized Mr. Murray by giving him a stage and deciding that "only then we can ask smart and devastating questions in return. That's one model, sure," he wrote, "but it's not the only one."[35]

Let's consider one kind of argument that could be framed around an incident like this:

1. Calling into question the dignity, humanity, or equal rights of minority groups is morally wrong. (That is, it's wrong to verbally stigmatize, inferiorize, or marginalize people because of their race, ethnicity, gender, etc.)
2. Any speaker who expresses such immoral views should not be given a platform to speak on campus.
3. Author X expresses such morally repugnant views.
4. Therefore, Author X should not be allowed to speak on campus.

This argument is valid, and let's assume premise 3 is true. Premise 1 is also true, but what makes it true is unstated and needs to be brought into the open. Premise 2 is the heart of the argument and needs to be defended, for even if expressing the reprehensible views is wrong, it does not follow that the speaker must be banned from campus.

The most straightforward reason for thinking that expressing the bigoted views is wrong is that they violate the fundamental moral principles of respect for persons and justice. Violation of these principles alone would be reason enough to condemn the views and the speaker, even if his expressing them does not cause significant harm. Some would argue, however, that premise 1 is true because such bigoted speech does cause significant harm—psychological

Fig. 4.5 Students turn their backs to Charles Murray during his lecture at Middlebury College. Up to seventy students faced disciplinary measures over their disruption of his talk. A professor was injured in a melee afterward.

or dignitary harm, or the promotion of discrimination or violence, or the commission of a violent act (because oppressive speech just *is* violence). As noted previously, the nature and seriousness of speech harms are intensely debated among philosophers, psychologists, and other theorists.

Many would accept premise 2 because they believe the harms of denigrating and discriminatory speech are serious and that no one should be subjected to them, especially people who are already vulnerable and marginalized. They would contend that a platform should never be provided to a speaker who causes such harm.

Others would reject premise 2, but not because they think bigoted speech is harmless. They would argue that no platforming (or banning speech in other ways) would (1) ultimately threaten the free speech rights of everyone, including vulnerable and marginalized groups; (2) deprive students and faculty of the chance to evaluate, debunk, and disarm hateful speech; and (3) deny opportunities for students to develop their skills in analyzing, arguing, and shaping important moral and social issues. They would also likely hold that no platforming or censoring hateful ideas does nothing to eradicate them or lessen their impact. Bad ideas must be dragged out into the open and defeated.

It's worth noting that Murray's theory about race and intelligence was examined by scholars and critics who found his methodology to be seriously flawed and his conclusions unsupported. Middleburg had arranged for one of those critics (a faculty member) to interrogate Murray publicly about his views after his talk, but she never got the chance.

KEY TERMS

no platforming   **safe space**   **trigger warning**

 EXERCISES

Exercises marked with * have answers in "Answers to Exercises" (Appendix B).

Exercise 4.1: Review Questions

1. What is academic freedom? Why is it essential to higher education?
2. How does the AAUP distinguish between education and indoctrination?
3. What are trigger warnings? Are they sometimes justified? Never justified?
*4. What is a safe space?
5. In what sense should every space on campus be a safe space?
*6. What is no platforming?
7. What is Ruth Simmons's advice to students who seek ideological comfort and safety on campus?
*8. What is Ben-Porath's distinction between dignitary safety and intellectual safety?
9. What is Simpson and Srinivasan's argument for no platforming?
10. What is Moody-Adams's argument against the notion of the university as a home?

Exercise 4.2: Moral Arguments

1. Should a professor who holds racist views but does not demonstrate racist or discriminatory behavior in the classroom be fired? Why or why not?
2. Should a university dismiss a physics professor whose teaching is considered exemplary by both colleagues and students but who tweets baseless conspiracy theories about liberals (or conservatives)? Explain.
3. Do students have right not to be offended? Why or why not?

4. Should (protected) speech on campus be restricted if it makes some students feel unsafe? Explain.

5. What is Ulrich Baer's argument for no platforming? Do you agree? Why or why not?

Notes

1. Jonathan Zimmerman, *Campus Politics: What Everyone Needs to Know* (New York: Oxford University Press, 2016), 58.

2. Ann Franke, "Academic Freedom Primer," Association of Governing Boards of Universities and Colleges (AGB), July/August 2011, http://agb.org/sites/default/files/legacy/u1525/Academic%20Freedom%20Primer.pdf.

3. Benjamin Daniels and Catherine Baiocchi, "Academic Freedom: Whose Right Is It Anyway?" *The National Law Review*, May 31, 2019, https://www.natlawreview.com/article/academic-freedom-whose-right-it-anyway.

4. Cary Nelson, "Defining Academic Freedom," *Inside Higher Ed*, December 21, 2010, https://www.insidehighered.com/views/2010/12/21/defining-academic-freedom.

5. Sigal R. Ben-Porath, *Free Speech on Campus* (Philadelphia: University of Pennsylvania Press, 2017), 87.

6. Daniels and Baiocchi, "Academic Freedom."

7. Colleen Flaherty, "Unacademic Freedom?," *Inside Higher Ed*, March 1, 2016, https://www.insidehighered.com/news/2016/03/01/does-academic-freedom-protect-falsehoods.

8. Flaherty, "Unacademic Freedom?"

9. Divya Kumar, "UCF Denounces Professor's Twitter Posts on Race; Petition Calls for His Firing," *Tampa Bay Times*, June 5, 2020, https://www.tampabay.com/news/education/2020/06/05/ucf-denounces-professors-twitter-posts-on-race-petition-calls-for-his-firing/.

10. Michael Levenson, "University to Investigate Professor Who Tweeted about 'Black Privilege'" *New York Times*, June 5, 2020, https://www.nytimes.com/2020/06/05/us/ucf-professor-charles-negy-race.html?searchResultPosition=3.

11. Martin E. Comas, "UCF Protesters Demand Professor Be Fired for Racist Tweets," *Orlando Sentinel*, June 14, 2020, https://www.orlandosentinel.com/news/seminole-county/os-ne-ucf-professor-negy-racist-tweets-20200614-pqznqgsafnhqbd36eb2pign4si-story.html.

12. AAUP, "Freedom in the Classroom," June, 2007, https://www.aaup.org/AAUP/comm/rep/A/class.htm.

13. AAUP, "Freedom in the Classroom."

14. AAUP, "Freedom in the Classroom."

15. Michele Moody-Adams, "Is There a 'Safe Space' for Academic Freedom?" in *Academic Freedom*, ed. Jennifer Lackey (New York: Oxford University Press, 2018), 37.

16. Moody-Adams, "Is There a 'Safe Space' for Academic Freedom?," 39.

17. AAUP, "On Trigger Warnings," August, 2014, https://www.aaup.org/report/trigger-warnings.

18. Moody-Adams, "Is There a 'Safe Space' for Academic Freedom?," 39–40.

19. Sigal R. Ben-Porath, *Free Speech on Campus*, 92–93.

20. Michele Moody-Adams, "Is There a 'Safe Space' for Academic Freedom?," 45–46.

21. Erwin Chemerinsky and Howard Gillman, *Free Speech on Campus* (New Haven, CT: Yale University Press, 2017), 138.

22. Michael S. Roth, "Don't Dismiss 'Safe Spaces,'" *New York Times*, August 29, 2019, https://www.nytimes.com/2019/08/29/opinion/safe-spaces-campus.html.

23. Roth, "Don't Dismiss 'Safe Spaces,'"

24. Moody-Adams, "Is There a 'Safe Space' for Academic Freedom?," 40.

25. Ruth Simmons, "Text of President's Opening Convocation Address," September 4, 2001, https://www.brown.edu/Administration/News_Bureau/2001-02/01-014t.html.

26. Ulrich Baer, *What Snowflakes Get Right: Free Speech, Truth, and Equality on Campus* (New York: Oxford University Press, 2019), 80, 94.

27. Samantha Harris, "The Misguided Movement to 'No Platform' Steve Bannon," *The Fire*, February 2, 2018, https://www.thefire.org/the-misguided-movement-to-no-platform-steve-bannon/.

28. Chemerinsky and Gillman, *Free Speech on Campus*, 11.

29. Ben-Porath, *Free Speech on Campus*, 62.

30. Harris, "The Misguided Movement to 'No Platform' Steve Bannon."

31. Barack Obama, Commencement Address at Rutgers University, May 20, 2016, https://singjupost.com/transcript-president-obamas-full-speech-at-rutgers-commencement-2016/?singlepage=1.

32. Robert Mark Simpson and Amia Srinivasan, "No Platforming," in *Academic Freedom*, ed. Jennifer Lackey (New York: Oxford University Press, 2018), 195–196.

33. Chemerinsky and Gillman, *Free Speech on Campus*, 72–73.

34. Scott Jaschik, "Shouting Down a Lecture," *Inside Higher Ed*, March 3, 2017, https://www.inside-highered.com/news/2017/03/03/middlebury-students-shout-down-lecture-charles-murray.

35. Brock Read, "A Scuffle and a Professor's Injury Make Middlebury a Free-Speech Flashpoint," *The Chronicle of Higher Education*, March 5, 2017, https://www.chronicle.com/article/a-scuffle-and-a-professors-injury-make-middlebury-a-free-speech-flashpoint/?cid=gen_sign_in.

Race, Racism, and Justice 5

Issues of race and racial justice have been simmering on campuses for decades, but they have recently boiled over as many students demanded racial equity and as incidents outside the university have shown that racial reckonings in America are way past due. The most infamous of these recent incidents was the May 2020 death of George Floyd, a forty-six-year-old black man killed by a Minneapolis police officer who pinned him to the street by jamming a knee into his neck for almost nine minutes as Floyd gasped, "I can't breathe." His death launched massive public protests in thousands of US cities and provoked demonstrations throughout the world. On many campuses minority students have reported a culture of racism, encounters with students using racial slurs, widespread acceptance of racial stereotypes, and racial inequities in the way colleges and universities function.

Harvard professor of law Randall Kennedy describes some of the racial tensions:

> Recently, chairs of African American studies departments at Georgetown, Notre Dame, Fordham, and other Catholic universities and colleges asserted that "systemic racism and white supremacy are problems" at their campuses. "Symbolic statements, marches, token town halls, or other typical measures to pacify our campus communities," they warned, are insufficient "while grave inequities persist." A letter to the trustees and president of Dartmouth from professors and staff there called for the dismantling of "structures that implicitly or explicitly work against and devalue Black, Brown, and other people of color at Dartmouth." Faculty and staff members at the University of Chicago set forth "a set of specific and immediate actions the [university] must take to begin to repair and redress its

long history of willingly enabling and directly contributing to structural racism." If their requirements remain unmet, they said, they will decline to participate in university affairs, urge colleagues at other institutions to boycott the university, and prevent the university from using their accomplishments to launder the "neglect and derision of people of color and scholarship and teaching on race."

These and similar protests are part of an international eruption of outrage against racism and an insistence that positive change—*real* change—be pursued immediately. That dissent is splendid in many respects, displaying creativity, persistence, and bravery in demanding the redress of long-neglected racial wrongs. After all, according to virtually every indicator of well-being imaginable—life expectancy, wealth, income, access to education and health care, risk of victimization by violent criminality, likelihood of being arrested or incarcerated—a distinct, adverse gap separates Blacks from whites. The dissidents and their allies have refused to allow business to proceed as usual. They have pushed racial inequity to the front of popular consciousness. They have crammed into a couple of months more public education about matters of race than has taken place in years. They have been the heroes of the George Floyd moment.[1]

To understand such racial ills and to try to remedy them, we must be clear about the nonmoral facts of racism and race (a point that Kennedy emphasized)

Fig. 5.1 In downtown Miami, Florida, crowds of white and black people protest the police killing of George Floyd.

as well as the right and wrong of racial beliefs, actions, and motivations. What is racism? Why is it morally wrong? Does systemic racism exist? Do races even exist? Who is guilty of racism? Philosophers, sociologists, and other scholars have been carefully examining these questions and are articulating coherent answers.

Race and Racism

The basic presupposition of racism is that there are in fact such things as races—the notion that there are discrete groups of people who share certain essential, inherent characteristics. The traditional idea is that race is a matter of heritable *biological* features common to all members of a racial group and that these features explain the psychological and cultural traits of those members. Race scholar Lawrence Blum points out that the popular idea of race generally omits the biological element but keeps the idea of *inherency*—the notion that "certain traits of mind, character, and temperament are inescapably part of a racial group's 'nature' and hence define its racial fate."[2] A group's nature is supposed to be permanent and unchanging. On this conception of race, whites are just naturally that way; blacks are naturally this way; Jews have these inherent traits; Asians have these inherent characteristics; Native Americans have this inherent disposition. Racism, then, presupposes the idea that distinct races exist and that important, inherent differences among them can be distinguished. This presupposition alone, however, does not constitute racism. **Racism** is the additional belief that some races are inferior in these important ways or are otherwise deserving of dislike or hostility.

The two essential elements in this definition are what Blum calls *inferiorization* and *antipathy*. All forms of racism, he says, can be identified by reference to one or both of these concepts:

> Inferiorization is linked to historical racist doctrine and racist social systems. Slavery, segregation, imperialism, apartheid, and Nazism all treated certain groups as inferior to other groups . . .
>
> Though race-based antipathy is less related to the original concept of "racism," today the term unequivocally encompasses racial bigotry, hostility, and hatred. Indeed, the racial bigot is many people's paradigm image of a "racist." . . .
>
> Historical systems of racism did of course inevitably involve racial antipathy as well as inferiorization. Hatred of Jews was central to Nazi philosophy; and it is impossible to understand American racism without seeing hostility to blacks and Native Americans as integral to the nexus of attitudes and emotions that shored up slavery and segregation.[3]

Racism is morally wrong, and shortly we'll examine exactly why that is. But racism is also empirically wrong—it is based on assumptions about the world that science has shown to be unfounded. The consensus among scientists and scholars is that the traditional view of races—that there are distinct groups of people sharing significant biological characteristics—is false. Race, in other words, has no physical scientific basis. Sociologist Tanya Maria Golash-Boza explains:

> Race is a social construction, an idea we endow with meaning through daily interactions. It has no biological basis. This might seem odd to read, as the physical differences between a Kenyan, a Swede, and a Han Chinese, for example, are obvious. However, these physical differences do not necessarily mean that the world can be divided into discrete racial groups. If you were to walk from Kenya to Sweden to China, you would note incremental gradations in physical differences between people across space, and it would be difficult to decide where to draw the line between Africa and Europe and between Europe and Asia. There may be genetic differences between Kenyans and Swedes, but the genetic variations within the Kenyan population are actually greater than those between Swedes and Kenyans. Although race is a social, as opposed to a biological, construction, it has a wide range of consequences in our society, especially when used as a sorting and stratifying mechanism.[4]

> Philosopher of race Naomi Zack sums up the science like this:

> There are no general genes for race, such that, once identified, their presence could be used to predict more specific, or secondary, racial characteristics. None of the physical differences associated with racial difference in society is correlated with any important difference in human talent, function, or skill. . . . To conclude, there is no foundation in science for racial difference, either on the basis of physical traits that in American society are believed to indicate biological racial membership, or on the basis of any traits that may be presumed to determine mental and psychological capabilities.[5]

If races don't exist in any biological sense—if there is no physical basis for sorting people into recognizable racial categories—then the central assumption underlying the traditional form of racism collapses.

Many people assume that the idea of race has been around since the dawn of history, but this assumption is incorrect. Historically, the idea that people can be divided into discrete groups based on their common biological and cultural traits is relatively new. In the ancient world, people did not think to categorize humanity into exclusive racial groups. They recognized that cultures might differ in various ways—in skin color, for example—but they did not lump all persons of a particular skin tone into a single social classification. The idea of race arose in different forms over time beginning only around the sixteenth century. Historians and sociologists maintain that as Europeans subjugated and enslaved Africans and native peoples in the Americas, the idea of inferior and superior

Fig. 5.2 Naomi Zack, philosopher of race and the editor of *The Oxford Handbook of Philosophy and Race*.

races developed and was used to rationalize the unequal status and ill treatment of whole cultures. According to the American Anthropological Association's "Statement on Race":

> Today scholars in many fields argue that "race" as it is understood in the United States of America was a social mechanism invented during the 18th century to refer to those populations brought together in colonial America: the English and other European settlers, the conquered Indian peoples, and those peoples of Africa brought in to provide slave labor. . . .
>
> [Race] subsumed a growing ideology of inequality devised to rationalize European attitudes and treatment of the conquered and enslaved peoples. Proponents of slavery in particular during the 19th century used "race" to justify the retention of slavery. The ideology magnified the difference among Europeans, Africans, and Indians, established a rigid hierarchy of social exclusive categories, underscored and bolstered unequal rank and status differences, and provided the rationalization that the inequality was natural or God-given. . . .
>
> As they were constructing US society, leaders among European-Americans fabricated the cultural/behavioral characteristics associated with each "race," linking superior traits with Europeans and negative and inferior ones to blacks and Indians.[6]

In the nineteenth and early twentieth centuries, scientifically minded thinkers sought to prove that there were indeed separate races, that race could explain the basic differences among people, that some races were superior to others, and that the white European race was superior to all. These endeavors came to be known as *scientific racism,* and they have been largely discredited by modern science. Starting from dubious assumptions and drawing from data such as skull and brain measurements and "intelligence" tests, these early investigators argued that European men were biologically more advanced and more intelligent than any other racial group and that these advantages explained their dominance in the world. Scientific research in later decades, however, debunked these conclusions by showing that they were based on obvious biases, faulty assumptions, methodological errors, and motivated reasoning.

So if race is a social construction, should we discard the concept of race altogether? Many who have studied this question are reluctant to do that. The political scientist Michael James, for example, says,

> Race constructivists accept the skeptics' dismissal of biological race but argue that the term still meaningfully refers to the widespread grouping of individuals into certain categories by society, indeed often by the very members of such racial ascriptions. Normatively, race constructivists argue that since society labels people according to racial categories, and since such labeling often leads to race-based differences in resources, opportunities, and well-being, the concept of race must be conserved, in order to facilitate race-based social movements or policies, such as affirmative action, that compensate for socially constructed but socially relevant racial differences.[7]

Even though races in the biological sense don't exist, "racialized groups"— groups that people *believe* are discrete races and treat as such—do. Scholars contend that despite the nonexistence of biological race, giving up entirely our ability to talk and think about racialized groups and racial realities would have disastrous effects—which is why so many observers condemn the notion of racial color blindness. As Blum says,

> [J]ettisoning race in the two ways I've mentioned (racial language and racial thinking) would have important moral costs as well. Many would be misled into thinking that if there are no races, there can be no racism, no groups to be its target. But to be a target of racism requires only that a group is racialized, not that it is actually a race.
>
> More fundamentally, race is part of our history and our current social arrangements. Groups defined by race are continuing targets of discrimination, inferiorizing, and stigmatizing. These groups, especially blacks, Native Americans, and some Latino/Hispanic groups, also live with accumulated deficits from even more horrendous injustices in the past. Whites possess a range of unearned advantages in virtually every major domain of social existence—education, jobs,

health care, and political power; and often they harbor subtle assumptions that they are "all right" while other groups are defective in some way. If we give up race entirely, we abandon the ability to name these racial wrongs. . . . Color blindness has assumed the status of an almost absolute principle that further motivates whites to be blind to continuing racial discrimination and injustice.[8]

So racism involves either the idea that some racial groups are inferior to others or that some deserve dislike or hostility. It can be manifested in personal beliefs, attitudes, and actions, or in the activities, rules, or policies of governments and organizations. It is widely regarded as a kind of moral failing, something that most people would want never to be guilty of and never to be called a racist, whether or not they are guilty of the charge.

Racism is morally wrong. But why?

Inferiorizing racism is morally wrong mainly because it is a violation of fundamental moral principles (discussed in Chapter 1). It violates the principle of *respect for persons*, the precept that persons are possessors of ultimate inherent worth and should be treated as such. Persons have rights—the rights of free expression, choice, and privacy, the right not to be coerced, enslaved, cheated, or discriminated against. This form of racism also violates the *principle of justice*, the idea that people should get what is fair or what is their due or, more generally, that equals should be treated equally. People should be treated the same unless there is a morally relevant reason for treating them differently—and racial difference is *not* morally relevant.

Having racist beliefs and attitudes is wrong, and acting on them is, of course, morally worse. According to Blum, these wrongs take on an additional weight of immorality because they are racial:

> What is it about racially-based violations of these human norms that intensifies the moral wrong involved?
>
> The additional opprobrium is racism's integral tie to the social and systematic horrors of slavery, apartheid, Nazism, colonialism, segregation, imperialism, and the shameful treatment of Native Americans in the United States—all race-based systems of oppression. U.S. law recognizes that racially based wrongs are more serious than other similar wrongs by calling race a particularly "invidious" distinction.[9]

Antipathy racism is morally blameworthy because hatred, hostility, and bigotry are vices, especially when they are directed against people who have been made to suffer solely because of their membership in a racial group. Antipathy racism, like the inferiorizing kind, has led to, and still leads to, racial conflict, suffering, injustice, and violence.

For many ethicists, racism is morally wrong simply because it hurts people. This is an appeal to another moral principle, the principle of *utility*, which says we should produce the most favorable balance of benefit over harm for all concerned.

It is obvious that racist beliefs, words, and actions can do harm or lead to harm, and the harm is magnified when racism operates through organizations, corporations, governments, and the law.

Racism Past and Present

In North America the injustice and pain of racism has been a story about African Americans, indigenous Americans, Hispanic/Latino Americans, Asian Americans, and white Americans. Here we will focus on African Americans because so much of the psychological, social, and moral trauma of racial conflict in the United States flows from black experience, beginning with the institution of black slavery in the seventeenth century.

In the United States misconceptions about racism are widespread, robust, and abiding. Many believe that the original racist sin, slavery, was an unfortunate footnote in American history that has no relevance today, that we now live in a postracial world where racial injustice has been nearly eradicated, that racism is just a belief or attitude of (bad) persons, that current inequalities between whites and people of color are not the result of racism, and that systemic racism in the criminal justice system does not exist. A multitude of historians, sociologists, and other scholars have shown these beliefs to be false.

Fig. 5.3 This painting by Sidney King depicts Virginia in 1619 as a Dutch frigate docks at Point Comfort bringing twenty African slaves to be traded to the settlers for food.

Racism today is inextricably linked to the history of American slavery, a brutal institution that was legal for 246 years. It has not been *illegal* for nearly that long. English colonists brought the first African slaves to the colony of Jamestown in 1619. During the following two and a half centuries, hundreds of thousands of Africans were dragged from their homes and chained together on ships for the journey to America under conditions so cruel that thousands of them died on the way. At the end of the trip in the New World, they were bought and sold as property—men, women, and children—torn from their families, bound to masters who worked them, often whipped them, sometimes sexually abused them, and occasionally killed them.

In the late 1700s, the United States' founding document, the Constitution, established a new nation but granted no rights to slaves. Almost half the men who crafted the Constitution owned slaves. Thomas Jefferson argued that Africans and their descendants were less than human.

Between 1861 and 1865, Americans slaughtered each other in the Civil War, the deadliest conflict ever waged on American soil, with at least 620,000 soldiers killed and millions wounded. The main cause of this bloody tragedy was slavery. In 1865, slavery was officially abolished, but racist doctrines that justified slavery and the lower status of blacks were widespread. In the next fifteen years, the Ku Klux Klan, a terrorist organization known as "The Invisible Empire of the South," beat, tortured, and hanged black Americans for asserting their rights or for simply being black. In the 1880s, former Confederacy states enacted Jim Crow laws—legislation designed to deny black citizens the right to vote and to ensure unequal segregation in virtually every area of public life. Jim Crow laws didn't exist in Northern states, but widespread racial discrimination did. In 1896, the Supreme Court's ruling in *Plessy v. Ferguson* permitted increased segregation and Jim Crow practices.

Between 1875 and 1950, over four thousand black men, women, and children were murdered in racial terror lynchings. They were hanged, burned alive, and hacked to death. In the 1960s, blacks were discriminated against in restaurants, restrooms, classrooms, lunch counters, hospitals, theaters, train cars, at cemeteries, and on buses. Killings and beatings of peaceful black protestors and their white supporters shocked the nation with their brutality and frequency. In 1965, the Voting Rights Act passed, allowing the federal government to intervene to help blacks vote.

Historians think most Americans don't have a good understanding of the history of American slavery and what a powerful effect it has had—and still has—on the country. They contend that our ignorance of this history has several causes, including inadequacies in how it is taught. Scholars explain the problem in a recent report:

> Slavery is hard history. It is hard to comprehend the inhumanity that defined it. It is hard to discuss the violence that sustained it. It is hard to teach the ideology of white supremacy that justified it. And it is hard to learn about those who abided it.

We the people have a deep-seated aversion to hard history because we are uncomfortable with the implications it raises about the past as well as the present. . . .

But our antipathy for hard history is only partly responsible for this sentimental longing for a fictitious past. It is also propelled by political considerations. In the late 19th and early 20th centuries, white Southerners looking to bolster white supremacy and justify Jim Crow reimagined the Confederacy as a defender of democracy and protector of white womanhood. To perpetuate this falsehood, they littered the country with monuments to the Lost Cause.

Our preference for nostalgia and for a history that never happened is not without consequence. We miseducate students because of it. Although we teach them that slavery happened, we fail to provide the detail or historical context they need to make sense of its origin, evolution, demise and legacy. And in some cases, we minimize slavery's significance so much that we render its impact—on people and on the nation—inconsequential. As a result, students lack a basic knowledge and understanding of the institution, evidenced most glaringly by their widespread inability to identify slavery as the central cause of the Civil War. . . .

Understanding American slavery is vital to understanding racial inequality today. The formal and informal barriers to equal rights erected after emancipation, which defined the parameters of the color line for more than a century, were built on a foundation constructed during slavery. Our narrow understanding of the institution, however, prevents us from seeing this long legacy and leads policymakers to try to fix people instead of addressing the historically rooted causes of their problems.[10]

Fig. 5.4 Vintage engraving of a mother and daughter being sold at slave auction in the 1860s South.

In the report, scholars and educators identified key concepts that people must grasp to have a full understanding of slavery and its contemporary influence. In their investigations they found that the concepts were too often not covered by teachers, textbooks, and educational standards—and frequently not comprehended by students. Following are some of the essential ideas:

- Slavery, which was practiced by Europeans prior to their arrival in the Americas, was important to all of the colonial powers and existed in all of the European North American colonies.
- Slavery and the slave trade were central to the development and growth of the economy across British North America and, later, the United States.
- Protections for slavery were embedded in the founding documents; enslavers dominated the federal government, Supreme Court, and Senate from 1787 to 1860.
- "Slavery was an institution of power," designed to create profit for the slaveholder and break the will of the enslaved and was a relentless quest for profit abetted by racism.
- Enslaved people resisted the efforts of their enslavers to reduce them to commodities in both revolutionary and everyday ways.
- The experience of slavery varied depending on time, location, crop, labor performed, size of slaveholding, and gender.
- Slavery was the central cause of the Civil War.
- Slavery shaped the fundamental beliefs of Americans about race and whiteness, and white supremacy was both a product of, and legacy of, slavery.
- Enslaved and free people of African descent had a profound impact on American culture, producing leaders and literary, artistic, and folk traditions that continue to influence the nation.[11]

Many today believe that slavery is old news and that racism and racial discrimination, despite a few racist incidents here and there, are a thing of the past. But most experts who have studied racism and race relations would strongly disagree. They say racism is indeed a significant problem in America, as evidenced by widespread racial inequalities at nearly every level of society. The philosopher Naomi Zack, editor of *The Oxford Handbook of Philosophy and Race*, asks,

> How is it that in a post–civil rights age of racial equality, people of color are disproportionately undereducated, poor, incarcerated, and more likely to be treated violently by police? The contradiction between equality as stated in law and humanitarian and scientific consensus versus the reality of social inequality and injustice cannot be adequately addressed as a psychological or ethical issue, on the level of individuals. Deeper cultural, political, and economic analyses are required to explain why and how people behave in ways that appear to violate their highest and most general legal and moral principles.[12]

Here's a sketch of some of the more striking examples of racial inequality today, from the social scientist and race scholar Eduardo Bonilla-Silva:

> Blacks and dark-skinned racial minorities lag well behind whites in virtually every area of social life; they are about three times more likely to be poor than whites, earn about 40 percent less than whites, and have about an eighth of the net worth that whites have. They also receive an inferior education compared to whites, even when they attend integrated institutions. In terms of housing, black-owned units comparable to white-owned ones are valued at 35 percent less. Blacks and Latinos also have less access to the entire housing market because whites, through a variety of exclusionary practices by white realtors and homeowners, have been successful in effectively limiting their entrance into many neighborhoods. Blacks receive impolite treatment in stores, in restaurants, and in a host of other commercial transactions. Researchers have also documented that blacks pay more for goods such as cars and houses than do whites. Finally, blacks and dark-skinned Latinos are the targets of racial profiling by the police, which, combined with the highly racialized criminal court system, guarantees their overrepresentation among those arrested, prosecuted, incarcerated, and if charged for a capital crime, executed. Racial profiling on the highways has become such a prevalent phenomenon that a term has emerged to describe it: driving while black. In short, blacks and most minorities are "at the bottom of the well."[13]

How do we explain these inequalities? And how is it that many whites claim not to see racism? According to Bonilla-Silva,

> Nowadays, except for members of white supremacist organizations, few whites in the United States claim to be "racist." Most whites assert they "don't see any color, just people"; that although the ugly face of discrimination is still with us, it is no longer the central factor determining minorities' life chances; and, finally, that, like Dr. Martin Luther King Jr., they aspire to live in a society where "people are judged by the content of their character, not by the color of their skin." More poignantly, most whites insist that minorities (especially blacks) are the ones responsible for what "race problem" we have in this country. . . . Most whites believe that if blacks and other minorities would just stop thinking about the past, work hard, and complain less (particularly about racial discrimination), then Americans of all hues could "all get along."[14]

If whites do see contemporary racial inequality, says Bonilla-Silva, they are likely to blame it on nonracial factors:

> [W]hites rationalize minorities' contemporary status as the product of market dynamics, naturally occurring phenomena, and blacks' imputed cultural limitations. For instance, whites can attribute Latinos' high poverty rate to a relaxed work ethic ("the Hispanics are mañana, mañana, mañana —tomorrow, tomorrow, tomorrow") or residential segregation as the result of natural tendencies among

groups ("Does a cat and dog mix? I can't see it. You can't drink milk and scotch. Certain mixes don't mix.").[15]

For many people, racism is basically **individual racism**, person-to-person acts of intolerance or discrimination. But a prevalent, seldom-acknowledged kind of racism is **institutional** or **structural racism**, unequal treatment that arises from the way organizations, institutions, and social systems operate. This is inferiorizing or antipathy racism that functions almost unseen in corporations, government agencies, schools, the labor market, and systems of health care, housing, and criminal justice. The people who work within such systems may or may not be racially prejudiced, but the systems themselves cause racial discrimination and inequality through their policies and procedures.

REMOVING CONFEDERATE MONUMENTS

Confederate monuments—viewed by some as memorials to Southern heritage and by others as symbols of slavery, racism, and white supremacy—have been controversial ever since they were erected. Debates about their removal intensified in 2015 after the mass shooting of African Americans at the historic "Mother

Fig. 5.5 In July 2020, a worker attaches a rope as they prepare to remove the statue of Confederate General Stonewall Jackson from its pedestal on Monument Avenue in Richmond, Virginia.

Emanuel" church in Charleston, South Carolina. The shooter was a white supremacist fond of the Confederacy and its symbols. Debates flared up again in 2017
after white nationalists rallied in Charlottesville, Virginia, yelling racial slurs and
displaying Confederate flags and Ku Klux Klan symbols. They were protesting
the removal of a statue dedicated to the memory of Robert E. Lee. Violence broke
out, and a woman was killed and several others injured when a white supremacist drove his car into a crowd of counterprotesters. Protests swept the country
in 2020 after the police killing of George Floyd, hastening efforts to remove the
monuments that now stand on college campuses and in public spaces.

   In recent years Confederate statues have been violently torn down, vandal-
ized, and officially moved or removed. After years of conflict over the issue,
the University of Mississippi took down its thirty-foot Confederate statue that
had stood for over a hundred years in the heart of the campus. Duke University
removed its statue of Robert E. Lee, and the University of Texas at Austin removed
its statues of Lee and three other Confederate leaders.

   Confederate monuments—which number in the hundreds—were created
not merely to commemorate the Confederate war dead or to honor the Southern
way of life. The consensus among historians is that most of the monuments were
erected, often decades after the Civil War, to justify Jim Crow laws, perpetuate white supremacy, resist desegregation, and spread discredited Lost Cause
mythology (which said, among other things, that the South's pro-slavery cause
was just and that black people were enslaved for their own good). It should not
be surprising, then, that white supremacists regard Confederate monuments as
sacred, as symbols of the true path that America should follow but sadly does not.

   Those who oppose removing the monuments argue that the statues symbolize the history and heritage of our country, which should not be erased, no
matter how messy or unpleasant. Or they insist the monuments are not racist
but are intended to honor the bravery and sacrifice of those who fought to preserve Southern values and way of life. Some treat the controversy as a free speech
issue, declaring that people have a right to hold controversial opinions and to
build monuments to express and venerate those views. Or they offer a slippery-
slope argument: if we tear down monuments to Robert E. Lee, should we also
remove statues to George Washington and Thomas Jefferson because they also
owned slaves, despite their role in founding the country and its democratic ideals? Where do we draw the line?

   Many argue that Confederate monuments should be removed because they
celebrate not the ideals of democracy, freedom, and diversity but the values of
cruelty, hate, and exploitation. They honor men who advocated and perpetuated
an immoral, barbaric system of human bondage. They pay homage to a shameful
racist past that should be resisted and repudiated.

   One of the strongest arguments for getting rid of campus Confederate monuments is based on the concept of dignitary harm. Recall from the discussion of
free speech that dignitary harm is done when people are made to feel they are not

fully accepted, equal members of society. This argument says that Confederate monuments on campus cause dignitary harm by being symbols of racism. They are racist because they symbolize the Confederacy, a vicious defender of slavery, and thus directly or indirectly portray blacks as inferior or as deserving of hatred or dislike. The monuments—as university-sponsored symbols of racism—convey the idea that African American students are not fully accepted, equal members of the community and should therefore be removed.

Statements and symbols can be racist apart from the motivations that produced them. So a Confederate statue on the quad or in the chapel can be racist even if the school does not intend that meaning.

Both individuals and systems can perpetuate racial prejudice or racial discrimination. **Racial prejudice** is antipathy toward a racial group based on a faulty view of that group. **Racial discrimination** is unfavorable treatment of people because of their race. Of course, prejudice and discrimination can be directed at traits other than race, including sexual orientation, age, gender, ethnicity, religion, and national origins.

Overt, individual racism (the kind voiced publicly in racial slurs, for example) may be less common these days, but scholars insist that institutional or structural racism is common and nearly invisible. According to Bonilla-Silva:

[C]ontemporary racial inequality is reproduced through "new racism" practices that are subtle, institutional, and apparently nonracial. In contrast to the Jim Crow era, where racial inequality was enforced through overt means (e.g., signs saying "No Niggers Welcomed Here" or shotgun diplomacy at the voting booth), today racial practices operate in a "now you see it, now you don't" fashion. For example, residential segregation, which is almost as high today as it was in the past, is no longer accomplished through overtly discriminatory practices. Instead, covert behaviors such as not showing all the available units, steering minorities and whites into certain neighborhoods, quoting higher rents or prices to minority applicants, or not advertising units at all are the weapons of choice to maintain separate communities. In the economic field, "smiling face" discrimination ("We don't have jobs now, but please check later"), advertising job openings in mostly white networks and ethnic newspapers, and steering highly educated people of color into poorly remunerated jobs or jobs with limited opportunities for mobility are the new ways of keeping minorities in a secondary position. Politically, although the civil rights struggles have helped remove many of the obstacles for the electoral participation of people of color, racial gerrymandering, multimember legislative districts, election runoffs, annexation of predominately white areas, at-large district elections, and anti-single-shot devices (disallowing concentrating votes [on] one or two candidates in cities using at-large elections) have become standard practices to disenfranchise people of color.[16]

Today blacks fare much worse than whites in income, wealth, education, employment, health, and home ownership. These inequalities are caused by racist policies and conditions of the past, and they have in most cases been allowed to continue or been made worse by inequalities in the present.

A good example is racial inequalities in wealth. Income is the money an individual earns from work, but wealth consists of a person's total assets—cash and property (land, houses, cars, savings, investments), minus debt. In the United States, in 2016, the typical black household could claim just $13,024 in wealth, while a typical white household had $149,703.[17] The vast difference can be explained by a history of official and unofficial anti-black discrimination. According to Golash-Boza:

> One of the main reasons for the inability of blacks to build wealth has been the creation of housing segregation within U.S. cities. . . .
>
> A combination of three forces led to residential segregation: collective racial violence carried out by whites, federal housing programs and policies that exclusively benefited whites, and practices created and reinforced by the nascent real estate industry. . . .
>
> The Federal Housing Administration (FHA) was established in 1934 with the purpose of bolstering the economy and, in particular, the construction industry. . . . The FHA created the conditions under which banks could loan people money to purchase homes with small down payments and at reasonable interest rates. . . .
>
> Banks used FHA guidelines to decide who should be permitted to borrow money. The 1938 *Underwriting Manual* of the FHA stated that "if a neighborhood is to retain stability, it is necessary that properties shall continue to be occupied by the same social and racial classes." . . . The *Manual* also endorsed a practice known as *redlining*, in which communities where loans were not recommended were outlined in red on a map. Those communities where loans were denied were primarily black.
>
> Between 1933 and 1978, U.S. government policies enabled over 35 million families to increase their wealth through housing equity. As homeowners, millions of American were able to begin to accumulate tax savings, home equity, economic stability, and other benefits associated with homeownership. White Americans benefited disproportionately from this shift for two primary reasons: (1) it was easier for white people to purchase homes, and (2) the homes that whites bought increased in value more rapidly than those purchased by blacks because of the perceived desirability of all-white neighborhoods. . . .
>
> The final factor that contributed to residential segregation was *racially restrictive covenants*—contractual agreements that prevent the sale or lease of property

within an area to non-whites—created and enforced by the real estate industry. By the 1920s, deeds in nearly every new housing development in the northern United States prevented the ownership or rental of houses in the development by anyone who was not white. . . .

In 1948, the Supreme Court declared racially restrictive covenants unenforceable. And in 1968, the passage of the Fair Housing Act made these covenants illegal. Once the covenants became illegal, real estate agents developed new tactics to preserve residential segregation. One of the most common activities was *steering*, in which real estate agents would show homes in white neighborhoods only to whites and homes in black neighborhoods only to blacks. For these and other reasons, over sixty years after the passage of the Fair Housing Act, we still have high levels of residential segregation, exacerbating wealth inequality.[18]

Racial disparities in education have also been linked to racial segregation, prejudice, and discrimination—while many whites incorrectly assume the inequalities are due to minority children's mental deficiencies. Most scholars reject this psychological explanation, as Lawrence Blum explains:

The idea that conventionally defined racial groups differ in intelligence has been largely discredited by contemporary science, and popular adherence to it has declined sharply. But it has by no means entirely disappeared in popular thought, and a more statistically based form has arisen in genetic science as well. In the United States, both forms are encouraged by a basic fact on the ground in education—often referred to as the "achievement gap"—that by almost every plausible measure, black, Native American, and Latino students do not do as well in school as white and Asian students. This gap encourages the view that there is something educationally deficient about black, Latino, and Native American students. Racial achievement gaps can be explained by a range of factors, most of which concern black and Latino students' circumstances rather than their innate capacities—poorer health among disadvantaged racial minorities; less parental education, which disadvantages students in various different ways; lower parental socio-economic status (SES), often leading to unstable home and living situations and moving from school to school; stress from not having decent and regular employment; teacher racial prejudice, ignorance and insensitivity; living in neighborhoods of concentrated disadvantage; and cultural factors relating to school engagement among minority youth.[19]

Researchers maintain that racial disparities are also widespread in the criminal justice system. For example, according to Golash-Boza,

Racial inequalities in law enforcement are institutionalized at every level of the criminal justice process, from stops to arrests to charges to sentencing to release. Blacks and Latinos are more likely to be arrested than whites. They are more

"WHITE PRIVILEGE" AND ITS PROBLEMS

White privilege refers to the advantages or benefits that whites enjoy simply because they are white. Blum says there are two distinct forms of white privilege:

> One is simply that of being spared racial discrimination, stigmatizing, indignities, stereotyping, and other race-based wrongs. . . . A second, however, consists in material benefits accruing to whites because of discrimination against racial minorities. When a black is denied a job because of discrimination, there is one more job available to a non-black (usually a white). When poor schooling leaves many blacks and Latinos inadequately prepared for higher education or the job market, jobs and places in colleges become more available to whites (and to others, such as some Asian groups, positioned to take advantage of these opportunities).[20]

These advantages of racial privilege can seem almost invisible. As Golash-Boza says,

> If you are white, it can be difficult to notice that you are not being followed around the store [by security]; that people are smiling at you on the street instead of clutching their purses; that not one asks you if you speak English; that you are not asked for identification when paying with a credit card. Instead, you are likely to think that these things are normal—that this is simply how things are.[21]

Philosopher and race scholar Shannon Sullivan concurs:

> One of the main features of racial inequality after the end of de jure Jim Crow is its relative invisibility. Today white advantages often are subtle, even hidden, and they frequently are difficult to prove empirically or pinpoint with certainty. When they can be demonstrated, as in the case of institutional racial biases against people of color, they often are explained away as the result of something other than racial bias. . . . In other cases, racial inequalities benefitting white people operate without explicitly mentioning race or whiteness at all. K-12 school suspension rates, for example, tend to be extremely imbalanced, penalizing black students disproportionately, but they often are discussed as race-neutral matters of "zero tolerance" of "disruptive" and "insubordinate" behavior. . . . Practices such as these tend to camouflage race and white advantage, making it all too easy for white (and other) people to deny that they exist and for racial inequality to hum along unchallenged.[22]

Does having or benefiting from white privilege make you a racist? Blum argues that it's a mistake to conflate white privilege with personal racism:

> The whole point of the idea of white privilege is that it does *not* depend on the attitudes of its beneficiaries toward disadvantaged racial groups; nonracists still partake of white privilege. . . . What is so disturbing about white privilege is that you need not be in any way personally blameworthy for having it, but it is still

unfair that you do. It is not personally racist to have white privilege. . . . [W]hite privilege is a different sort of racial ill than personal racism. But it is morally wrong to be complacent about or accepting of racial privileges once one knows one possesses them; one is (often) thereby being complicit with injustice.[23]

"White privilege" can help us identify a type of racial ill, scholars say, but the concept is easily misused. Sullivan argues that it can, unfortunately, distract white people from the more important task of working toward racial justice:

> Removing the feeling of being accused and blamed for situations that one did not choose can make it psychologically easier for white people to see how whiteness privileges them despite their intentions. And yet this benefit is simultaneously a problem. The notion of white privilege can funnel white people's attention and energy into mere introspection and conscious raising. White people's critical self-examination is not problematic in and of itself. . . . However, as some philosophers have charged, white self-examination through the concept of white privilege can become an end in itself, rather than a means toward racial justice for people of color. Instead of leading to political and other forms of action against racism, white privilege discourse often bogs down white people in anguished personal and confessional soul searching, leaving them floundering in their guilty awareness of their privileges.[24]

Zack has similar misgivings:

> [White privilege discourse] goes too far in blaming all whites for all forms of racism and it does not go far enough in directly addressing injustice against nonwhites. . . . [W]hite privilege discourse may miss the importance of racial injustice and degenerate into just another display of the advantages that white people have of not being required to respond to racial injustice against their racial group. . . . Yes, whites are privileged, but no amount of exhortation to "check" their privilege or confessional discourse in response will correct the legal injustice of police homicide based on racial profiling.[25]

likely to be charged, more likely to be convicted, more likely to be given a longer sentence, and more likely to face the death penalty. The cumulative effect of these disparities at each stage of the process creates a situation in which black men are seven times more likely than white men to be put behind bars.[26]

Golash-Boza is one of many scholars to argue that the criminal justice system is infected with systemic racism. "Systemic racism" does not mean that all those in the system are racists—only that institutional racism is at work, where the system produces racial inequalities through its procedures and structure independently of people's racial attitudes.

A long line of scientific studies suggests that this systemic racism does in fact exist. Here's a snapshot of some of the more recent research:

- A massive study published in May 2020 of ninety-five million traffic stops by fifty-six police agencies between 2011 and 2018 found that while black people were much more likely to be pulled over than whites, the disparity lessens at night, when police are less able to distinguish the race of the driver. The study also found that blacks were more likely to be searched after a stop, though whites were more likely to be found with illicit drugs. The darker the sky, the less pronounced the disparity between white and black motorists. The study also found that in states that had legalized marijuana, the racial disparity narrowed but was still significant.

- A 2020 report on 1.8 million police stops by the eight largest law enforcement agencies in California found that blacks were stopped at a rate 2.5 times higher than the per capita rate of whites. The report also found that black people were far more likely to be stopped for "reasonable suspicion" (as opposed to actually breaking a law) and were three times more likely than any other group to be searched, even though searches of white people were more likely to turn up contraband.

- An August 2019 study published by the National Academy of Sciences based on police-shooting databases found that between 2013 and 2018, black men were about 2.5 times more likely than white men to be killed by police, and that black men have a 1-in-1,000 chance of dying at the hands of police. Black women were 1.4 more times likely to be killed than white women. Latino men were 1.3 to 1.4 times more likely to be killed than white men. Latino women were between 12 percent and 23 percent less likely to be killed than white women.

- According to the Justice Department, between 2012 and 2014, black people in Ferguson, Missouri, accounted for 85 percent of vehicle stops, 90 percent of citations, and 93 percent of arrests, despite comprising 67 percent of the population. Blacks were more than twice as likely as whites to be searched after traffic stops, even though they proved to be 26 percent less likely to be in possession of illegal drugs or weapons. Between 2011 and 2013, blacks also received 95 percent of jaywalking tickets and 94 percent of tickets for "failure to comply." The Justice Department also found that the racial discrepancy for speeding tickets increased dramatically when researchers looked at tickets based on only an officer's word versus tickets based on objective evidence, such as radar. Black people facing similar low-level charges as white people were 68 percent less likely to see those charges dismissed in court. More than 90 percent of the arrest warrants stemming from failure to pay/failure to appear were issued for black people.

- A 2020 ACLU report found that even in the era of marijuana reform, black people are more than 3.5 times more likely to be arrested for marijuana offenses than whites. The report also found that "in every state and in over 95% of counties with more than 30,000 people in which at least 1% of the residents are Black, Black people are arrested at higher rates than white people for marijuana possession." This, again, despite ample data showing both races use the drug at similar rates.

- A survey of data from the US Sentencing Commission in 2017 found that when black men and white men commit the same crime, black men on average receive a sentence almost 20 percent longer. The research controlled for variables such as age and prior criminal history.
- A study published in May 2018 found that when a white person and a black person are convicted of similar crimes, Republican-appointed judges sentence the black person to three months longer in prison.
- A 2014 study looking at thirty-three years of data found that after adjusting for variables such as the number of victims and brutality of the crimes, jurors in Washington State were 4.5 times more likely to impose the death penalty on black defendants accused of aggravated murder than on white ones.
- A 2006 Stanford report found that when a black person was accused of killing a white person, defendants with darker skin and more "stereotypically black" features were twice as likely to receive a death sentence. When the victim was black, there was almost no difference.
- Black people are also more likely to be wrongly convicted of murder when the victim was white. Only about 15 percent of people killed by black people were white, but 31 percent of black exonerees were wrongly convicted of killing white people. More generally, black people convicted of murder are 50 percent more likely to be innocent than white people convicted of murder. [27]

Racist or Not?

On campus and off, the term "racist" is being applied to numerous individuals, actions, policies, institutions, and systems. We are morally obligated to be clear about exactly who or what deserves the label. As Blum argues, racism involves either antipathy or inferiorization directed at a racial group. Racial antipathy is revealed in attitudes and actions expressing contempt, disrespect, and hostility, and racial inferiorization is embodied in attitudes and actions that treat one racial group as somehow inferior to another. Actions (like statements) can be racist, and attitudes (like motives) can be racist, but racism in the former does not necessarily involve racism in the latter.

If this analysis of racism is correct, then many things are clearly racist, but many other things are clearly not. As Blum says,

> Some feel that the word [racist] is thrown around so much that anything involving "race" that someone does not like is liable to castigation as "racist." . . . A local newspaper called certain blacks "racist" for criticizing other blacks who

Fig. 5.6 Lawrence Blum, professor of philosophy and author of *"I'm Not a Racist, But...": The Moral Quandary of Race.*

supported a white over a black candidate for mayor. A white girl in Virginia said that it was "racist" for an African American teacher in her school to wear African attire. . . . Merely mentioning someone's race (or racial designation), using the word "Oriental" for Asians without recognizing its origins and its capacity for insult, or socializing only with members of one's own racial group are called "racist." . . .

Not every instance of racial conflict, insensitivity, discomfort, miscommunication, exclusion, injustice, or ignorance should be called "racist." Not all *racial* incidents are *racist* incidents. We need a more varied and nuanced moral vocabulary for talking about the domain of race. . . . All forms of racial ills should elicit concern from responsible individuals. If someone displays racial insensitivity, but not racism, people should be able to see that for what it is.[28]

Many statements are unequivocally racist: a white person calls a black person the n-word, a white man tells a racist joke that demeans blacks, an Asian American blurts out "goddamn white people," a black person says Latinos are lazy, a white woman asserts that Mexicans are rapists and murderers. These statements would be racist even if the person making them did not bear any antipathy or inferiorizing attitude toward the targeted group. Whether the person making the racist statement is in fact a racist is a separate issue. Someone who harbors no animosity or inferiorizing attitude toward a racial group but who nevertheless utters a racist statement is no racist—but instead may be racially insensitive, ignorant, uncomfortable, or self-deceived.

According to Naomi Zack, it is possible for whites to hold or act on racist beliefs about non-whites without realizing that their beliefs are racist. She calls this "unacknowledged racism":

> For example, someone who thinks that most black men are dangerously violent, and as a result fears and regards with hostility any black male stranger, knows that they hold the generalization about black male violence, but fails to acknowledge that it is a negative racial stereotype, and racist on that count.
>
> Another kind of unacknowledged racism, which has been mistakenly called "unconscious," occurs when people unreflectively put racist beliefs and assumptions that they have not critically examined into practice, through habit, obedience to custom, or early childhood training. . . . [For example] a small business owner who always hired whites for a particular job because that is what his father did and what his customers expect.[29]

Zack argues that people should be held morally responsible for their unacknowledged racism.

Racism should be of concern to everyone, but we must be morally mature enough to recognize that racism comes in degrees. The most evil manifestations of racism are slavery, segregation, apartheid, massacres, lynchings, and mass incarcerations. But beyond these extremes, there are gradations to take into account. Clearly, racist violence is worse than preaching racist violence. Believing that another race is inferior or that it deserves to be hated is not as morally heinous as trying to harm that group. Having unexpressed racist attitudes is not as morally bad as trying to convince others to have them. Telling a racist joke about a racial group is not as bad as discriminating against that group in business or employment. An artistic creation—a movie, painting, song, or book—can be slightly racist or savagely racist in the way it depicts people of color. Racism is a serious moral matter, but we need to address each instance with the degree of seriousness and moral censure that it deserves. Otherwise we risk treating racism simplistically and distorting much needed conversations about it.

Microaggressions are commonplace slights or insults conveyed intentionally or unintentionally by words or actions to disadvantaged groups. Some microaggressions are racist; many are not. But they all can cause harm. A single microaggression may by itself amount only to a minor irritation, but cumulatively such occurrences can be seriously detrimental to those affected. Microaggressions can be subtle, ambiguous, hardly noticed—but injurious over time. People are said to be guilty of racial microaggressions when, for example, they . . . .

- Ask an Asian American classmate, "Where are you from?" (Implying that the student is an outsider, not a true American.)
- Say to a black person, "You are so articulate." (Implying that black people are usually not linguistically competent.)
- Ask a black classmate, "What is the black view of rap music?" (Which amounts to a failure to respect the student's individuality and to wrongly assume that all black people share the same views.)
- Question how a black student could have gotten an A on a tough exam. (Implying that black people are academically inferior.)
- Say to a black male, "You're really un-intimidating for a black guy." (Implying that all black males must be intimidating or aggressive.)
- Ask a black male who attends an Ivy League school, "So you play football?" (Implying that a young black male couldn't attend an elite university except on a sports scholarship.)

While acknowledging that cumulative slights or insults can be harmful, and that even subtle forms of prejudice should be addressed, some scholars argue that using the concept of microaggression can itself be confusing, harmful, or counterproductive. Conor Friedersdorf, for example, says the term "microaggression" is inapt:

> To be sure, there are minor, objectionable, cumulatively burdensome actions that can accurately be called "aggressive." Catcalling is a familiar example. A man who crowds alongside a woman for a half-block while trying to get her phone number is behaving aggressively. . . . But a well-intentioned white or black student asking an Asian American classmate, "What country are you from?" is unfortunate even as it is unaggressive.
>
> Aggression is "hostility" or "violent behavior" or "the forceful pursuit of one's interests." If there's going to be a term for behavior that is burdensome partly because the often well-intentioned people who do it are blind to its wrongness and cumulative effect, baking "aggression" into that term is hugely confusing. What's more, the confusion seems likely to needlessly increase the tension between the person experiencing the grievance and the person who is ostensibly responsible.[30]

Michele Moody-Adams sees a peculiar difficulty in the way some people construe microaggressions:

> The problem is that those who make these claims describe most of the phenomena they address as mainly a matter of "unconscious" or "automatic" stereotypes and bias, yet they typically see nothing objectionable in the effort to punish those who display these unconscious or automatic attitudes. Some influential contributors to the scholarly literature on microaggressions have become critical of this attitude, suggesting that it is neither defensible nor productive to seek to punish microaggressions that are truly unintentional.[31]

RESPONDING TO MICROAGGRESSIONS

Kevin Nadal, a professor of psychology at John Jay College of Criminal Justice, is an author and leading researcher on microaggressions. Here he describes how people of color, women, LGBT persons, and others can react effectively to micro-aggressions by asking themselves three questions.

Did this microaggression really occur?

Sometimes microaggressions may be flagrantly obvious that a person can identify them effortlessly. For instance, when a man of color notices that a white woman clutches her purse as he enters an elevator, he may be able to identify this as a microaggression immediately. This has happened hundreds of times in his life and he is confident that she is assuming him to be a criminal. Similarly, when a person says "That's so gay!" in front of an LGBT person, the LGBT individual recognizes that the person is clearly using homophobic language.

With some encounters, an individual may question whether a microaggression has happened. For example, if a woman hears someone whistle as she walks down a street, she may think, "Did that really just happen or am I hearing things?". . .

When there are people around (particularly people who the individual trusts) to verify and validate the microaggression, it makes it easier for the individual to definitively label the event as a microaggression. When there is no one around, it may be helpful to seek support from loved ones. For instance, with modern technology, people can easily call, text, email, or communicate with their social media networks about microaggressions. I myself have seen many people update their status on Facebook, describing microaggressions that happened to them on the subway or on the sidewalks. Most of the time, people respond in supportive ways.

Should I respond to this microaggression?

If an individual is certain (or moderately certain) that a microaggression did in fact occur, she or he has to ponder the potential risks or consequences of responding or not responding. Some questions include:

1. If I respond, could my physical safety be in danger?
2. If I respond, will the person become defensive and will this lead to an argument?
3. If I respond, how will this affect my relationship with this person (e.g., coworker, family member, etc.)?
4. If I don't respond, will I regret not saying something?
5. If I don't respond, does that convey that I accept the behavior or statement?

How should I respond to this microaggression?

If individuals do decide to take action, they must contemplate how to react. First, they can approach the situation in a passive-aggressive way. For instance, perhaps the victims make a joke or a sarcastic comment as a way of communicating that they are upset or annoyed. Perhaps the victims respond by rolling their eyes or sighing. Or, they do nothing in that moment and decide to talk to others about it first, in the hopes that it will get back to the perpetrator.

Second, victims can react in a proactive way. This might be effective when the victim simply does not have the energy to engage the perpetrator in a discussion. Sometimes individuals who experience microaggressions regularly may feel so agitated that they just want to yell back. For some individuals, an active response may be a therapeutic way of releasing years of accumulated anger and frustration.

Finally, an individual may act in an assertive way. This may include calmly addressing the perpetrator about how it made him or her feel. This may consist of educating the perpetrators, describing what was offensive about the microaggression. Oftentimes the perpetrator will become defensive, which may lead to further microaggressions (particularly microinvalidations). It may be important to use "I" statements (e.g., "I felt hurt when you said that."), instead of attacking statements (e.g., "You're a racist!"). It also may be important to address the behavior and not the perpetrator. What this means is that instead of calling the perpetrator "a racist," it might be best to say that the behavior he or she engaged in was racially charged and offensive. People don't like being called a racist, sexist or homophobe, so if you want to have an effective dialogue with a person without being defensive, it may be best to avoid using such language.

When the entire interaction is over, it is important for the victim of the microaggression to seek support. Seeking support can include practical support (e.g., if someone experiences microaggressions at a workplace, she or he can file a complaint with Human Resources). Individuals can also seek social support (e.g., talking to your loved ones or peers with similar identities who can validate your experiences).[32]

Argument Analysis

Consider this argument about removing a Confederate monument from a university campus:

1. It is morally permissible to display symbols of cultural or historical significance on university campuses.
2. Existing symbols of cultural or historical significance should be respected (they should not be removed).
3. The statue of Confederate general Robert E. Lee on the quad is a symbol of cultural and historical significance.
4. Therefore, the Robert E. Lee statue should not be removed.

This argument is valid, but each premise is problematic. Premise 1 is false since it is a generalization likely to have exceptions. It cannot be the case that displaying *any* symbol of cultural or historical significance on campus is morally acceptable. Many historical events and cultural practices are too gruesome, cruel, or wicked to commemorate.

Premise 2 is also a false generalization. It cannot be the case that merely because a formerly venerated statue has stood on campus for a hundred years it should never be removed. We constantly evaluate the past in light of the present, and sometimes we rightly judge that an old symbol must go. Appealing to tradition alone to support a view is a logical fallacy.

Strictly speaking, premise 3 is true, but simplistic. To some, a Confederate statue like that of a famous general is a symbol of Southern heritage or way of life, not racism. But symbols can have more than one meaning. To others, Confederate monuments are unequivocally racist because they symbolize the Confederacy, a system that defended and maintained a way of life whose central pillar was slavery. They honor men who fought hard to retain a barbaric order built on racial suffering. Those who want to remove the statue of Robert E. Lee can argue that by being a symbol of racism, it causes dignitary harm, sending the message that African Americans are less than fully equal members of the university community.

The argument, then, against removing the statue in the quad fails.

KEY TERMS

individual racism	microaggression	racial prejudice
institutional or structural racism	racial discrimination	racism

---

 ## EXERCISES

Exercises marked with * have answers in "Answers to Exercises" (Appendix B).

Exercise 5.1: Review Questions

1. How does Lawrence Blum define racism? In his definition, what is inferiorization? What is antipathy?
*2. What do most historians say was the central cause of the Civil War?
3. What is the basic presupposition of racism?

4. According to historians and sociologists, how was the idea of inferior and superior races used in the Americas against Africans and native peoples?
5. What is scientific racism? How did later scientific research debunk it?
*6. Why is inferiorizing racism morally wrong? Why is antipathy racism wrong?
7. Is it the case that we now live in a postracial world where racial injustice has been nearly eradicated? Why or why not?
*8. What is institutional racism? What is racial prejudice?
9. How did the Federal Housing Administration help ensure wealth inequality among blacks?
10. What is white privilege?

Exercise 5.2: Moral Arguments

1. Do you agree that systemic racism exists in the criminal justice system? Why or why not?
2. Why does Conor Friedersdorf think the term *microaggression* is inapt? Do you agree? Explain.
3. Does having or benefiting from white privilege make you a racist? Why or why not?
4. Does uttering a racist statement make you a racist? Why or why not?
5. What is "racism without racists"? Give two examples of this phenomenon.

Notes

1. Randall Kennedy, "How Racist Are Universities, Really?," *The Chronicle of Higher Education*, August 12, 2020, https://www.chronicle.com/article/how-racist-are-universities-really?cid=gen_sign_in.
2. Lawrence Blum, *"I'm Not a Racist But . . .": The Moral Quandary of Race* (Ithaca, NY: Cornell University Press, 2002), 133.
3. Blum, *"I'm Not a Racist But . . .,"* 8–9.
4. Tanya Maria Golash-Boza, *Race and Racisms: A Critical Approach* (New York: Oxford University Press, 2016), 3.
5. Naomi Zack, "Race and Racial Discrimination," in *The Oxford Handbook of Practical Ethics*, ed. Hugh LaFollette (Oxford: Oxford University Press, 2003), 259, 263.
6. American Anthropological Association, "AAA Statement on Race," May 17, 1998, https://www.americananthro.org/ConnectWithAAA/Content.aspx?ItemNumber=2583.
7. Michael James, "Race," in *Stanford Encyclopedia of Philosophy*, Spring 2017 ed., ed. Edward N. Zalta, https://plato.stanford.edu/archives/spr2017/entries/race/.
8. Blum, *"I'm Not a Racist But . . .,"* 165.
9. Blum, *"I'm Not a Racist But . . .,"* 27.
10. Hasan Kwame Jeffries, "Teaching Hard History," Southern Poverty Law Center, January 31, 2018, https://www.splcenter.org/20180131/teaching-hard-history.
11. Southern Poverty Law Center, "Teaching Hard History."
12. Naomi Zack, "Introduction," *The Oxford Handbook of Philosophy and Race* (New York: Oxford University Press, 2019), 5–6.
13. Eduardo Bonilla-Silva, *Racism without Racists* (Lanham, MD: Rowman and Littlefield, 2018), 2.

14. Bonilla-Silva, *Racism without Racists*, 1.
15. Bonilla-Silva, *Racism without Racists*, 2.
16. Bonilla-Silva, *Racism without Racists*, 3.
17. Heather Long and Andrew Van Dam, "The Black-White Economic Divide Is as Wide as It Was in 1968," *Washington Post*, June 4, 2020.
18. Golash-Boza, *Race and Racisms*, 199–201.
19. Lawrence Blum, "Race and K-12 Education," in *The Oxford Handbook of Practical Ethics*, ed. Naomi Zack (Oxford: Oxford University Press, 2003), 436–437.
20. Blum, *"I'm Not a Racist But . . .,"* 110.
21. Golash-Boza, *Race and Racisms*, 3.
22. Shannon Sullivan, "White Privilege," in *The Oxford Handbook of Philosophy and Race*, ed. Naomi Zack (New York: Oxford University Press, 2019), 332.
23. Blum, *"I'm Not a Racist But . . .,"* 73, 76.
24. Sullivan, White Privilege," 334.
25. Naomi Zack, "Uses and Abuses of the Discourse of White Privilege," *Philosopher* (blog), June 24, 2016, https://politicalphilosopher.net/2016/06/24/featured-philosopher-naomi-zack/.
26. Golash-Boza, *Race and Racisms*, 233.
27. Radley Balko, "There's Overwhelming Evidence That the Criminal Justice System Is Racist. Here's the Proof," *Washington Post*, June 10, 2020.
28. Blum, *"I'm Not a Racist But. . .,"* 1–2.
29. Zack, "Race and Racial Discrimination," in *The Oxford Handbook of Practical Ethics*, ed. Naomi Zack (Oxford: Oxford University Press, 2003), 255.
30. Conor Friedersdorf, "Why Critics of the 'Microaggression' Framework Are Skeptical," *The Atlantic*, September 14, 2015, https://www.theatlantic.com/politics/archive/2015/09/why-critics-of-the-microaggressions-framework-are-skeptical/405106/.
31. Michele Moody-Adams, "A 'Safe Space' for Academic Freedom?" in *Academic Freedom*, ed. Jennifer Lackey (Oxford: Oxford University Press, 2018), 52.
32. Kevin L. Nadal, "A Guide to Responding to Microaggressions," *CUNY Forum* 2, no. 1 (2014): 71–76, ELAMICRO A_Guide_to_Responding_to_Microaggressions.pdf (advancingjustice-la.org).

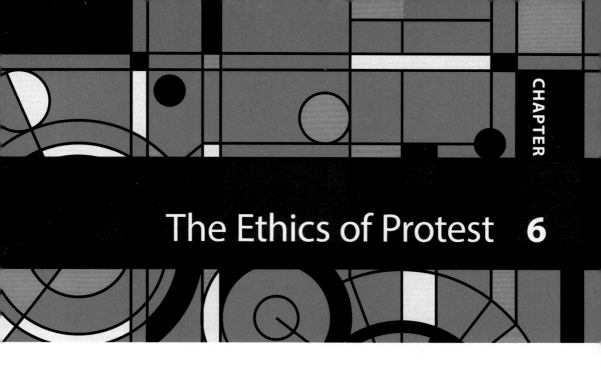

The Ethics of Protest 6

Protests have been mighty forces for change in American history, from the Boston Tea Party to the suffragette campaigns to the civil rights movement to the Black Lives Matter demonstrations that swept the country (and the world) after the police killing of George Floyd. The participation of students in such stories of resistance and dissent has been extensive and influential.

We can trace modern episodes of student activism from the four black college students in 1960 Greensboro, North Carolina, who sat at a whites-only Woolworth's lunch counter and refused to leave (they inspired other sit-ins in over fifty cities). The following years saw student demonstrations *against* the Vietnam War, sexual violence, and police misconduct and *for* the rights of minorities, LGBTQ persons, women, and immigrants. In more recent history, we have witnessed the 2011 Occupy Wall Street protests at multiple campuses, the 2013 student debt protests at New York University, the 2014 student rallies at St. Louis University condemning the police killing of Michael Brown in Ferguson, the 2014 sexual assault awareness protest at Columbia University, the 2015 University of Missouri series of protests against racism, the 2020 tuition strike at Columbia University and other institutions, and the 2020 one-hundred-plus "car caravan" at Northern Vermont University that braved the COVID-19 pandemic to oppose a proposal that would close three Vermont college campuses.

A **protest** is a public demonstration of dissent, disapproval, or resistance against policies, actions, or ideas deemed to be morally wrong or unjust. The aim is usually to draw attention to a problem, influence public opinion, or force change. Protests can be peaceful or evolve into violence. They can have little or no effect, or they can change the world. They can have right on their side or be morally suspect or ambiguous, resulting in a better state of affairs or something worse.

Fig. 6.1 African American students (from left: Joseph McNeil, Franklin McCain, William Smith, and Clarence Henderson) holding a sit-in at a Woolworth's lunch counter in Greensboro, North Carolina, February 2, 1960.

Questions about the ethics of protesting arise everywhere. Is there a moral right to protest? If so, does this moral right supersede laws? What protest tactics are morally permissible? Hanging policymakers in effigy? Risking the safety of bystanders, university officials, and opposing protesters? Interfering with the free speech rights of others? Heckling or harassing political or academic leaders at their homes, in restaurants, at concerts and theaters? Resorting to physical violence and intimidation?

Just as we can make moral judgments about someone's intentions, we can also assess the aims and motivations behind protests. We can ask, What is the purpose of this sit-in, petition, or rally? Is it to promote justice, to focus attention on a problem, to try to set things right—or to vent frustrations, exact revenge, or punish people we hate?

There will probably always be student protests, but their numbers, focus, and tactics will likely vary over time, as they have in the past. In the 1960s and 1970s, protests erupted in over half of American campuses, mostly over the issues of race and the war in Vietnam. Since then the number of campus protests has risen and fallen (mostly fallen), other issues have demanded attention, and the realities of a new era have set in. These realities include a large percentage of students who cannot or will not participate in campus protests because they are career-minded and have no time for politics, because they have children to care for or work part-time, or they live off-campus. Health guidelines for dealing with the COVID-19 pandemic have limited or ruled out protest gatherings and forced protesters to find new ways to make themselves heard. And many of these ways have evolved online.

The Right to Protest

The First Amendment guarantees our right to assemble and to communicate our opinions through protest, a right that is essential for a viable democracy. The government through the police and other officials, however, can legally restrict this right in some narrowly defined ways, and law enforcement officers have sometimes violated the right by trying to suppress legal protests.

More fundamentally, the freedom to protest is a moral right supported by several moral values and theories, including the principles of justice and respect for persons. Moral standards also apply to why and how protests are conducted. Thus, we can judge a protest to be morally justified or unjustified (whether or not it is legal), prompted by morally good or bad motives, and carried out in morally right or wrong ways.

The First Amendment right to protest is circumscribed by laws and competing rights that limit how and where protesters can exercise their right. The American Civil Liberties Union (ACLU) explains:

- Your rights are strongest in what are known as "traditional public forums," such as streets, sidewalks, and parks. You also likely have the right to speak out on other public property, like plazas in front of government buildings, as long as you are not blocking access to the government building or interfering with other purposes the property was designed for.
- Private property owners can set rules for speech on their property. The government may not restrict your speech if it is taking place on your own property or with the consent of the property owner.
- Counterprotesters also have free speech rights. Police must treat protesters and counterprotesters equally. Police are permitted to keep antagonistic groups separated but should allow them to be within sight and sound of one another.
- When you are lawfully present in any public space, you have the right to photograph anything in plain view, including federal buildings and the police. On private property, the owner may set rules related to photography or video.
- You don't need a permit to march in the streets or on sidewalks, as long as marchers don't obstruct car or pedestrian traffic. If you don't have a permit, police officers can ask you to move to the side of a street or sidewalk to let others pass or for safety reasons.
- Certain types of events may require permits. These include a march or parade that requires blocking traffic or street closure; a large rally requiring

the use of sound amplifying devices; or a rally over a certain size at most parks or plazas.

- While certain permit procedures require submitting an application well in advance of the planned event, police can't use those procedures to prevent a protest in response to breaking news events.
- Restrictions on the route of a march or sound equipment might violate the First Amendment if they are unnecessary for traffic control or public safety, or if they interfere significantly with effective communication to the intended audience.
- A permit cannot be denied because the event is controversial or will express unpopular views.[1]

How does the First Amendment apply to campus protests? The Foundation for Individual Rights in Education (FIRE), a long-time defender of students' right to free speech, has provided some useful answers with this Q&A:

Q: I go to a public college. Can I protest on campus?
A: Yes. Public universities are government entities that are bound by the Constitution, so students on public campuses have free speech rights protected by the First Amendment.

Q: I go to a private college. Can I protest on campus?
A: Probably. Even though private institutions are not required to honor constitutional rights, most private colleges promise their students the right to free speech. . . .

Q: Can my school shut down our protest because they don't like what we're saying?
A: No. Under the First Amendment, you may not be censored or punished because of your opinion. This means that students have the right to express even the most controversial viewpoints. There are very limited exceptions to this rule—including threats to harm another person or inciting imminent violence or destruction of property—that can legitimately lead to arrest or disciplinary action under your school's student conduct code.

Q: Are all forms of protest protected?
A: No. While the First Amendment protects your right to speak your mind with only limited exceptions, public colleges are allowed to maintain reasonable time, place, and manner restrictions—in other words, viewpoint-neutral rules on where, when, and how you can demonstrate on campus—in order to prevent disruption of the educational environment. For example, a college can prohibit loud amplification near school buildings during hours that classes are in session. But the rule has to be applied even-handedly. The school can't allow the College Republicans to use a megaphone but forbid the College Democrats from doing so—or vice versa. Keep in mind that these rules also have to be reasonable. A college does not need to, say, limit all demonstrations to a tiny corner of campus on weekdays between 4:00 p.m. and 5:00 p.m. to keep campus running smoothly. . . .

Q: Is my right to protest the same indoors as outdoors?

A: No. Because of concerns about disruption, noise, and even fire safety, colleges generally impose much more restrictive rules on what students can do inside a building than outside—and the law very often backs them up. By contrast, colleges have very little justification for suppressing a peaceful student protest on the quad or in other open, public areas of campus—and the law very often backs up students in those circumstances.

Q: I want to occupy an administrative building. Can I do that?

A: If you do, be aware that you may be arrested or face punishment through your college's disciplinary process. The First Amendment does not protect civil disobedience—nonviolent unlawful conduct undertaken intentionally as a form of protest. Examples might include occupying a campus building or participating in a "die-in" that blocks traffic on a campus street. Such forms of protest may be a violation of criminal law (e.g., trespassing or disorderly conduct) or a violation of the student conduct code, so you should be prepared to face potential punishment from either or both systems.

Q: Can I get in trouble for other things while I'm protesting?

A: Yes. The First Amendment does not protect unlawful conduct. If you engage in conduct that violates criminal law—such as violence, vandalism, or underage drinking—while protesting, you can be arrested and/or face campus disciplinary proceedings.

Q: Do I give up all my free speech rights if I participate in civil disobedience?

A: No. Even though the police or college can remove and possibly punish you for disruptive activity, like blocking traffic or interrupting classes, they can't do so because they don't like your message or point of view.[2]

Civil Disobedience

Protests can take several forms, both legal and illegal, civil and uncivil, conscientious and not. Legal protests try to get their point across without law-breaking—that is, without unlawfully impeding traffic, interfering with lawful activities, or violating the rights of others. Legal protesters may march, picket, rally, or speak out in public spaces or online.

Other kinds of protests involve disobedience to laws or policies. The justification for the disobedience derives ultimately from a fact discussed in Chapter 1: morality and the law are distinct, and when they conflict, the former can override the latter. There is disagreement among philosophers about the precise moral underpinnings of disobedience to legal or political rules, but most agree that people have a right, in certain situations, to conscientiously disobey.

The kind of disobedient protest known as **conscientious objection** consists of a refusal to comply with a directive or legal order for reasons of personal morality. Protesters practice conscientious objection not to change the law or policy or to publicize its unfairness but to avoid participating in something they think is bad or wrong. The most common example of conscientious objection

Fig. 6.2 Occupy Wall Street activists hold their ground in the early morning when New York City Mayor Michael Bloomberg threatened to remove them.

is the pacifist who refuses to obey a conscription order to serve in the military. But the term may also apply to, say, a physician who refuses to perform a legal abortion or a citizen who refuses to pay taxes because the revenue will be used to support an unjust war.

Civil disobedience is deliberate lawbreaking designed to bring about change in a law or government policy. A protester violates a particular law while showing respect for the law in general by willingly accepting punishment for the violation. In *direct* civil disobedience, protesters break the law they are against; in *indirect* civil disobedience, for practical reasons, they break an alternative law to show opposition to the law they actually oppose. Well-known instances of civil disobedience include Gandhi's resistance to British rule in India, the civil rights movement led by Martin Luther King, Jr., the refusal of Rosa Parks to relinquish her bus seat in the segregated South, Nelson Mandela's resistance to apartheid in South Africa, and student sit-ins against the Vietnam War.

In classic civil disobedience (defended by both the philosopher John Rawls and Martin Luther King, Jr.), a central characteristic is *conscientiousness*—the willingness of protesters to breach the law out of sincere moral conviction and in the interests of society. Combined with conscientiousness is the element of *communication*—protesters conveying through their disobedience their disapproval of the law and their desire for the public to change it. Another factor is *publicity*—ensuring that the disobedient acts are not covert but are done in the open so their point and impact are clear. Probably the most notable feature is *nonviolence*—a commitment not to harm or injure others while breaking the law. Acts of violence violate the civil liberties of others and thus interfere with the protesters' appeal to the public's own sense of justice. Civil disobedience is intended to send a message, and violence is thought to dilute that message. As John Rawls says, "To engage in violent acts likely to injure and hurt is incompatible with civil disobedience as a mode of address. Indeed, any interference with the civil liberties of others tends to obscure the civilly disobedient quality of one's act."[3]

You can see these elements in many of King's expositions of civil disobedience (what he called "nonviolent resistance"). For example:

> The alternative to violence is nonviolent resistance. This method was made famous by Mohandas K. Gandhi, who used it to free India from the domination of the British empire. Five points can be made concerning nonviolence as a method in bringing about better racial conditions.
>
> First, this is not a method for cowards: it *does* resist. The nonviolent resister is just as strongly opposed to the evil against which he protests as is the person who uses violence. His method is passive or nonaggressive in the sense that he is not physically aggressive toward his opponent. But his mind and emotions are always active, constantly seeking to persuade the opponent that he is mistaken. This method is passive physically but strongly active spiritually; it is nonaggressive physically but dynamically aggressive spiritually.
>
> A second point is that nonviolent resistance does not seek to defeat or humiliate the opponent, but to win his friendship and understanding. The nonviolent resister must often express his protest through noncooperation or boycotts, but he realizes that noncooperation and boycotts are not ends themselves; they are merely means to awaken a sense of moral shame in the opponent. The end is redemption and reconciliation. . . .
>
> A third characteristic of this method is that the attack is directed against forces of evil rather than against persons who are caught in those forces. It is evil we are seeking to defeat, not the persons victimized by evil. . . .
>
> A fourth point that must be brought out concerning nonviolent resistance is that it avoids not only external physical violence but also internal violence of spirit. At the center of nonviolence stands the principle of love. In struggling for human dignity the oppressed people of the world must not allow themselves to become bitter or indulge in hate campaigns. To retaliate with hate and bitterness would do nothing but intensify the hate in the world. Along the way of life, someone must have sense enough and morality enough to cut off the chain of hate. This can be done only by projecting the ethics of love to the center of our lives. . . .
>
> Finally, the method of nonviolence is based on the conviction that the universe is on the side of justice. It is this deep faith in the future that causes the nonviolent resister to accept suffering without retaliation. He knows that in his struggle for justice he has cosmic companionship.[4]

Theorists disagree about the importance of adhering to all the features of the classic conception of civil disobedience. Some say, for example, that in certain circumstances, limited amounts of violence may be the best way to communicate disapproval of a law or policy. As Kimberley Brownlee says,

> [A]lthough the word *violence* has negative connotations, it includes a wide range of acts and events, major and minor, intended and unintended, that sometimes cause, but other times only *risk* damage or injury. It is implausible to say that every modest, non-injurious act of violence in the course of disobedience is, by definition, uncivil and at odds with respect for basic needs and rights.[5]

Likewise, it's thought that the publicity requirement can sometimes undermine the protester's attempt to communicate:

> [P]ublicity sometimes detracts from or undermines the attempt to communicate through civil disobedience. If a person publicises her intention to breach the law, then she provides both political opponents and legal authorities with the opportunity to abort her efforts to communicate. For this reason, unannounced or (initially) covert disobedience is sometimes preferable to actions undertaken publicly and with fair warning. Examples include releasing animals from research laboratories or vandalising military property; to succeed in carrying out these actions, disobedients would have to avoid publicity of the kind Rawls defends. Such acts of civil disobedience nonetheless may be regarded as "open" when followed soon after by an acknowledgment of the act and the reasons for acting. Openness and publicity, even at the cost of having one's protest frustrated, offer ways for disobedients to show their willingness to deal fairly with authorities.[6]

Civil disobedience as a mode of political and moral protest has had both exponents (such as Rawls, King, and Gandhi) and detractors. This is how Harvard philosopher Peter Suber responds to some of the more well-known objections:

> **Objection:** Civil disobedience cannot be justified in a democracy. Unjust laws made by a democratic legislature can be changed by a democratic legislature. The existence of lawful channels of change makes civil disobedience unnecessary.
> **Reply:** Thoreau, who performed civil disobedience in a democracy, argued that sometimes the constitution is the problem, not the solution. Moreover, legal channels can take too long, he argued, for he was born to live, not to lobby. His individualism gave him another answer: individuals are sovereign, especially in a democracy, and the government only holds its power by delegation from free individuals. Any individual may, then, elect to stand apart from the domain of law. Martin Luther King, Jr., who also performed civil disobedience in a democracy, asks us to look more closely at the legal channels of change. If they are open in theory, but closed or unfairly obstructed in practice, then the system is not democratic in the way needed to make civil disobedience unnecessary. Other activists have pointed out that if judicial review is one of the features of American democracy which is supposed to make civil disobedience unnecessary, then it ironically subverts this

Fig. 6.3 Rosa Parks was arrested for civil disobedience on December 1, 1955. Her crime was disobeying an Alabama law that required black people to give up seats to white people when the bus was full.

goal; for to obtain standing to bring an unjust statute to court for review, often a plaintiff must be arrested for violating it. Finally, the Nuremberg principles require disobedience to national laws or orders which violate international law, an overriding duty even in (perhaps especially in) a democracy.

Objection: Even if civil disobedience is sometimes justified in a democracy, activists must first exhaust the legal channels of change and turn to disobedience only as a last resort.

Reply: Legal channels can never be "exhausted." Activists can always write another letter to their congressional delegation or to newspapers; they can always wait for another election and cast another vote. But justice delayed, King proclaimed, is justice denied. After a point, he argued, patience in fighting an injustice perpetuates the injustice, and this point had long since been passed in the 340-year struggle against segregation in America. In the tradition which justifies civil disobedience by appeal to higher law, legal niceties count for relatively little. . . .

Objection: We must obey the law under a contract with other members of our society. We have tacitly consented to the laws by residing in the state and enjoying its benefits.

Reply: Obviously this objection can be evaded by anyone who denies the social contract theory. But surprisingly many disobedient activists affirm that theory, making this an objection they must answer. Socrates makes this objection to Crito who is encouraging him to disobey the law by escaping from prison before he is executed. Thoreau and Gandhi both reply (as part of larger, more complex replies) that those who object deeply to the injustices committed by the state can, and should, relinquish the benefits they receive from the state by living a life of voluntary simplicity and poverty; this form of sacrifice is in effect to revoke one's tacit consent to obey the law. Another of Thoreau's replies is that consent to join a society and obey its laws must always be express, and never tacit. But even for Locke, whose social contract theory introduces the term "tacit consent," the theory permits disobedience, even revolution, if the state breaches its side of the contract. A reply from the natural law tradition, used by King, is that an unjust law is not even a law, but a perversion of law (Augustine, Aquinas). Hence, consent to obey the laws does not extend to unjust laws. A reply made by many Blacks, women, and native Americans is that the duty to obey is a matter of degree; if they are not fully enfranchised members of American society, then they are not fully bound by its laws.

Objection: What if everybody did it? Civil disobedience fails Kant's universalizability test. Most critics prefer to press this objection as a slippery slope argument; the objection then has descriptive and normative versions. In the descriptive version, one predicts that the example of disobedients will be imitated, increasing lawlessness and tending toward anarchy. In the normative version, one notes that if disobedience is *justified* for one group whose moral beliefs condemn the law, then it is justified for any group similarly situated, which is a recipe for anarchy.

Replies: The first reply, offered in seriousness by Thoreau and Gandhi, is that anarchy is not so bad an outcome. In fact, both depict anarchy as an ideal form of society. However, both are willing to put off the anarchical utopia for another day and fight in the meantime for improved laws; consequently, this strand of their thinking is often overlooked. Another reply is a variation on the first. Anarchy may be bad, but despotism is worse (Locke instead of Hobbes). If we face an iniquitous law, then we may permissibly disobey, and risk anarchy, in order to resist the tendency toward the greater evil of despotism. A. J. Muste extended this line of thinking to turn the slippery slope objection against itself. If we let the state conscript young men against their wills to fight immoral wars, then what will the state do next? For Muste, conscription puts us on a slippery slope toward despotism, and obedience would bring us to the bottom.

Utilitarians observe that disobedience and obedience may both be harmful. The slippery slope objection falsely assumes that the former sort of harm always outweighs the latter. In the case of an iniquitous law, the harm of disobedience can be the lesser evil. This utilitarian reply is sometimes found to coexist with a complementary deontological reply, for example in Thoreau: one simply must not lend one's weight to an unjust cause.

Ronald Dworkin replies, in effect, that the descriptive version of the argument is false and the normative version irrelevant. There is no evidence that civil disobedience, even when tolerated by legal officials, leads to an increase in lawlessness. Moreover, rights trump utility. Since (for Dworkin) there is a strong right to disobey certain kinds of unjust laws, and since the slippery slope argument points only to the disutility of disobedience, this is a case of a right in conflict with utility; hence the right to disobey must prevail.[7]

IS IT PROTECTED SPEECH OR CIVIL DISOBEDIENCE?

Free speech and civil disobedience are often confused. Philosopher Martha C. Nussbaum tries to disentangle these two ideas by focusing on a well-publicized incident that occurred at her school:

[Consider] a letter of protest signed by over 150 members of the faculty of my own university, the University of Chicago, in a case involving then-pending disciplinary action against student body president Tyler Kissinger in May 2016. Kissinger and a group of student and non-student protesters had occupied Levi Hall, the university's administration building. Kissinger had gotten past security by claiming official business as student body president. He hid in a bathroom for a time, then used his backpack to prop open one of the locked doors of the building to let in the other protesters (thus bypassing the usual security and ID procedure). The protesters went to the fifth floor and sat in the lobby of the president's office. The demands of the protesters were heterogeneous, including a $15-per-hour minimum wage for campus workers, more accountability from campus police, and divestment from fossil fuels. The protest ended when the university threatened to have the protesters arrested and expelled if they remained in the building after its 5 p.m. closing time. While university disciplinary proceedings—which might have prevented Mr. Kissinger from graduating a few days later—were in the offing, the faculty letter of June 9 asked for the dismissal of all charges, saying that Kissinger's actions were protected by a "right to engage in peaceful protest." "Free speech, free access to university space, and dialogue among students, faculty, and administrators are essential to the university's educational mission." A university spokesman had already expressed a different view of the case: "Freedom of expression and dissent are fundamental values of the University of Chicago. The University's policies do not prevent students from engaging in protest, and the university does not discipline students for speaking out on any issue." Mr. Kissinger, the statement continued, had been charged with "premeditated and dishonest behavior to gain entry into Levi Hall, creating an unsafe situation." Kissinger himself, speaking to the *New York Times* (before the faculty letter was drafted), took the same position as the faculty letter, conflating speech with illegal protest actions: "If they are cracking down on people who are protesting, I don't understand what the university means by free expression."

I shall argue that Kissinger's acts are not protected speech, in the sense that they are protected by the First Amendment. . . . His acts may or may not count as acts of civil disobedience—we'll see that there are some problems, given the protesters' heterogeneous aims, the looseness of the connection between their actions and their goals, and their apparent lack of awareness of the illegality of their actions (trespass, creating a security problem). Basically, however, the university spokesperson is absolutely correct: the actions are illegal, and they are not protected free speech. . . .

Kissinger . . . did not frame his acts as civil disobedience, for which he expected to pay the legal penalty. Indeed, he told the *New York Times* that his acts were protected speech, and seemed surprised and offended by the prospect of a legal penalty. Second, his acts were furtive rather than public and honest, as the classic definition requires. Third, Kissinger's demands were highly heterogeneous. . . .[This] extreme heterogeneity is not simply a strategic issue: it also compromises the very claim (had such a claim been made) that the protesters are targeting an urgent issue of justice with the aim to awaken the conscience of the community.[8]

Uncivil Disobedience

Civil disobedience is a widely acknowledged, if controversial, form of protest, often thought to be both morally justified and strategically effective. But consider these examples of a different kind of disobedient protest:

> Protesters gathered outside the home of Fox News host Tucker Carlson in Northwest Washington on Wednesday evening, calling him racist and chanting "we know where you sleep at night," the latest in a string of similar episodes in which prominent conservatives have been aggressively confronted in their private lives.
>
> Carlson, who is often denounced by liberal critics for his rhetoric about immigrants and minorities, was not home at the time, at about 6:30 p.m., and nor were his children. But his wife was there, and according to Carlson, she locked herself in the pantry and called 911 out of fear of a home invasion.
>
> "Tucker Carlson, we are outside your home," one person can be heard saying in a video of the incident that was posted to social media and has since been deleted. . . .
>
> The protesters were scattering by the time police arrived. No one was arrested and the confrontation, which is thought to have involved about 20 people, is being investigated as a suspected hate crime, according to a police report.
>
> Smash Racism DC, the anti-fascist group that helped organize the protest, was unapologetic Thursday, writing on Facebook: "Fascists are vulnerable. Confront them at their homes!"
>
> In June, amid national debate over the separation of migrant children from their parents at the southern U.S. border, Homeland Security Secretary Kirstjen Nielsen was heckled as she ate at a Mexican restaurant in D.C. In September, in an episode Smash Racism DC also helped organize, protesters shouted Sen. Ted Cruz (R-Tex.) and his wife out of an upscale restaurant, castigating the lawmaker for supporting the nomination of Brett M. Kavanaugh to the Supreme Court.[9]

> Last Saturday night, a Fox News contributor names Kat Timpf was at a bar in Brooklyn. As she recounted the incident to *National Review,* a man asked her where she worked. A while later, she said, a women began "screaming at me to get out." Timpf walked away, but the woman followed her around the bar while other patrons laughed. Fearing physical attack, Timpf left. She told *National Review* and *The Hill* that it was the third time she has been harassed since 2017. A few months earlier, a woman yelled at her during dinner at a Manhattan restaurant. The year before, while she was about to give a speech, a man dumped water on her head. . . .
>
> Conservatives, of course, aren't the only ones who endure intimidation in their personal lives. Since Christine Blasey Ford's testimony against Brett Kavanaugh, harassment has forced her family to move four times, prevented her from returning to work, and required her to hire private security.[10]

Such actions have been called **uncivil disobedience**, lawbreaking protest that (unlike civil disobedience) shuns publicity, evades lawful penalty, is morally offensive, or is potentially violent. These protests earn the applause of those who dislike the victims and their politics, but they provoke the condemnation of most others, both from the Left and the Right. Regarding the Carlson protest, former Fox host Megyn Kelly tweeted, "This has to stop . . . He does not deserve this. It's stomach-turning." CNN host S. E. Cupp said, "This is not okay. By the political left, the political right or the deranged. Don't do this." Stephen Colbert, host of the Late Show, said "Fighting Tucker Carlson's ideas is an American right. Targeting his home and terrorizing his family is an act of monstrous cowardice. Obviously don't do this, but also, take no pleasure in it happening. Feeding monsters just makes more monsters."[11]

The terms "civil disobedience" and "uncivil disobedience" can be misleading since, historically, acts of civil disobedience have always been considered uncivil and offensive in some quarters, and occurrences of civil disobedience were never meant to be models of decorum.

The question is, Can uncivil disobedience (as defined here) be morally justified? Some philosophers think it can be, under certain conditions. Even so, many commentators are not likely to approve of incidents like those just described. These two philosophers, for example, would probably condemn the actions as both morally and strategically flawed:

Charles Watson

We live in a weaponized moment, yet going to someone's home is highly problematic. You immediately cast them in the position of self-defense. They feel a visceral threat. This isn't a moment of political activism. It's intimidation and coercion. There is no way we are having a conversation when you are threatening my home.

What is the end goal other than coercion and threat? Why involve someone's spouse and children? If you use fear to coerce me, it does not create a strong bond, because the minute you turn your back, our alliance is tenuous. Strategically, all these methods do is give you a short-term fix, a euphoria. These actions will not create deep loyalty. They will not create understanding or a lasting bond.

Always ask the question: "Whose interests are served?" Arguments are not pure and free. What interests are served by violence and intimidation? What agenda does violence advance? Primal impulses are served, but what else? How can we advocate for the vulnerable by trammeling others and making *them* vulnerable?

Sarah Holtman

If my reason for engaging in more extreme forms of protest is simply to do to another what they have done to me, that is revenge. It is not using the principles of justice to address a wrong. That steps outside the human aspiration to come together and agree on moral standards to govern our behavior. As Rousseau observed, what is right or just is conceptually distinct from (and opposed to) what someone achieves through might or power. If my reason for choosing violent protest is that it will give me the power to make your decisions for you, then I am appealing to power, not justice, and my reasoning conflicts with the aim of living together under shared laws and institutions that all of us can endorse.

I'm personally someone who believes in vigorous protest—we are morally warranted in seeking to make people deeply uncomfortable in order to awaken them to injustice and get them to act. But political protest needs to be designed to show people in the community—people who may be less familiar with the issues at hand—what needs fixing and why. Going to personal homes or engaging in violence to property may not help the cause even if they are otherwise justifiable.[12]

Candice Delmas, author of *A Duty to Resist: When Disobedience Should Be Uncivil*, argues that we have a moral duty to resist injustice not just through civil disobedience and legal actions but also through uncivil disobedience and defiance. "I aim to show," she says, "that some types of uncivil disobedience, including political riots, vigilante self-defense, whistleblowing, sanctuary assistance, and graffiti street art, can be justified—not in exceptional circumstances but systematically, and even in supposedly legitimate, liberal democratic states."[13]

Delmas contends that the traditional arguments used against civil and uncivil disobedience can be turned around and used instead to justify principled disobedience, including the uncivil kind:

[The] objection that unlawful resistance involves making oneself an exception or free-riding on others' compliance and thereby failing to treat others as equals does not withstand scrutiny. Agents often resort to disobedience because they, or those on whose behalf they act, or with whom they stand in solidarity, are marginalized and excluded, deprived of a say in the decisions that affect them. The oppressed are the ones treated as less than equals, and therefore disobedience intended to protest this inferior treatment cannot reasonably be thought of as violating mutual reciprocity.

Noncommunicative uncivil disobedience, such as direct action, however, calls for a different kind of response to the free-riding objection, since it does not necessarily seek to denounce the marginalization of some members of the community. For instance, agents providing covert assistance to migrants or engaged in vigilante self-defense aim first and foremost to prevent harms. Their apparent disregard for laws and the outcomes of democratic processes may seem like an assertion of moral superiority, a way to say, "I know better than everyone else what is right and wrong."

But this objection conceals the targets' own responsibility for the harms agents seek to prevent. When disobedients are justified, it is typically because the state endangers or harms some people or unjustly fails to protect them from harm. Thus the Lavender Panthers existed only because—and so long as—the San Francisco police did not intervene to protect gays from homophobic violence. The first sanctuary movement grew in the 1980s to help refugees from Central America who, although they were fleeing civil conflicts partly caused and sustained by the

United States, were refused asylum in the country. Judging them as presumptuous and self-righteous seems misguided and unfounded. . . .

Another objection is that any disobedience—be it criminal or principled, civil or uncivil—sows anarchy and invites violence. A society where everyone disobeys all laws they find unjust would be no better than the state of nature, where everyone individually decides what is right and wrong. States cannot tolerate such exercise of discretionary judgment. . . .

In response, republican and liberal theorists have argued that, far from undermining the stable system of rights, civil disobedience can instead strengthen it. . . . Scheuerman argues that, far from undermining it, "civil disobedience buttresses the rule of law," as "fidelity to the law" demands "of conscientious political actors that they push for dramatic change that might deepen both law's legitimacy and its efficacy." Beyond the particulars of these arguments, the potential of civil disobedience to protect rather than undermine the rule of law is now widely accepted in the literature, and to a lesser extent in public discourse.

What about uncivil disobedience, though? Can it also exemplify respect for the rule of law and serve to bolster law's integrity? I believe it can. Consider one type of uncivil principled disobedience purporting to preserve the rule of law: government whistleblowing, defined as unauthorized seizure and disclosure of state-classified information.

There are many plausible candidates for unauthorized whistleblowing that strengthened the rule of law: Daniel Ellsberg's leaks of the Pentagon Papers, which uncovered the state's commission of war crimes in Vietnam, Cambodia, and Laos, as well as deception at home; Deep Throat's leaks about the Watergate scandal, which resulted in punishment for others' lawbreaking; and Snowden's whistleblowing on the NSA's massive, unconstitutional domestic surveillance program.

Leaks of this nature, which expose serious wrongdoing and abuses, promote the rule of law. While many people describe instances of government whistleblowing they approve of as civil disobedience, in part because of their common potential to support the rule of law, it is important not to confuse the two. Government whistleblowing usually fails to adhere to norms of civility (especially publicity and non-evasiveness) and poses threats to national security by irreversibly undoing the secrecy the state had determined appropriate or necessary. Through their disclosure, government whistleblowers thus usurp the power of the state to determine, and to have exclusive authority over, the boundaries around state secrets. Government whistleblowing is thus typically uncivil in some ways, but it can be justified, like civil disobedience, on the grounds that it strengthens the rule of law.[14]

Delmas recognizes, however, that there are some basic constraints that must apply to any principled lawbreaking, especially to uncivil disobedience:

Resistors must act with respect for other people's interests, including, but not limited to, their basic interests in life and bodily integrity; their interests in non-domination and in choosing the values that shape their lives; and their interest in protection by a stable, secure system of rights. That is, these basic human interests constrain both the legitimate goals and the appropriate means of resistance, and one should accept and seek to protect these basic interests when engaging in principled disobedience. . . .

Resistors should generally seek the least harmful course of action feasible to achieve their (legitimate) goal, that is, from among those courses of action that have a reasonable chance of success. This constraint does not rise to the level of necessary condition for the justification of principled disobedience, in part because agents may sometimes justifiably settle for second or third best if, say, *the* least harmful course of action demands too much sacrifice on their part. That the course of action should have a reasonable chance of achieving the goal of resistance should not be misunderstood: it does not require that every act lead directly to reform or directly lessen oppression. Recall the variety of goals that may motivate resistance. A small act of everyday resistance, such as confronting a man's catcall or misogynist tweet, may only get one harassed; it certainly will not, in itself, change sexist mores. Yet its aim may simply be to force this man to reflect on his treatment of women. And it may be that an aggressive confrontation, likely to further antagonize the man, would not have a reasonable chance of succeeding at making him think, but that it would be successful if the goal is simply for the woman to assert her dignity and express anger at being objectified. In short, the success of resistance should not be measured solely in terms of the (good) social consequences it brings about (through direct action or policy reform): it may instead be measured by whether and how well it gets its message across to its intended audience (including, at the limit, oneself).[15]

SHOULD STUDENTS BE PUNISHED FOR DISRUPTING SPEECH?

Punishments for student hecklers have gained support at some universities, and several states have passed laws that require schools to penalize disruptions. Recently the board of regents of the University of Wisconsin voted for rules requiring mandatory punishments for students found to have disrupted others' free speech. The rules would require students who have "materially and substantially disrupted the free speech of others" to be suspended after two violations and to be expelled after three. According to one news report,

> Students, faculty, lawmakers and civil liberties organizations have vocally opposed the disciplinary sanctions for years. At a public hearing March 5, five UW-Madison students and a professor called the policy vague and "draconian." The Board also received 14 written comments, 12 of which opposed the rule, according to meeting materials.
>
> One commenter said the rule would have the opposite effect and chill free speech, intimidating "students from protest policies that could be detrimental to campus life," according to meeting materials. Another said that it removes individual schools' freedoms, "eliminating any autonomy that each campus currently has to adjust for the different learning and social environments present."

But supporters of disciplinary sanctions have said they will prevent student protesters from shutting down speakers or opinions they disagree with.[16]

In a report published before the rules were approved, they were decried by both liberals and conservatives:

> Two free-speech experts said they oppose the shouting down of campus speakers, but they don't see mandatory punishments as the best way to deal with students who do that. Such policies "tie the hands of individual decision makers—administrators who are better equipped to determine the context, what actually happened, and mete out a punishment accordingly," said Will Creeley, vice president for legal and public advocacy at the Foundation for Individual Rights in Education. . . .
>
> Determining whether speech crosses a line into disruption is a tricky business, said Nadine M. Strossen, a professor at New York Law School and former president of the American Civil Liberties Union.
>
> Strossen has spent much of her career defending the speech rights of extremists, even neo-Nazis. But Wisconsin's policy, she said, would have the effect of privileging their right to speak over students' right to demonstrate against them.
>
> When students shouted down the homeland-security secretary at Georgetown on Monday, the failure of university officials to act was unacceptable, Strossen said. The students should have been escorted out of the auditorium. But that doesn't mean they should be expelled, she said.[17]

Argument Analysis

Suppose fifteen university students carry out an act of uncivil disobedience off-campus. They gather one evening outside the residence of the secretary of the US Department of Homeland Security who had instituted harsh procedures for the processing of migrant children at the US-Mexico border. (Children were separated from their frantic parents, sheltered in barely adequate conditions, and then returned to their parents after a month.) The students shout threats at the secretary (who was home at the time with his wife and children), pound on the door and windows, spray-paint anti-government slogans on the exterior walls, and leave after an hour before the police arrive.

Suppose also that the leader of the student protesters later posts an argument on Facebook to justify their actions, an argument that can be broken down like this:

1. The secretary of Homeland Security is guilty of mistreating and terrorizing innocent migrants, including children.
2. He and his family deserve to be subjected to the same kind of terror that he has inflicted on many other families. He should be shown what it feels like.
3. Our protest was meant to deter future mistreatment of migrants.
4. Therefore, our act of uncivil disobedience was morally justified.

This argument is not valid—that is, even if the premises are true, it does not follow that the conclusion is true. It may be possible to show that the students' actions were morally justified, but this argument doesn't do it.

We can grant premise 1: the secretary did not personally mistreat the migrants, but he did authorize and direct his department to do so.

Premise 2 is problematic for at least two reasons. First, even if the secretary deserves to be threatened and frightened, it does not follow that his family deserves such treatment. Second, civil disobedience seems morally justified at times because it aims to change an unjust law or policy and to send a message to others about that injustice. But the aim of the protesting students seems to be revenge or punishment. Revenge is generally regarded as an emotional response that has very little, if anything, to do with justice. According to many philosophers, retributive punishment can be morally justified but only if it is administered as part of a deliberative process sanctioned by the state. To these thinkers, personal revenge is immoral as well as detrimental to civil society.

Premise 3 may be true but misguided strategically. Since the protest is directed at the secretary and his family instead of at the government agency directly responsible for the migrants' mistreatment or to the public who might be moved to address the mistreatment, the protest seems ineffective and possibly counterproductive. This instance of uncivil disobedience seems very unlikely to deter any ill treatment of migrants.

KEY TERMS

civil disobedience	protest
conscientious objection	uncivil disobedience

 EXERCISES

Exercises marked with * have answers in "Answers to Exercises" (Appendix B).

Exercise 6.1: Review Questions

1. What are some of the ways that the First Amendment right to protest is limited by laws and competing rights?
*2. What is conscientious objection? How does it differ from civil disobedience?
3. What four elements are essential to classic civil disobedience?
*4. What is Peter Suber's response to those who say civil disobedience cannot be justified in a democracy?
5. What is uncivil disobedience? How does it differ from civil disobedience?

*6. Why are the terms "civil disobedience" and "uncivil disobedience" sometimes considered misleading?

7. What is Candice Delmas's view of uncivil disobedience?

8. What is Martha Nussbaum's view of the Tyler Kissinger case at the University of Chicago? Does she think his actions amounted to protected speech?

9. On a university campus, are all forms of protest protected? Explain.

10. Can schools shut down a protest because they don't like what the protesters are saying? Why or why not?

Exercise 6.2: Moral Arguments

1. Were the uncivil protests that targeted Tucker Carlson at his home in Washington, DC, morally justified? Why or why not?

2. Under what circumstances is civil disobedience justified? Give two examples.

3. Is uncivil disobedience ever justified? If so, in what situations? If not, why not?

4. Do students have a right to interfere with the free speech of other students? If so, under what circumstances? If not, why not?

5. Does the owner of a restaurant have a right to refuse to serve a politician whose polices she finds repugnant? If so, why? If not, why not? Would such an action be considered conscientious objection or uncivil disobedience?

Notes

1. ACLU, "Know Your Rights: Protesters' Rights," http://www.aclu.org.
2. Foundation for Individual Rights in Education, "FIRE's FAQ for Student Protests on Campus," http://www.thefire.org.
3. John Rawls, *A Theory of Justice* (Cambridge, MA: Harvard University Press, 1999), 321.
4. Martin Luther King Jr., "Violence and Racial Justice," in *A Testament of Hope*, ed. James Melvin Washington (New York: Harper and Row, 1986), 7–9.
5. Kimberley Brownlee, *Conscience and Conviction: The Case for Civil Disobedience* (Oxford: Oxford University Press, 2012), 198.
6. Kimberley Brownlee, "Civil Disobedience," *The Stanford Encyclopedia of Philosophy* (Fall 2017 edition), ed. Edward N. Zalta,//plato.stanford.edu/archives/fall2017/entries/civil-disobedience/.
7. Peter Suber, "Civil Disobedience," in *Philosophy of Law: An Encyclopedia* (Shrewsbury, MA: Garland Press, 1999), II.110–113 http://nrs.harvard.edu/urn-3:HUL.InstRepos:4725008.
8. Martha C. Nussbaum, "Civil Disobedience and Free Speech in the Academy," in *Academic Freedom*, ed. Jennifer Lackey (New York: Oxford University Press, 2018), 170–171, 181.
9. Allyson Chiu, Perry Stein, and Emma Brown, "Anti-Fascist Protesters Target Tucker Carlson's Home," *The Washington Post*, November 8, 2018.
10. Peter Beinart, "Left-Wing Protests Are Crossing the Line," *The Atlantic*, November 16, 2018.
11. Brian Stelter, "Police Launch Investigation after Antifa Activists Descend on Fox Host Tucker Carlson's Home," CNN Business, November 8, 2018. www.cnn.com.

12. Camille Gage, "The Ethics of Protesting: How Far Is Too Far in Getting Your Message Across," *Minnesota Reformer*, October 2, 2020. https://minnesotareformer.com.

13. Candice Delmas, *A Duty to Resist: When Disobedience Should Be Uncivil* (New York: Oxford University Press, 2018), 48.

14. Delmas, *A Duty to Resist*, 52–55.

15. Delmas, *A Duty to Resist*, 49–50.

16. Yvonne Kim, "UW Regents Approve Changes to Require Student Punishments for Disrupting Free Speech," *The Cap Times*, April 3, 2020, https://madison.com/ct/news/local/education/uw-regents-approve-changes-to-require-student-punishments-for-disrupting-free-speech/article_0b94bc03-b99e-5009-9333-1311a0344403.html.

17. Sarah Brown, "To Protect Free Speech, U. of Wisconsin Is Poised to Double Down on Punishing Disruptive Protesters," *Chronicle of Higher Education*, October 10, 2019, https://www.chronicle.com/article/to-protect-free-speech-u-of-wisconsin-is-poised-to-double-down-on-punishing-disruptive-protesters/?cid=gen_sign_in.

The Ethics of Belief Online   7

We were wrong about the Internet. The technology that was supposed to make us smarter, friendlier, better informed, more tolerant, and more open-minded. Digital access was supposed to deliver us from our narrow views of the world, spread democracy, and set our imaginations free. But in many ways, the technology's powerful advantages have been turned against us, helping to make our view of the world narrower, darker, and dumber. Like every other major technological advance of the past, it has become a source of both moral good and bad—but this time on a scale that few could have imagined. The problem is, the good and bad are not in the flying zeros and ones, not in the billion apps and links, but in ourselves.

Moral questions arise in every corner of the infosphere, ranging from minor ones (like, Is it okay to ghost someone after sending them super-friendly vibes? or Is it wrong to give a high rating to a product you actually thought was terrible?) to those concerning serious, potentially tragic consequences. In this latter category are questions about our participation in or response to misogyny (hatred of or prejudice against women), LGBTQ bigotry, racism, harassment, threats, trolling, bullying, cyberstalking, doxing (the malicious publication of a person's personal information online), and revenge porn (sexually explicit images of someone posted online without their consent for the purpose of causing them psychological or social anguish). With a few keystrokes, people can wreck a person's life, silence them as brutally as a chokehold, and inflict on them psychological pain that's as agonizing as a knife wound.

The most interesting question about these actions is not, Are they morally wrong? Of course, they are wrong. They are condemned by moral principles and virtually every moral theory. The more trenchant moral question is, How should

Fig. 7.1 Amnesty International has reported that a poll it commissioned in 2017 "showed that nearly a quarter (23%) of the women surveyed across the eight countries said they had experienced online abuse or harassment at least once, including 21% of women polled in the UK and 1/3 (33%) of women polled in the US. In both countries, 59% of women who experienced abuse or harassment said the perpetrators were complete strangers."

we respond to them—both when they happen to us and when they happen to others? Plenty of thoughtful people continue to work on providing answers and devising practical solutions to the problems, even though many of the wrongs are rooted in cultural myths and ideological dogmas that predate the Internet by hundreds of years.

There are questions, however, that are even more philosophically basic than these, questions that relate to virtually everything we do online. They are about not the ethics of acting or doing, but of *believing*. Philosophers ask: *What is morally permissible to believe, to disbelieve, and to encourage others to believe?* Is it wrong to believe something without justification or evidence, to risk error or harm involving ourselves or others? Is it wrong to share information—memes, posts, blogs, news—that may be false, fake, or dangerous? What if we *know* it's false, fake, or dangerous? Do we share some responsibility if it leads to heartache or catastrophe? Of course, much depends on the stakes involved. It's one thing to knowingly share misinformation about a celebrity's fashion choices, but it is quite another to spread misinformation about the coronavirus vaccine or to repeat a rumor about a classmate cheating on their partner.

Beliefs have consequences, especially now in the roiling storm of the information age when misinformation and propaganda flow into our lives like a river

24/7, when what we say can fly around the world in half a second and help or harm hundreds, when believing preposterous things can lead to personal, social, or national tragedy. If so, our beliefs about important things—beliefs embodied in our online thinking, arguing, sharing, and persuading—must matter morally. We can sensibly ask, Am I right to believe this and to urge others to believe it?

Believing

A fundamental philosophical principle (and the essence of critical thinking) is that only if your beliefs are based on adequate evidence are you justified in believing them. Some philosophers have asserted that believing also has a moral dimension: it is *morally wrong* to believe a proposition without adequate evidence. One of these thinkers is the famous biologist Thomas Henry Huxley (1825–1895). Another is mathematician W. K. Clifford (1845–1879). This is how Clifford states his view:

> It is wrong always, everywhere, and for anyone, to believe anything upon insufficient evidence. If a man, holding a belief which he was taught in childhood or persuaded of afterwards, keeps down and pushes away any doubts which arise about it in his mind . . . and regards as impious those questions which cannot easily be asked without disturbing it—the life of that man is one long sin against mankind.[1]

Clifford thinks that belief without evidence is immoral because our actions are guided by our beliefs, and if our beliefs are unfounded, our actions (including morally relevant actions) are likely to be imprudent. He tells a story to illustrate his point. Once upon a time a ship owner decided to sell tickets for a transatlantic voyage. It occurred to him, though, that the ship might be unsafe: it was old, not well built, and often had to be repaired. These doubts ate at him, and he considered having the ship overhauled and refitted, but he knew the repairs would cost him dearly. So he pushed all these doubts and misgivings aside and persuaded himself to see everything in a more positive light. By the time the ship sailed, he had achieved a confident and sincere conviction that the vessel was safe and seaworthy. The ship owner, Clifford says, got his insurance money "when she went down in mid-ocean and told no tales."

The ship owner based his belief on wishful thinking, not on adequate evidence. Therefore, Clifford says, he did wrong; he was morally responsible for the death of the passengers. Even if the ship had not gone down, the ship owner still did wrong because "he had no right" to believe based on such flimsy evidence.

Clifford's view is absolute; he thinks it is "always, everywhere, and for anyone" wrong to believe without sufficient evidence. Contemporary philosophers don't take such a strict position. When not much is at stake in ordinary situations—for example, the belief that a houseplant needs watering or that the kitchen faucet is leaking—such strictness is not required. Nevertheless, when there is a risk of significant harm, injury, or injustice, we do seem to have a strong moral duty to believe as the evidence warrants. This echoes a point made in Chapter 1: moral judgments are based on both moral principles and propositions about nonmoral facts. If we are mistaken about the facts, then our moral judgments will also be mistaken—and we may very well do wrong as a result.

In the digital era, believing responsibly has never been more important—and more challenging. As you surely know by now, a massive share of online information is suspect, false, misleading, self-serving, biased, and crazy. A vast trove of it is generated by seriously uninformed people, nasty trolls, and partisan fanatics. Social media, blogs, and websites have made every person a potential publisher who can say almost anything online. But unlike traditional publishers, these writers typically have no one—no fact-checkers, no editors, no peer reviewers—to help ensure factual accuracy and to question their version of the facts. Too many of them are well-meaning but unaware, passionate but vile, interesting but unhinged.

Few things on the Internet seem to challenge the morality of our beliefs more than the phenomenon of fake news. **Fake news** is deliberately false or misleading news stories that masquerade as truthful reporting. In modern media, the term has been used as a warning about misinformation, as an accusation against adversaries, and as an incantation that's supposed to make objective truth disappear. Liberals have used it to accuse conservatives of promoting misinformation and half-truths, while conservatives have wielded it to charge liberals with trying to unfairly discredit views on the Right. Some conservatives have claimed that fact-checking, which has often resulted in a charge of fake news against them, is a left-wing conspiracy, and some liberals have argued that conservatives undermine legitimate journalism by falsely labeling real news as fake. We can see these crosscurrents of skepticism in two extreme modes of thinking: the acceptance of claims coming only from one's own partisan tribe, or the rejection of all claims from all other partisan tribes. As one observer puts it,

> Fake news, and the proliferation of raw opinion that passes for news, is creating confusion, punching holes in what is true, causing a kind of fun-house effect that leaves the reader doubting everything, including real news.
>
> That has pushed up the political temperature and increased polarization. No longer burdened with wrestling with the possibility that they might be wrong, people on the right and the left have become more entrenched in their positions, experts say. In interviews, people said they felt more empowered, more attached to their own side and less inclined to listen to the other. Polarization is fun, like cheering a goal for the home team.[2]

Much of the fake news we see is LOL funny or ridiculous, but a great deal of it is harmful, destructive, and dangerous. Fake news has sewn distrust among people, pushed political conflict to the boiling point, exaggerated disagreements and social conflicts, and incited confrontation and violence by proclaiming the reality of imaginary events. Conspiracy theorists and their accomplices have, in the aftermath of mass shootings and other tragedies, posted fake news designed

Fig. 7.2 Evidence shows that the pro-Trump Capitol riot of January 6, 2021, was propelled in large part by massive amounts of online misinformation, conspiracy theories, and fake news.

to incite fear, suspicion, and hate. Even before the flames are extinguished and the victims are counted, conspiracy theories fly around the Internet to blame the innocent, point fingers randomly, or declare that the innocent victims were really actors. Elections have been violently contested, the Capitol has been breached and ransacked, millions of people have taken to the streets in a rage because they believe an election has been stolen—and fake news helped light the fuse.

Fake news, whether real or imagined, whether soothing or vexing, is bad for intelligent discourse, bad for the pursuit of knowledge, bad for sane politics, and bad for democracy. And believing it for no good reason—especially when the stakes are high—can be regarded as a serious moral failing.

Critical thinking offers our most important defense against fake news (and all other forms of misinformation). It helps us proportion our beliefs to the evidence. By using critical thinking, we can confidently believe because we have good reason to believe, and by having good reasons for our belief, we are doing the right thing.

A prerequisite for critical thinking is adopting an attitude of *reasonable skepticism*. This attitude entails that we give up the habit of automatically accepting claims in the media, that we reject the questionable assumption that most of what's said online is true, that we stop taking the word of online sources on faith. Above all, reasonable skepticism means that we *do not believe a claim unless there are legitimate reasons for doing so*. Legitimate reasons are those that increase the likelihood of a claim being true. Such reasons come from reliable evidence, trustworthy sources, and critical reasoning. The problem is that we too often reach for illegitimate reasons, those that are *irrelevant* to the truth of a claim. Here are some illegitimate reasons for accepting or rejecting claims from a media source:

- My group (political faction, fans of politician X or pundit Y, online community, etc.) trusts this source. (So I will, too.)
- This source contradicts my beliefs. (If I disagree with it, it must be fake news.)
- An opposing group rejects this source. (So I will accept it because I hate the opposing group.)
- This source reinforces what I'd like to believe. (So I will believe it without question.)
- I reject any claim that comes from sources I don't like. (Because nothing they say can be right.)
- The claims made by this source *feel* true; therefore, they must actually *be* true. (Because my feelings alone can certify claims.)
- I have faith in my leader, and he or she hates this source. (So I will hate it, too, because I believe whatever he or she says.)
- Believing this claim or source makes me feel good. (And feeling good is what matters.)
- I let my intuition or gut tell me whether to trust a source. (It saves time and energy.)

There are times when it's perfectly rational to believe a claim just because a source says it's true. But that attitude is appropriate only when you have previously verified the reliability of the source by checking for legitimate reasons supporting the source's claims.

Maybe you're already a skeptic: you mistrust *all sources* in the mainstream media. Perhaps you're right to do so. Or not. In any case, the crucial question to ask is, again, What are the legitimate reasons for your view? Just saying that the mainstream media is untrustworthy does not relieve you of the duty to apply critical thinking to the claim.

When critically evaluating media (mainstream or otherwise) for trustworthiness, there is no way around the hard work of checking for good reasons to believe or disbelieve. And there is no denying that doing this often takes tremendous courage. Remember, *a good critical thinker is prepared to believe almost anything—given enough good reasons.*

Fortunately even in the Wild West of the infosphere, there are helpful strategies we can employ to discern what's real, what's fake, and what's worth our time. Here are a few of them:

Read laterally. When professional fact-checkers want to know whether a website is a reliable source of information, they read *laterally*—they leave the site after a quick look and see what other sources have to say about the person or organization behind the site. They don't just read *vertically*—they don't stay within the site and let themselves be distracted by features that are not sure indicators of reliability (like the site's layout, design, and authoritative-sounding name). Thus, good fact-checkers are more likely than others to reach accurate conclusions about a site's reliability and to do so more quickly.

So by reading laterally, you can quickly do at least three things:

(1) determine who is really behind the information you're seeing,
(2) uncover the purpose or motivation behind the information (is it to sell you something, persuade you to support a cause, push political views, report the news, or entertain you?), and
(3) find out how credible the source of the information is.

Reading laterally is about comparing sources, and that's especially important in debates about political or social questions. Consulting a variety of sources helps you put the information in proper perspective, uncover errors and bias, pinpoint consensus and disagreement among experts, and find out where the preponderance of evidence points. Certainly your hunt for sources should be carefully planned and limited, but examining too few of them can lead to views that are one-sided, incomplete, and wrong.

How can you tell if the news you're getting is incomplete, if there's important news or facts you're not seeing? You can't, unless you check alternative news sources for any missing stories. Reading a variety of newspapers, newsmagazines, blogs, websites, and journals of opinion is the best way to ensure that you're getting the big picture.

A useful aid in comparing perspectives is the website AllSides.com. Using reasonable criteria, it rates the political biases of hundreds of media outlets and writers and then, for particular news stories, provides articles that cover those stories from multiple political perspectives, ranging from left to center to right. Another reliable site that also covers multiple perspectives on controversial issues is ProCon.org.

Read critically. Ultimately, the credibility of websites, social media, and other sources of information comes down to the truth of the claims. Critical thinking tells us that it is reasonable to

(1) accept claims that are supported independently by reliable authorities, evidence, or other claims that you know to be true;
(2) accept claims that are adequately supported by the source itself through citations to other credible sources (experts, research, reports, etc.) or through references to supporting facts;
(3) reject claims when there is good reason for believing them false; and
(4) suspend judgment on claims that you are unsure of, for it is unreasonable to accept a claim without good reasons, and the only cure for uncertainty about a source's claims is further research and reflection.

The key questions to ask:

- *Are the claims plausible?* Do the claims make sense on their face? If a blogger says that one hour of sunlight on your skin each day can inoculate you against COVID-19, you would be smart to be skeptical of this claim because no evidence at all supports it and it conflicts with everything science knows about sunlight, viruses, and human skin. If a post or website announces that a UFO landed on the White House lawn yesterday, you would be right to doubt the claim because, among other things, such outrageous assertions are common on the Internet, no UFO claims have ever been proven, no reputable news organization has ever reported an actual UFO landing, and scientists and competent investigators have never authenticated even one UFO case, and so on. If a claim doesn't seem plausible to you, don't believe it, unless you have verified it.
- *What is the support for the claims?* Check if they are supported by references to trustworthy websites or news organizations, scientific research, legitimate experts, or polls by reputable organizations. See if the arguments are solid—that is, whether the supporting premises are true and the conclusions follow logically from the premises. If photos are offered as evidence, check them out: do a reverse-image search on images.google.com or TinEye.com.
- *Have reliable fact-checking organizations examined the claims?* Viral stories are often fact-checked by at least one of the top fact-checkers—including Snopes.com, FactCheck.org, PolitiFact.com, TruthorFiction.com, Hoax-Slayer.com, and *Washington Post*'s Fact Checker.

Use Google and Wikipedia carefully. Skilled researchers use Google and Wikipedia—but they do so sensibly. When you type questions or key words into Google, the first sources listed will almost certainly be sponsored sources—ads—which are likely to be biased or misleading. Other results at the top of the list will be chosen by Google's algorithms or by others who want their websites listed first. Thus, the first results will not necessarily be reliable or relevant.

But Google can still be a useful research tool if you know how to employ it. Try these tips:

- Search with Google Scholar (scholar.google.com). It will retrieve links only to trustworthy scholarly journals, papers, and books.
- Narrow your searches to domains most likely to yield reliable information—that is, to domains ending in.edu (educational sites), .gov (official governmental agencies at national, state, and local levels), and .org (non-profit and for-profit entities including schools and communities).
- To better zero in on your topic and to avoid getting a lot of extraneous hits, use quotation marks around words that should be searched as a unit:

YOUR BRAIN ON SOCIAL MEDIA

Online we are subject to a long list of cognitive biases that can distort our think-ing and lead us to believe something without legitimate reasons. Consider these:

Mere Exposure Effect

What if all the garbage we encounter online—all the lies, come-ons, fake news, misinformation, trivia, and rants—could affect our thinking without our con-scious awareness, even after we dismiss what we read as so much bunk? Research has shown that this is a real phenomenon that happens often. It's called the **mere exposure effect**, the idea that just being exposed repeatedly to words or images (even without registering them consciously) can induce a favorable or comfort-able feeling toward them, whether or not there is any good reason for doing so. This means you could end up liking or feeling positive toward a viral meme or nonsensical theory without knowing why. The element that makes the mere exposure effect work is familiarity with the thing exposed.

Illusion-of-Truth Effect

If there's one constant on social media, it's repetition: the same lies, ads, rants, bad arguments, and fervid affirmations hitting you again and again, day after day. Research reveals that these repeat performances can be more than just annoying. They can alter your perception of what is true. This is called the **illusion-of-truth effect**, a phenomenon in which you come to believe that a false claim is actually true simply because it is familiar. In a typical study of the effect, scientists showed people statements without any indication of whether they were true or not. Then days later, the researchers showed them the statements again mixed in with new statements. When asked to assess the statements' truth, the people judged the original state-ments as truer than the new ones—just because the earlier statements felt familiar. They had seen them before. But, of course, familiarity is no guarantee of truth.

The worrisome part is that the illusion-of-truth effect can happen even when we know better—that is, even when we have the opportunity to draw upon our store of knowledge. Too often, people don't apply what they know, and they allow familiarity to decide for them. Lies repeated are many times taken as truth—simply because they are repeated. Repetition and familiarity should cue our skepticism and remind us to look closer.

False Consensus Effect

Social media is the best incubator ever devised for what psychologists call **false consensus effect**, the tendency to overestimate the degree to which other people share our opinions, attitudes, and preferences. We like to think that most people agree with us (on a single issue or all issues), believe what we believe, have the same values, and look at the world the same way we do. We especially want to believe that attractive and respected people have the same beliefs we do. Thinking that many others agree with us gives us confidence that we are right, reasonable, smart, worthy, or sane. Our views aren't eccentric or beyond the pale; they are part of the consensus.

The problem is that we are often wrong about how widely our beliefs and attitudes are shared by others. We might say "everyone knows this" or "most people believe this," but there's a good chance that our estimates of how many concur are a huge exaggeration. There is little doubt that false consensus effect contributed to people's shocked reactions to the results of the 2016 US presidential election. Filter bubbles and social media communities, of course, generate internal consensus, but this internal agreement leads members to think that the consensus also exists outside the groups.

The Dunning-Kruger Effect

This scenario happens online every day: the least informed person in a discussion decides to educate everyone else on the topic, confidently lecturing on the fine points and presuming to correct people's "obvious" misconceptions, never doubting for a minute his own grasp of the facts and his own superior understanding, while gushing forth a lot of bad information, misjudgments, and non sequiturs. The problem here (other than the obnoxiousness of the gusher) is not just that he is ignorant, but that he doesn't know how ignorant he is. This is the **Dunning-Kruger effect**, the well-researched phenomenon of being ignorant of how ignorant we are.

So how can we avoid the Dunning-Kruger trap? Here's the advice of Guy Harrison, the author of *Think Before You Like*:

> Having the mere awareness and understanding that all people—yourself included—struggle to accurately assess competency levels can inspire the crucial and necessary pause, that moment of reflection before speaking, writing, clicking, liking, or swiping. Prior to declaring the "obvious answer" to gun violence, racism, sexism, or poverty—and then digging in to defend it—we must recall that confidence is not the same thing as knowledge. The Dunning-Kruger effect explains much of the loud, proud folly you find on social media.[3]

- • Type: "John Carson" novelist Chicago
- • Instead of: John Carson novelist Chicago
- Search *inside* specific websites with the syntax "site:" For example, to find an article in *USA Today* on refugees, type: site:usatoday.com refugees
- Search for websites similar to one you're interested in with the syntax "related:" For example, type: related:artvoice.com.my

Wikipedia articles are user created and thus considered by scholars and journalists to be not as consistently accurate or dependable as reference works from well-known reputable publishers. This is why citing a Wikipedia article as a source in an academic paper is so often frowned on. Nevertheless, Wikipedia is a very useful place to *start* a research project. The extensive lists of resources at the end of articles can point you to huge troves of authoritative books, essays, reference materials, experts, and websites. Starting at these resource lists, you can follow where your research leads, checking out the reliability and suitability of the resources as you go.

Sharing

Online, believing is one thing. Sharing is another. Both have moral implications. For example, since fake news is a lie (an intentionally told falsehood), communicating it is morally problematic. A common argument in ethics goes like this: a lie is wrong because it violates or undermines people's autonomy, their rational capacity for self-governance or self-determination, their ability to direct their own lives and choose for themselves. When we lie to people, we violate their autonomy by interfering with or thwarting their ability to choose their own paths and make their own judgments.

Autonomy involves the capacity to make personal choices, but choices cannot be considered entirely autonomous unless they are fully informed. When we make decisions in ignorance—without relevant information or blinded by misinformation—our autonomy is diminished just as surely as if someone physically manipulated us.

If this is correct, then concocting fake news or automatically sharing it after receiving it is possibly immoral. (This judgment, of course, would not apply to jokes, satire, and any other obviously unserious content.) This means that when the fake news we share causes harm (by, for example, provoking violence, harassment, or emotional distress), we would bear some responsibility for that harm. If we share it only with friends, we still may not be off the hook because they may also share it—and who knows where the sharing will end? Sharing information that we *know* is fake news is worse than sharing it when we are not sure, but most ethicists would probably condemn both actions.

In sharing fake news and other misinformation, there are gradations of moral wrong and thus degrees of deserved blame. Consider, for example, the problem of misinformation in the COVID-19 pandemic. The pandemic is not just a public health crisis that challenges our medical, scientific, and political resources. It is also a moral challenge because people are dying, and what we do, what we believe, and what we *say* we believe can alter the magnitude of the tragedy. In the age of social distancing, we are wirelessly huddled together closer than ever, nudging each other by our words toward higher or lower risk, safety or peril, comfort or terror. Our moral obligations to speak responsibly do not disappear just because we communicate digitally and impersonally. Under pressure from the pandemic, our duties have become weightier than ever.

In 2020, many people (including President Trump) promoted an unproven treatment for the virus; an armchair epidemiologist offered bogus proof that the danger had been hyped by the mainstream media; social media posts urged people not to seek treatment or to get the vaccine; and a church touted a cure that consists of toxic chemicals used to clean swimming pools. Such messages likely had disastrous consequences, and so we might rightly judge the messengers as having acted not just rashly or recklessly but immorally. We can assign to them varying degrees of blame depending on their motives, awareness of their actions, and the degree of harm done.

The worst offenders are the *deliberate deceivers*, those who knowingly traffic in pandemic lies to score partisan points, show support for their tribe, troll the opposition, exact revenge, or make a buck. They are morally akin to the knave who knows the village's drinking water has been poisoned but still declares the water to be perfectly safe—or hawks snake oil to those seeking protection from the poison. People may die, but that's none of his concern.

Next on the scale of culpability are the *self-deceivers*. Philosophers define self-deceivers as people who are motivated to hold false beliefs despite contrary evidence and who may betray through their behavior some awareness of the truth. The obvious examples of the self-deceived are partisans who denied the severity of the COVID-19 threat because it made their favorite political leader look clueless, decreased their party's electoral chances, or conflicted with the party line.

Can self-deceivers (like Clifford's ship owner) be held morally responsible for their own deception and for pushing the resulting falsehoods? The question comes down to whether self-deceivers have some control over their acquiring and sustaining self-deceptive beliefs. On most philosophical accounts, self-deceivers can indeed possess the requisite control, either because they intended to acquire the false beliefs in the first place or because they can recognize and resist the desires and emotions that distort their thinking. If this is the case, then the self-deceiving commentators who urged people to forgo face masks and social distancing because COVID-19 was "no more serious than the flu" bear some moral responsibility for the catastrophe that followed. They are like the town crier who suspects the drinking water may be poisoned but convinces himself that it is not and tells no one because the news would put his boss, the mayor, in a bad light.

It can often be difficult to tell whether someone is deliberately deceiving or is self-deceived, whether the offender is a verbal mugger or an informational drunk driver. Either way, people can be harmed, and when they are, someone is to blame.

Mixed in with the deceivers and self-deceivers are what the philosopher Harry G. Frankfurt calls *bullshitters*—people who don't care whether what they say is true or false but who intend to deceive their audience about their motives. They might blather to make themselves look good or to present themselves as something they are not. Bullshitters, of course, are everywhere online. Because of their frequent fabrications and their disregard for evidence and accuracy, many politicians, TV commentators, and inflammatory bloggers have been accused of

TRUSTWORTHY FACT-CHECKERS

Fact-checking websites rate the reliability of sources and the truth of claims, but who rates the trustworthiness of the fact-checkers? Fortunately the best, most reliable fact-checker organizations share certain characteristics that we can readily identify: (1) They are nonpartisan, and their funding is fully disclosed; (2) they explain their fact-checking methodology and disclose their sources; (3) they use nonpartisan and primary sources whenever possible and are appropriately skeptical of strongly biased information; (4) they employ neutral wording and minimize appeals to emotions, stereotypes, and logical fallacies; (5) they avoid partisan considerations in selecting topics to cover; (6) they promptly correct errors after publication; and (7) they have a solid track record in accurate reporting. Here are four top sites that meet all or almost all of these criteria.*

Snopes.com—One of the oldest and possibly the most trusted of fact-checking sites. For years it has been rendering definitive verdicts on urban legends, rumors, myths, and fake news. Factual accuracy: high.
PolitiFact.com—The best site for checking the accuracy of political claims. Won the Pulitzer Prize. Factual accuracy: high.
FactCheck.org—Like Politifact, this site strives to decrease deception and misinformation in American politics. Checks the accuracy of political statements in speeches, TV ads, news releases, interviews, and more. Factual accuracy: very high.
TruthOrFiction.com—Similar to Snopes, this site fact-checks urban legends, myths, Internet rumors, and other questionable claims but typically focuses on recurring stories rather than on those arising from current events. Factual accuracy: very high.

Other recommended sites: Fact Checker at the *Washington Post*, AP Fact Check (https://www.apnews.com/APFactCheck), NPR Fact Check (npr.org), The Sunlight Foundation (sunlightfoundation.com), the Poynter Institute (poynter. org), AllSides.com, FlackCheck.org, and OpenSecrets.org.

* The source for these judgments is MediaBiasFactCheck.com, the authoritative rater of bias and accuracy in traditional and online news sources. MediaBiasFactCheck.com itself meets all seven criteria noted earlier. Some recommended fact-checkers such as Snopes.com and FactCheck.org are also signatories to the International Fact-Checking Network (IFCN) code of principles (https://www.poynter.org/ifcn-fact-checkers-code-of-principles/).

being supreme bullshitters who often got the pandemic facts wrong. But there was plenty of blame to go around. Many played the same game when online they skipped critical thinking and thoughtlessly shared pandemic fake news, propaganda, viral rumors, and conspiracy theories. They were therefore at least partly responsible when they helped spread misinformation that sent someone down a path that ended in a hospital bed, or the morgue.

Arguing

If, when stakes are high and issues are important, we have a moral obligation to believe responsibly, we must surely have a duty to *argue* responsibly. That is, we must be obligated to seek good evidence to support our premises, to reason carefully to solid conclusions, and to not fall for bad arguments.

Here's one way to explain the difference between responsible and irresponsible arguing. Online, there is arguing, and then there is arguing. Or, to be more precise, there is Arguing 1 and Arguing 2. Arguing 2 is arguing in the usual sense of arguing—not as the offering of well-supported statements, but as a pointless back-and-forth of unsupported assertions, or as a tense attack and counterattack of words, which at its worst degrades into accusations, name-calling, ridicule, insults, and rage. Arguing 2 has very little to do with critical thinking and logical argument and everything to do with satisfying the needs of the perpetrators—needs to be noticed, to feel powerful and in control, to feel better about themselves, to be entertained, to strike a blow for their side. Generally, they cannot be reasoned with, and in arguing with them, you usually learn nothing. Nobody wins in Arguing 2, and cyberspace is filled from end to end with this kind of fake arguing.

Arguing 1 is arguing in the critical thinking sense, the morally responsible way. It is logical argument. It involves making a statement and trying to show that the statement is true by offering reasons and evidence to support it. Arguing 1 is about establishing what is and is not reasonable to believe. This is the kind of arguing that prevails among serious thinkers of all stripes, all political persuasions, and all levels of education. When they argue, they strive for an objective perspective, commit to following reason and evidence wherever they lead, try to understand and respect opposing views, and reject arguing that is personal, abusive, intolerant, and dishonest. The aim is understanding. Winning, conquering, impressing, or troubling the waters is beside the point. This is how critical thinkers have been pursuing knowledge in every field for at least two millennia. Arguing 1 does happen online; it takes place most often in serious and thoughtful blogs, websites, e-journals, and comment streams.

Suppose you go online intending to engage in some serious, honest, productive debate on an important issue. You want to do Arguing 1, and you want to avoid Arguing 2, the usual pointless, snarky, muddled back-and-forth that wastes people's time and brings out the worst in them. How do you do that? Here's how:

- Begin by avoiding people you suspect are interested only in scoring points, grandstanding, letting off steam, or trying to get a rise out of you. If halfway through the conversation you discover they are not interested in rational argument, say goodbye and leave. Gravitate toward forums where respectful, intelligent discussions are the norm.

- Keep the focus on the argument. Critique the argument's form or the truth of the premises, *not* the person. Making the debate personal sidetracks the debate, injects emotion into it, and adds nothing relevant.
- Try to understand the other person's point of view and what motivates it. By doing so you increase your chances of winning the argument, learning something you didn't know, and calming the discussion through your show of empathy. Appreciating your opponent's objections can help make your own argument stronger and demonstrate that you are serious and fair-minded.
- Show your opponent moral respect. Give her a fair hearing. Don't assume the worst about her motives, values, or background. Don't stereotype her based solely on her political leanings or affiliations. Avoid snarky comments, sarcasm, name-calling, and insults.
- Stay on point; don't veer off into irrelevant side issues or nitpicking. Pointing out your opponent's bad grammar and spelling errors does not advance your argument one bit and will likely put an end to any chance of rational discussion.
- Rein in your emotions. If you get angry, agitated, or exasperated, you won't be able to think as clearly as you should, you may start hurling insults instead of solid arguments, and your opponent will probably respond in kind.
- Know what you're talking about. Suppose you begin arguing for a position with someone only to discover that you are ignorant of the facts. But you keep insisting that you're right, because you're too embarrassed to admit you know nothing about the topic. This situation is a colossal waste of time. It's better to know the facts before you jump into the fray. Research the topic ahead of time, noting the arguments for and against the position in question.
- Think twice before trying to engage in a serious argument on a social media platform with a short character limit, like Twitter, for example. Twitter's character limit makes conversations about complex issues and long arguments difficult or pointless. And the back-and-forth becomes even more unwieldy when a half dozen people chime in to add their two cents.

Argument Analysis

Suppose Alex gets some amazing news on Facebook. The post says someone has discovered a cure for COVID-19. It's oleandrin, a chemical derived from the Oleander plant. There's no mention of any scientific research supporting the use of oleandrin to fight COVID-19, and he vaguely remembers a news report about safety concerns. He responds to the post by typing "Great News" and recommends oleandrin to all his friends. When someone complains that he shouldn't have promoted an unproven treatment, he responds with an argument like this:

1. There's no proof that oleandrin *doesn't* work.
2. I recommended it because I wanted to help people.
3. People have a right to know about this stuff, especially since scientists have yet to come up with a sure-fire cure for COVID-19.
4. Therefore, I did nothing wrong in spreading the word about this substance.

This argument is not valid: even if all three premises were true, the conclusion could still be false. Alex falls into the category of a self-deceiver. He has reason to believe that oleandrin may be unsafe, but he pushes that doubt aside and promotes it anyway. He also deceives himself about the effectiveness of oleandrin as a treatment. There's no evidence that it's effective; he has no idea whether it is or not. The absence of evidence showing that it doesn't work does not prove that it does (the fallacy of appeal to ignorance). But he enthusiastically recommends it anyway. Alex clearly was wrong to tout the chemical, and his benign motivation (expressed in premise 2) and people's right to know (premise 3) don't change that. The conclusion is false.

Note: Oleandrin is a real chemical that has been touted by some as a cure for the coronavirus. It is unproven, and experts have warned that it is dangerous and potentially fatal.

KEY TERMS

Dunning-Kruger effect	false consensus effect	mere exposure effect
fake news	illusion-of-truth effect	

 EXERCISES

Exercises marked with * have answers in "Answers to Exercises" (Appendix B).

Exercise 7.1: Review Questions

1. What is the fundamental philosophical principle about justified belief and evidence?
2. What is Clifford's view on believing on insufficient evidence?
*3. What is fake news?
4. Why is believing fake news regarded as a possible moral failing?

5. What is reasonable skepticism?

*6. What are three illegitimate reasons for accepting or rejecting claims?

7. What is reading laterally?

8. What are the key questions we must ask when we read critically?

*9. What is the mere exposure effect? The Dunning-Kruger effect?

10. What is the difference between deliberate deceivers, self-deceivers, and bullshitters?

Exercise 7.2: Moral Arguments

1. Do you agree that in Clifford's story about the ship lost at sea that the wishful-thinking ship owner did wrong? Why or why not? Do you agree that the ship owner would have done wrong even if the ship had not gone down? Explain.

2. Is it morally wrong to share fake news that you believe to be false? Why or why not?

3. Is it morally wrong to share fake news about COVID-19 when you aren't sure whether it is accurate? Explain.

4. Suppose someone posts misinformation about an unproven treatment for cancer (saying that it is safe and effective when it is not), and she is self-deceived about it. Has she done anything morally wrong? Why or why not?

5. Should those who campaign against the use of vaccines (anti-vaxxers) be held morally responsible when people heed their warning, forego vaccinations, and become seriously ill as a result? Explain.

Notes

1. W. K. Clifford, "The Ethics of Belief," in *The Rationality of Belief in God*, ed. George I. Mavrodes (Englewood Cliffs, NJ: Prentice-Hall, 1970), 159–160.

2. Sabrina Tavernise, "As Fake News Spreads, More Readers Shrug at the Truth," in *Fake News: Read All About It* (New York: The New York Times Company, 2017), 120-125.

3. Guy P. Harrison, *Think Before You Like* (Amherst, NY: Prometheus Books, 2017), 186–187.

For Further Reading

Chapter 1: Moral Reasoning on Campus

Audi, Robert. *Moral Knowledge and Ethical Character*. New York: Oxford University Press, 1997.

Cahn, Steven M., and Joram G. Haber. *Twentieth Century Ethical Theory*. Upper Saddle River, NJ: Prentice-Hall, 1995.

Fox, Richard M., and Joseph P. DeMarco. *Moral Reasoning*. 2nd ed. New York: Harcourt, 2001.

Frankena, William K. *Ethics*. 2nd ed. Englewood Cliffs, NJ: Prentice-Hall, 1973.

Gert, Bernard. *Morality: Its Nature and Justification*. New York: Oxford, 1998.

Harris, C. E. *Applying Moral Theories*. Belmont, CA: Wadsworth, 1997.

Nielsen, Kai. *Ethics Without God*. Buffalo, NY: Prometheus, 1973.

Pojman, Louis P. *Ethics: Discovering Right and Wrong*. 4th ed. Belmont, CA: Wadsworth, 2002.

Pojman, Louis P., and Lewis Vaughn, eds. *The Moral Life*. 3rd ed. New York: Oxford University Press, 2007.

Rachels, James. *The Elements of Moral Philosophy*. 4th ed. New York: McGraw-Hill, 2003.

Shafer-Landau, Russ. *Whatever Happened to Good and Evil?* New York: Oxford University Press, 2004.

Singer, Peter, ed. *A Companion to Ethics*. Cambridge: Blackwell, 1993.

Vaughn, Lewis. *Doing Ethics: Moral Reasoning and Contemporary Issues*. New York: W.W. Norton, 2008.

Vaughn, Lewis. *The Power of Critical Thinking*. 2nd ed. New York: Oxford University Press, 2008.

Wall, Thomas F. *Thinking Critically About Moral Problems*. Belmont, CA: Wadsworth, 2003.

Chapter 2: Free Speech, Equality, and Harm

Baer, Ulrich. *What Snowflakes Get Right: Free Speech, Truth, and Equality on Campus*. New York: Oxford University Press, 2019.

Ben-Porath, Sigal R. *Free Speech on Campus*. Philadelphia: University of Pennsylvania Press, 2017.

Chemerinsky, Erwin, and Howard Gillman. *Free Speech on Campus*. New Haven, CT: Yale University Press, 2017.

Fish, Stanley. *There's No Such Thing as Free Speech, and It's a Good Thing, Too*. New York: Oxford University Press, 1994.

Knight Foundation. "Free Expression on College Campuses." May 2019. https://kf-site-production. s3.amazonaws.com/media_elements/files/000/000/351/original/Knight-CP-Report-FINAL.pdf.

Lackey, Jennifer, ed. *Academic Freedom*. New York: Oxford University Press, 2018.

Strossen, Nadine. *Hate: Why We Should Resist It with Free Speech, Not Censorship*. New York: Oxford University Press, 2018.

Waldron, Jeremy. *The Harm of Hate Speech*. Cambridge, MA: Harvard University Press, 2012.

Zimmerman, Jonathan. *Campus Politics: What Everyone Needs to Know*. New York: Oxford University Press, 2016.

Chapter 3: Hate Speech and Speech Codes

Baer, Ulrich. *What Snowflakes Get Right: Free Speech, Truth, and Equality on Campus*. New York: Oxford University Press, 2019.

Ben-Porath, Sigal R. *Free Speech on Campus*. Philadelphia: University of Pennsylvania Press, 2017.

Chemerinsky, Erwin, and Howard Gillman. *Free Speech on Campus*. New Haven, CT: Yale University Press, 2017.

Fish, Stanley. *There's No Such Thing as Free Speech, and It's a Good Thing, Too*. New York: Oxford University Press, 1994.

Majeed, Azhar. "Defying the Constitution: The Rise, Persistence, and Prevalence of Campus Speech Codes." *Georgetown Journal of Law & Public Policy* vol. 7, no. 2, 2009.

Matsuda, Mari J. "Public Response to Racist Speech: Considering the Victim's Story." *Michigan Law Review* 87, no. 8, Legal Storytelling (Aug. 1989): 2320–2381.

Strossen, Nadine. *Hate: Why We Should Resist It with Free Speech, Not Censorship*. New York: Oxford University Press, 2018.

Waldron, Jeremy. *The Harm of Hate Speech*. Cambridge, MA: Harvard University Press, 2012.

Zimmerman, Jonathan. *Campus Politics: What Everyone Needs to Know*. New York: Oxford University Press, 2016.

Chapter 4: Academic Freedom

American Association of University Professors (AAUP) and the Association of American Colleges and Universities. *1940 Statement of Principles on Academic Freedom and Tenure*. https://www.aaup.org/report/1940-statement-principles-academic-freedom-and-tenure.

Baer, Ulrich. *What Snowflakes Get Right: Free Speech, Truth, and Equality on Campus*. New York: Oxford University Press, 2019.

Lackey, Jennifer, ed. *Academic Freedom*. New York: Oxford University Press, 2018.

Zimmerman, Jonathan. *Campus Politics: What Everyone Needs to Know*. New York: Oxford University Press, 2016.

Chapter 5: Race, Racism, and Justice

Alexander, Michelle. *The New Jim Crow*. New York: The New Press, 2012.

Altman, Andrew. "Discrimination." In *Stanford Encyclopedia of Philosophy*, Winter 2016 ed., edited by Edward N. Zalta. https://plato.stanford.edu/archives/win2016/entries/discrimination/.

Appiah, Kwame Anthony. "Racisms." In *Anatomy of Racism*, edited by David Theo Goldberg. Minneapolis: University of Minnesota Press, 1990, 3-17.

Blum, Lawrence. *"I'm Not a Racist But . . .": The Moral Quandary of Race*. Ithaca, NY: Cornell University Press, 2002.

Bonilla-Silva, Eduardo. *Racism without Racists*. 5th ed. Lanham, MD: Rowman and Littlefield, 2018.

Golash-Boza, Tanya Maria. *Racism and Racisms: A Critical Approach*. New York: Oxford University Press, 2016.

Rattansi, Ali. *Racism: A Very Short Introduction*. Oxford: Oxford University Press, 2007.

Sullivan, Shannon. *Good White People: The Problem with Middle-Class White Anti-Racism*. Albany, NY: SUNY Press, 2014.

Zack, Naomi. *The Ethics and Mores of Race: Equality after the History of Philosophy*. Lanham, MD: Rowman and Littlefield, 2011.

Zack, Naomi, ed. *The Oxford Handbook of Philosophy and Race*. New York: Oxford University Press, 2017.

Chapter 6: The Ethics of Protest

American Civil Liberties Union. "Know Your Rights: Protesters' Rights." http://www.aclu.org/know-your-rights/protesters-rights/.

Brownlee, Kimberley. "Civil Disobedience." In *Stanford Encyclopedia of Philosophy*, Fall 2017 edition, edited by Edward N. Zalta. https://plato.stanford.edu/archives/fall2017/entries/civil-disobedience/.

Delmas, Candice. *A Duty to Resist: When Disobedience Should Be Uncivil*. New York: Oxford University Press, 2020.

Nussbaum, Martha C. "Civil Disobedience and Free Speech in the Academy." In *Academic Freedom*, edited by Jennifer Lackey, 170–185. New York: Oxford University Press, 2018.

Smith, William, and Kimberley Brownlee. "Civil Disobedience and Conscientious Objection." May 24, 2017. *Oxford Research Encyclopedia of Politics*. https://doi.org/10.1093/acrefore/9780190228637.013.114.

Suber, Peter. "Civil Disobedience." In *Philosophy of Law: An Encyclopedia* II, 110–113. Shrewsbury, MA: Garland, 1999.

Zimmerman, Jonathan. *Campus Politics: What Everyone Needs to Know*. New York: Oxford University Press, 2016.

Chapter 7: The Ethics of Belief Online

Harrison, Guy P. *Think Before You Like: Social Media's Effect on the Brain and the Tools You Need to Navigate Your Newsfeed*. Amherst, NY: Prometheus Books, 2017.

McManus, John. *Don't Be Fooled: A Citizen's Guide to News and Information in the Digital Age*. Sunnyvale, CA: Unvarnished Press, 2012.

Manne, Kate. *Down Girl: The Logic of Misogyny*. New York: Oxford University Press, 2018.

Novella, Steven, et al. *The Skeptics' Guide to the Universe*. New York: Grand Central Publishing, 2018.

Schick, Theodore, and Lewis Vaughn. *How to Think about Weird Things*. 8th ed. New York: McGraw-Hill, 2019.

Singer, P. W., and Emerson T. Brooking. *LikeWar: The Weaponization of Social Media*. Boston: Houghton, Mifflin, Harcourt, 2018.

Sistare, Christine T., ed. *Civility and Its Discontents: Civic Virtue, Toleration, and Cultural Fragmentation*. Lawrence: University Press of Kansas, 2004.

Vaughn, Lewis. *Applying Critical Thinking to Modern Media*. New York: Oxford University Press, 2021.

Answers to Exercises

Chapter 1

Exercise 1.1

> **5.** We cannot infer what should be or ought to be from what is.
> **9.** Moral theories try to explain what makes an action right or what makes a person good.
> **13.** Principlism is a moral theory consisting of multiple moral principles that must be weighed and balanced against one another to determine right actions.

Exercise 1.2

> **1.** Nonmoral.
> **6.** Moral.
> **9.** Moral.

Exercise 1.3

> **4.** The Indian government posed an imminent threat to Pakistan and the world. When a foreign government poses an imminent threat to Pakistan and the world, Pakistanis are justified in attacking that government. So the Pakistanis were justified in attacking Indian troops.
> **9.** Hacking into a database containing personal information on thousands of people and invading their privacy is immoral. You hacked into a database containing personal information on thousands of people and invaded their privacy. Therefore, what you did was immoral.

Exercise 1.4

> **3.** Killing another human being in self-defense is morally permissible. So it is not the case that in all circumstances the killing of a human being is wrong.

7. If helping someone to commit suicide would somehow save the lives of millions of people, the act would seem to be morally permissible. So it is not the case that assisted suicide is never morally justified.

Chapter 2

1. Hateful, abusive, or discriminatory speech directed against a person or group because of their race, religion, sexual orientation, gender identity, ethnicity, or national origin.
7. The Constitution does not prohibit all hate speech, nor does it allow all hate speech.
10. The right of free speech, though extremely important, is not absolute. Like any other right, speech can be legitimately restricted when it conflicts with other important values in society. The US Supreme Court has consistently ruled that the government may punish certain kinds of speech that it deems harmful.

Chapter 3

1. A campus regulation that restricts, forbids, or punishes what is generally considered protected speech.
6. Hateful, abusive, or discriminatory speech directed against a person or group because of their race, religion, sexual orientation, gender identity, ethnicity, or national origin.

Chapter 4

4. An environment or atmosphere on campus thought to be a refuge or haven for students.
6. The policy or practice of barring someone from speaking on campus because of their expressed opinions.
8. Dignitary safety is the sense of being an equal member of the community and of being invited to contribute to a discussion as a valued participant. Intellectual safety is the refusal to listen to challenges to one's views or to consider opposing viewpoints.

Chapter 5

2. Slavery.
6. Inferiorizing racism is morally wrong mainly because it is a violation of fundamental moral principles. Antipathy racism is morally blameworthy because hatred, hostility, and bigotry are vices, especially when they are directed against people who have been made to suffer solely because of their

membership in a racial group. Antipathy racism, like the inferiorizing kind, has led to, and still leads to, racial conflict, suffering, injustice, and violence.

8. Institutional or structural racism is unequal treatment that arises from the way organizations, institutions, and social systems operate. Racial prejudice is antipathy toward a racial group based on a faulty view of that group.

Chapter 6

2. Conscientious objection consists of a refusal to comply with a directive or legal order for reasons of personal morality. Civil disobedience is deliberate lawbreaking designed to bring about change in a law or government policy.

4. Suber says that Thoreau argued that sometimes the Constitution is the problem, not the solution. Moreover, legal channels can take too long, he argued, for he was born to live, not to lobby. His individualism gave him another answer: individuals are sovereign, especially in a democracy, and the government only holds its power by delegation from free individuals. Any individual may, then, elect to stand apart from the domain of law. Martin Luther King, Jr., asks us to look more closely at the legal channels of change. If they are open in theory, but closed or unfairly obstructed in practice, then the system is not democratic in the way needed to make civil disobedience unnecessary.

6. The terms "civil disobedience" and "uncivil disobedience" can be misleading since, historically, acts of civil disobedience have always been considered uncivil and offensive in some quarters, and occurrences of civil disobedience were never meant to be models of decorum.

Chapter 7

3. Fake news is deliberately false or misleading news stories that masquerade as truthful reporting.

6. My group (political faction, fans of politician X or pundit Y, online community, etc.) trusts this source. (So I will, too.) This source contradicts my beliefs. (If I disagree with it, it must be fake news.) The claims made by this source *feel* true; therefore, they must actually *be* true. (Because my feelings alone can certify claims.)

9. The mere exposure effect is the idea that just being exposed repeatedly to words or images (even without registering them consciously) can induce a favorable or comfortable feeling toward them, whether or not there is any good reason for doing so. The Dunning-Kruger effect is the phenomenon of being ignorant of how ignorant we are.

Writing Argumentative Essays

Arguments and Argumentative Essays

As we note in Chapter 1, an argument is a group of statements in which some of them (the premises) are intended to support another of them (the conclusion). This configuration of statements-supporting-another-statement is not only the basic structure of an argument—it's the general design of an argumentative essay. An argumentative essay tries to support a particular conclusion or position on an issue by offering reasons to support that conclusion. Arguments (in the critical thinking sense) are not passionate exchanges of unsupported views, pointless contests of the is-too-is-not variety. And neither are argumentative essays. A mere sequence of statements expressing your views is not an argument, just as several pages of such statements do not constitute an argumentative essay.

So in an argumentative essay, your main task is to provide rational support for a claim. If you are successful, you will have shown that there are good reasons to accept your view of things. Readers who think critically may well be persuaded by your arguments. If you write well, you may be able to make your essay even more persuasive through rhetorical or stylistic devices that add emphasis, depth, and vividness to your prose. No one wants to read a boring essay. What you should not do, however, is rely entirely on nonargumentative elements to persuade your audience. Strong emotional appeals, for example, can indeed persuade some people, but they prove nothing. In truly effective argumentative essays, the primary persuasive device is critical reasoning.

Basic Essay Structure

Good argumentative essays generally contain the following elements, though not necessarily in the order shown here:

- Introduction (or opening)
- Statement of thesis (the claim to be supported)
- Argument supporting the thesis
- Assessment of objections
- Conclusion

In the *introduction*, you want to do at least two things: (1) grab the reader's attention and (2) provide background information for the thesis. Effective attention-grabbers include startling statistics, compelling quotations, interesting anecdotes, opinions of experts, shocking or unexpected claims, and vivid imagery. Whatever attention-grabbers you use, *they must relate to the topic of the essay.* No use telling a good story if it has nothing to do with your thesis. Providing background for your thesis often means explaining why your topic is important, telling how you became concerned, or showing that there is a problem to be solved or a question to be answered. Very often the introduction is laid out in the first paragraph of the essay, sometimes consisting of no more than a sentence or two. In general, the briefer the introduction, the better.

The *thesis statement* also usually appears in the first paragraph. It's the statement that you hope to support or prove in your essay, the conclusion of the argument that you intend to present. You want to state the thesis in a single sentence and do so as early as possible in the essay. Your thesis statement is like a compass to your readers, guiding them through your essay from premise to premise, showing them a clear path. It also helps you stay on course, reminding you to keep every part of the essay related to your single unifying idea. Your thesis statement should be restricted to a claim that can be defended in the space allowed (often only 750 to 1,000 words). Not restricted enough: "Tuition is too high." Better: "Tuition increases at Podunk College are unacceptable." Better still: "The recent tuition increase at Podunk College is unnecessary for financial reasons." (More on how to devise a properly restricted thesis statement in a moment.)

The main body of the essay is the fully developed argument supporting the thesis. This means that the basic essay structure consists of the thesis statement followed by each premise or reason that supports the thesis. Each premise in turn is clearly stated, sufficiently explained and illustrated, and supported by examples, statistics, expert opinion, and other evidence. Sometimes you can develop the essay very simply by devoting a single paragraph to each premise. At other times, each premise may demand several paragraphs. In any case, you should develop just one point per paragraph, with every paragraph clearly relating to the thesis statement.

A sketch of the argument for the Podunk College essay, then, might look like this:

Premise: If the college has a budget surplus, then a tuition increase is unnecessary.
Premise: The college has had a budget surplus for the last five years.
Premise: If the college president says that the school is financially in good shape and therefore doesn't need a tuition increase, then it's probably true that the school doesn't need a tuition increase.
Premise: In an unguarded moment, the president admitted that the school is financially in good shape and therefore doesn't need a tuition increase.
Thesis statement: Therefore, the recent tuition increase at Podunk College is probably unnecessary for financial reasons.

Good argumentative essays include an *assessment of objections*—an honest effort to take into account any objections that readers are likely to raise about the thesis statement or its premises. When you deal with such objections in your essay, you lend credibility to it because you're making an attempt to be fair and thorough. In addition, when you carefully examine objections, you can often see ways to make your argument or thesis statement stronger. It isn't necessary to consider every possible objection, just the strongest or the most common ones. Sometimes it's best to deal with objections when you discuss premises that relate to them. At other times it may be better to handle objections near the end of the essay after defending the premises.

Finally, your essay—unless it's very short—must have a *conclusion*. The conclusion usually appears in the last paragraph of the essay. Typically it reiterates the thesis statement (though usually not in exactly the same words). If the argument is complex or the essay is long, the conclusion may contain a summary of the argument. Good conclusions may reassert the importance of the thesis statement, challenge readers to do something about a problem, tell a story that emphasizes the relevance of the main argument, or bring out a disturbing or unexpected implication of a claim defended in the body of the essay.

Guidelines for Writing the Essay

1. *Determine your thesis statement.* Do not write on the first thesis idea that pops into your head. Select a topic you're interested in and narrow its scope until you have a properly restricted thesis statement. Research the topic to find out what issues are being debated. When you think you have an idea for a thesis statement, stop. Dig deeper into the idea by examining the arguments associated with that claim. Choose a thesis statement that you think you can defend. If you come to a dead end, start the process over.
2. *Create an outline.* Establish the basic framework of your outline by writing out your thesis statement and all the premises that support it. Then fill in the framework by jotting down what points you will need to make in defense of each premise. Decide on what objections to your argument you will consider and how you will respond to them.
3. *Write a first draft.* As you write, don't be afraid to revise your outline or even your thesis statement. Writing will force you to think carefully about the strengths and weaknesses of your argument. If need be, write a second draft and a third. Good writers aren't afraid of revisions; they depend on them.
4. *Stay on track.* Make sure that each sentence of your essay relates somehow to your thesis statement and argument.
5. *Zero in on your audience.* Determine for what audience your essay is intended, and write to them. Is it readers of the local paper? fellow students? people who are likely to disagree with you?

6. *Support your premises*. Back up the premises of your argument with examples, expert opinion, statistics, analogies, and other kinds of evidence.
7. *Let your final draft sit*. If possible, when you've finished writing your paper, set it aside and read it the next day. You may be surprised how many mistakes this fresh look can reveal. If you can't set the essay aside, ask a friend to read it and give you some constructive criticism.

From Issue to Thesis

For many students, the biggest challenge in writing an argumentative essay is deciding on an appropriate thesis—the claim, or conclusion, that the essay is designed to support or prove. Very often, when an essay runs off the track and crashes, the derailment can be traced to a thesis that was bad from the beginning.

Picking a thesis out of the air and beginning to write is usually a mistake. Any thesis statement that you craft without knowing anything about the subject is likely to be ill-formed or indefensible. It's better to begin by selecting an issue—a question that's controversial or in dispute—then researching it to determine what arguments or viewpoints are involved. To research it, you can survey the views of people or organizations involved in the controversy. Read articles and books, talk to people, go online. This process should not only inform you about various viewpoints but also tell you what arguments are used to support them. It should also help you narrow the issue to one that you can easily address in the space you have.

Suppose you begin with this issue: whether the United States has serious industrial pollution problems. After investigating this issue, you would probably see that it is much too broad to be addressed in a short paper. You should then restrict the issue to something more manageable—for example: whether recent legislation to allow coal-burning power plants to emit more sulfur dioxide will harm people's health. With the scope of the issue narrowed, you can explore arguments on both sides. You cannot examine every single argument, but you should assess the strongest ones, including those that you devise yourself. You can then use what you've already learned about arguments to select one that you think provides good support for its conclusion. The premises and conclusion of this argument can then serve as the bare-bones outline of your essay. Your argument might look like this:

[Premise 1] Excessive amounts of sulfur dioxide in the air have been linked to increases in the incidence of asthma and other respiratory illnesses.
[Premise 2] Many areas of the country already have excessive amounts of sulfur dioxide in the air.
[Premise 3] Most sulfur dioxide in the air comes from coal-burning power plants.
[Conclusion] Therefore, allowing coal-burning power plants to emit more sulfur dioxide will most likely increase the incidence of respiratory illnesses.

For the sake of example, the premises of this argument are made up. But your essay's argument must be for real, with each premise that could be called into question supported by an additional argument. After all, your readers are not likely to accept your argument's conclusion if they doubt your premises.

In some cases, your paper may contain more than one argument supporting a single conclusion, or it may offer a critique of someone else's argument. In either case, investigating an issue and the arguments involved will follow the pattern just suggested. In a critique of an argument (or arguments), you offer reasons why the argument fails and thus support the thesis that the conclusion is false.

This process of devising a thesis statement and crafting an argument to back it up is not linear. You will probably have to experiment with several arguments before you find one that's suitable. Even after you decide on an argument, you may later discover that its premises are dubious or that they cannot be adequately supported. Then you will have to backtrack to investigate a better argument. Backtracking in this preliminary stage is relatively easy. If you postpone this rethinking process until you are almost finished with your first draft, it will be harder—and more painful.

From Thesis to Outline

We have just seen that the second step in writing an argumentative essay (after determining your thesis statement, or conclusion) is creating an outline. Outlines are useful because, among other things, they help avert disaster in the essay-writing phase. Imagine writing two-thirds of your essay and then discovering that the second premise of your argument cannot be supported and is in fact false. You might have to throw out the whole argument and start over.

At the head of your outline, insert your thesis statement, articulating it as clearly and as precisely as possible. At every stage of outlining, you can then refer to the statement for guidance. The premises and conclusion of your argument (or arguments) will constitute the major points of your outline. The following, for example, is the preliminary outline for the essay discussed earlier:

> **THESIS:** Allowing coal-burning power plants to emit more sulfur dioxide will most likely increase the incidence of respiratory illnesses.
>
> I. Excessive amounts of sulfur dioxide in the air have been linked to increases in the incidence of asthma and other respiratory illnesses.
> II. Many areas of the country already have excessive amounts of sulfur dioxide in the air.
> III. Most sulfur dioxide in the air comes from coal-burning power plants.
> IV. Therefore, allowing coal-burning power plants to emit more sulfur dioxide will most likely increase the incidence of respiratory illnesses.

After you clearly state the premises, you need to ask yourself whether any of them need to be defended. As discussed earlier, any premise likely to be questioned by your readers will need support. That is, the premise itself will need arguments to back it up, and the supporting arguments should be indicated in your outline. (Some premises, though, may not need support because they are obvious or generally accepted.) You can support a premise (claim) through deductive or inductive arguments with premises made up of examples, analogies, empirical evidence (such as scientific research or trustworthy observations), and authoritative judgments (such as those from reliable experts). Here's how the preceding outline might look with (fictional) supporting arguments clearly shown:

THESIS: Allowing coal-burning power plants to emit more sulfur dioxide will most likely increase the incidence of respiratory illnesses.

I. Excessive amounts of sulfur dioxide in the air have been linked to increases in the incidence of asthma and other respiratory illnesses.
   A. EPA data show an association between high amounts of sulfur dioxide and increased respiratory illnesses.
   B. Cities that monitor air pollution have noted increases in hospital admissions for asthma and other respiratory ills when sulfur dioxide emissions are high.

II. Many areas of the country already have excessive amounts of sulfur dioxide in the air.
   A. Scientists have reported high levels of sulfur dioxide in the air in fifteen major cities.

III. Most sulfur dioxide in the air comes from coal-burning power plants.
   A. Many environmental scientists assert that coal-burning power plants are the source of most sulfur dioxide.
   B. A few owners of coal-burning power plants admit that their plants emit most of the sulfur dioxide in their region.

IV. Therefore, allowing coal-burning power plants to emit more sulfur dioxide will most likely increase the incidence of respiratory illnesses.

You should expand your outline until you've indicated how you intend to provide support for each claim that requires it. This level of detail helps ensure that you will not encounter any nasty surprises in the writing phase.

Your essay should somehow address objections or criticisms that your readers are likely to raise, and your outline should indicate how you intend to do this. Answering objections can make your case stronger and lend credibility to you as the writer. Sometimes it's best to address objections where they are likely to arise—in connection with specific premises or arguments. At other times, your essay may be more effective if you deal with objections at the end of it, near the conclusion.

As you work through your outline, don't be afraid to rework your thesis statement or to make changes in arguments. Satisfy yourself that the outline is complete and that it reflects a logical progression of points.

From Outline to First Draft

If you have developed a detailed outline, then you have a path to follow as you write. And while you're writing an argumentative essay, having a path is much better than searching for one. Your outline should make the writing much easier.

No outline is a finished work, however. As you write, you may discover that your arguments are not as strong as you thought, or that other arguments would be better, or that changing a point here and there would make an argument more effective. If so, you should amend your outline and then continue writing. The act of writing is often an act of discovery, and good writers are not afraid of revisions or multiple drafts.

Start your draft with a solid opening that draws your readers into your essay and prepares the way for your arguments. Good openings are interesting, informative, and short. Grab the attention of your readers with a bold statement of your thesis, a provocative quote, a compelling story, or interesting facts. Prepare the way for your arguments by explaining why the question you're addressing is important, why you're concerned about it, or why it involves a pressing problem. Don't assume that your readers will see immediately that the issue you're dealing with is worth their time.

Include a clear statement of your thesis in your opening (in the first paragraph or very close by). In many cases, you will want to tell the reader how you plan to develop your argument or how the rest of the essay will unfold (without going into lengthy detail). In any case, by the time your audience reads through your opening, they should know exactly what you intend to prove and why.

Consider this opening for our imaginary essay on air pollution:

> Respiratory experts at the National Institutes of Health say that sulfur dioxide in the air is a poison that we should avoid. Yet the current administration wants to loosen environmental rules to allow coal-burning power plants to emit more sulfur dioxide than they already do. That's a bad idea. The latest evidence shows that letting the plants emit more of this poison will most likely increase the incidence of respiratory illnesses in hundreds of communities.

This opening gets the reader's attention by sounding the alarm about a serious health hazard. It provides enough background information to help us understand the seriousness of the problem. And the thesis statement in the last sentence announces what the essay will try to prove.

The body of your essay should fully develop the arguments for your thesis statement, or conclusion. You should devote at least one paragraph to each premise, though several paragraphs may be necessary. You may opt to deal with objections to your argument as you go along, perhaps as you put forth each premise, or at the end of the essay just before the conclusion. Each paragraph should develop and explain just one idea, which is usually expressed in a topic sentence.

Each sentence in each paragraph should relate to the paragraph's main idea. Any sentence that has no clear connection to the main idea should be deleted or revised. Link paragraphs together in a logical sequence using transitional words and phrases or direct references to material in preceding paragraphs.

Here are two paragraphs that might follow the air pollution opening:

> Scientists used to wonder whether there is a connection between airborne sulfur dioxide and respiratory illness—but no more. Research has repeatedly shown a strong link between high levels of sulfur dioxide in the air and diseases that affect the lungs. For example, data from studies conducted by the Environmental Protection Agency (EPA) show that when levels of airborne sulfur dioxide in urban areas reach what the EPA calls the "high normal" range, the incidence of respiratory illnesses increases dramatically. According to several EPA surveys of air quality, many major cities (not just Los Angeles) often have high normal levels of sulfur dioxide in the air. In addition, data from health departments in large cities show that when levels of airborne sulfur dioxide are at their highest, hospital admissions for asthma and other respiratory ills also increase.
>
> These findings, however, tell only half the story. Many parts of the country have more than just occasional surges in levels of airborne sulfur dioxide. They must endure unsafe levels continuously. New studies from the National Institutes of Health demonstrate that in at least ten major cities, the amount of sulfur dioxide in the air is excessive all the time.

In this passage, a single paragraph is devoted to each premise. Each paragraph develops a single idea, which is stated in a topic sentence. (The topic sentence for the first paragraph: "Research has repeatedly shown a strong link between high levels of sulfur dioxide in the air and diseases that affect the lungs." The second paragraph: "[Many parts of the country] must endure unsafe levels continuously.") Each sentence in each paragraph relates to the topic sentence, and the relationships among the sentences are clear. Likewise the connection between the discussion in the first paragraph and that of the second is apparent. The transitional sentence in the second paragraph ("These findings, however, tell only half the story") helps bridge the gap between the paragraphs. Both of them help support the thesis statement.

How you end your essay is often as important as how you start it. In short or simple essays, there may be no need for a conclusion. The thesis may be clear and emphatic without a conclusion. In many cases, however, an essay is strengthened by a conclusion, and sometimes a conclusion is absolutely essential. Often without an effective conclusion, an essay may seem to end pointlessly or to be incomplete. The typical conclusion reiterates or reaffirms the thesis statement without being repetitious. Or the conclusion of the essay's argument serves as the conclusion for the whole essay. In long or complex essays, the conclusion often includes a summary of the main points discussed.

Sometimes a conclusion is a call to action, an invitation to the reader to do something about a problem. Sometimes it relates a story that underscores the importance of the essay's argument. Sometimes it highlights a provocative aspect of a claim defended earlier. In all cases it serves to increase the impact of the essay.

The conclusion, however, is not the place to launch into a completely different issue, make entirely unsubstantiated claims, malign those who disagree with you, or pretend that your argument is stronger than it really is. These tacks will not strengthen your essay but weaken it.

Matters of Style and Content

1. *Write to your audience.* Almost everything you write—from college papers to love notes—is intended for a particular audience. Knowing who your audience is can make all the difference in what you say and how you say it. Unless things have gone terribly awry, you would not ordinarily address members of the town council the same way you would your one true love; nor your one true love as you would readers of the *New England Journal of Medicine*. You may wonder, then, who is the intended audience of your paper?

Your instructor, of course, may specify your audience and thus settle the issue for you. Otherwise, you should assume that your audience consists of intelligent, curious readers who are capable of understanding and appreciating clearly written, well-made papers on many subjects. Writing to your proper audience means that you will have to define unfamiliar terms, explain any points that may be misunderstood, and lay out your argument so that its structure and significance would be clear to any intelligent reader. This approach will both force you to attempt a better understanding of your subject and help you demonstrate this understanding through your writing.

2. *Do not overstate premises or conclusions.* Overstatement is the problem of exaggerating claims, of making an assertion sound stronger or more inclusive than it deserves. We are all guilty of overstatement, most often in everyday speech. We may say, "Everyone dislikes Professor Jones" or "Americans think the French are snobbish" when in fact only *some* students dislike Professor Jones and only *a few* of our American friends think that *some* French people are snobbish. In everyday conversation, such exaggerations are often understood as such and are used innocuously for emphasis. But too often the overstatements are simply distortions, assertions that claim too much and lead us into error or prejudice. To a disconcerting degree, assertions regarding opposing views in religion, politics, and morality are overstatements.

Overstatement can arise in at least two ways. First, particular statements—including premises—can be exaggerated. You may be tempted to assert that whatever issue you are addressing in your essay is "the most important issue of our time." You might declare that a premise is certainly or undoubtedly true (when in fact it is merely probable) or forgo important qualifiers such as "some," "perhaps," and "many." You may get carried away and say, for example, that killing another human being is *always* morally wrong, even though you would admit that killing in self-defense is morally permissible.

Second, the conclusions of arguments can be overstated: They can go beyond what logical inference would permit. Because of your commitment to your conclusion, you may overstate it. The result is an invalid or weak argument.

3. *Treat opponents and opposing views fairly.* Sometimes it seems that most of what people know about arguing a position they have learned from the worst possible teachers—partisan television and radio programs or attack-and-counterattack slugfests on social media. In these forums, the standard procedure is to attack the character and motivations of opponents, distort or misrepresent opposing views, and dismiss opponents' evidence and concerns out of hand. But in good writing, abusive or unfair tactics are out of order. They are also ineffective. When readers encounter such heavy-handedness, they are likely to be suspicious of the writer's motives, to wonder if the writer is close-minded, to question whether his or her assertions can be trusted, or to doubt the worth of arguments defended with such gratuitous zeal.

4. *Write clearly.* Being clear is a matter of ensuring that your meaning is understood by the reader. In most kinds of writing, clarity is almost always a supreme virtue.

Lack of clarity in your writing can occur in several ways. Inexperienced writers often produce some very murky papers because too often they assume that because they know what they mean, others will know, too. Typically, others do *not* know. The problem is that new writers have not yet developed the knack of viewing their own writing as others might. In other words, they fail to adopt an objective stance toward their own words. Good writers are their own best critics.

Trying to view your writing as others might takes practice. A trick that often helps is to not look at your writing for a day or two and then go back to it and read it cold. You may discover after you take this little break that some passages that seemed clear to you earlier are mostly gibberish. Another technique is to use peer review. Ask a friend to read your paper and pinpoint any passages that seem unclear.

5. *Be careful what you assume.* Behind every argument there are presuppositions that need not be made explicit because they are taken for granted by all parties. They may be too obvious to mention or in no need of justification. (They are distinct from implicit premises, which are essential to an argument and should be brought out into the open.) In arguments about the rights of hospital patients, for example, there would typically be no need to explain that a hospital is not a Chevrolet truck, or that patient rights have something to do with ethics, or that such rights may be important to patients. You should, however, be careful not to presuppose a claim that may be controversial among your readers. If you wish to establish that abortion is morally permissible, you should not assume your readers will agree that women have a right to choose abortion or that a fetus is not a person.

The Truth about Philosophy Majors

Here's the inaccurate, old-school way of thinking:

- Philosophy majors have no marketable skills; they are unemployable.
- They are unprepared for professional careers in anything but teaching philosophy.
- They are useless in an economy built on exploding tech, speed-of-light innovation, and market-wrenching globalization.
- They are destined to earn low salaries.

Here's the new reality: All these assumptions are FALSE.

CAREERS

A wide range of data suggest that philosophy majors are not just highly employable; they are thriving in many careers that used to be considered unsuitable for those holding "impractical" philosophy degrees. The unemployment rate for recent B.A. philosophy graduates is 4.3 percent, lower than the national average and lower than that for majors in biology, chemical engineering, graphic design, mathematics, and economics.[i]

Nowadays most philosophy majors don't get Ph.D.'s in philosophy; they instead land jobs in many fields outside academia. They work in business consulting firms, guide investors on Wall Street, lead teams of innovators in Silicon Valley, do humanitarian work for non-government organizations, go into politics, and cover the world as journalists. They teach, write, design, publish, create. They go to medical school, law school, and graduate school in everything from art and architecture to education, business, and computer science. (Of course, besides majoring in philosophy, students can also minor in it, combining a philosophy B.A. with other B.A. programs, or take philosophy courses to round out other majors or minors.)

Many successful companies—especially those in the tech world—don't see a philosophy degree as impractical at all. To be competitive, they want more than just engineers, scientists, and mathematicians. They also want people with broader, big-picture skills—people who can think critically, question assumptions, formulate and defend ideas, develop unique perspectives, devise and evaluate arguments, write effectively, and analyze and simplify complicated problems. And these competences are abundant in people with a philosophy background.

Plenty of successful business and tech leaders say so. Speaking of her undergraduate studies, philosophy major and eventual chief executive of Hewlett-Packard, Carly Fiorina says, "I learned how to separate the wheat from the chaff, essential from just interesting, and I think that's a particularly critical skill now when there is a ton of interesting but ultimately irrelevant information floating around."[ii]

Flickr co-founder Stewart Butterfield, who has both bachelor's and master's degrees in philosophy, says, "I think if you have a good background in what it is to be human, an understanding of life, culture and society, it gives you a good perspective on starting a business, instead of an education purely in business. You can always pick up how to read a balance sheet and how to figure out profit and loss, but it's harder to pick up the other stuff on the fly."[iii]

Sheila Bair got her philosophy degree from the University of Kansas and went on to become chair of the Federal Deposit Insurance Corporation from 2006 to 2011. She says that philosophy "helps you break things down to their simplest elements. My philosophy training really helps me with that intellectual rigor of simplifying things and finding out what's important."[iv]

PHILOSOPHY: A NATURAL SEGUE TO LAW AND MEDICINE

Law schools will tell you that a major in philosophy provides excellent preparation for law school and a career in law. Philosophy excels as a pre-law major because it teaches you the very proficiencies that law schools require: developing and evaluating arguments, writing carefully and clearly, applying principles and rules to specific cases, sorting out evidence, and understanding ethical and political norms. Philosophy majors do very well on the LSAT (Law School Admission Test), typically scoring higher than the vast majority of other majors.

Philosophy has also proven itself to be good preparation for medical school. Critical reasoning is as important in medicine as it is in law, but the study and practice of medicine requires something else—expertise in grappling with the vast array of moral questions that now confront doctors, nurses, medical scientists, administrators, and government officials. These are, at their core, philosophy questions.

David Silbersweig, a Harvard Medical School professor, makes a good case for philosophy (and all the liberal arts) as an essential part of a well-rounded medical education. As he says,

> If you can get through a one-sentence paragraph of Kant, holding all of its ideas and clauses in juxtaposition in your mind, you can think through most anything.… I discovered that a philosophical stance and approach could identify and inform core issues associated with everything from scientific advances to healing and biomedical ethics.[v]

Philosophy major and NBC journalist Katy Tur says, "I would argue that for the vast majority of people, an education of teaching you to think critically about the world you are in and what you know and what you don't know is useful for absolutely everything that you could possibly do in the future."[vi]

It's little wonder then that the top ranks of leaders and innovators in business and technology have their share of philosophy majors, a fair number of whom credit their success to their philosophy background. The list is long, and it includes:[vii]

Patrick Byrne, entrepreneur, e-commerce pioneer, founder and CEO of
    Overstock.com
Damon Horowitz, entrepreneur, in-house philosopher at Google
Carl Icahn, businessman, investor, philanthropist….
Larry Sanger, Internet project developer, co-founder of Wikipedia
George Soros, investor, business magnate
Peter Thiel, entrepreneur, venture capitalist, co-founder of PayPal
Jeff Weiner, CEO of LinkedIn

Of course, there are also many with a philosophy background who are famous for their achievements outside the business world. This list is even longer and includes:

Wes Anderson, filmmaker, screenwriter (*The Royal Tenenbaums*)
Stephen Breyer, Supreme Court justice
Mary Higgins Clark, novelist (*All By Myself, Alone*)
Ethan Coen, filmmaker, director
Stephen Colbert, comedian, TV host
Angela Davis, social activist
Lana Del Rey, singer, songwriter
Dessa, rapper, singer, poet
Ken Follett, author (*Eye of the Needle*)
Harrison Ford, actor
Ricky Gervais, comedian, creator of *The Office*
Philip Glass, composer
Rebecca Newberger Goldstein, author (*Plato at the Googleplex*)
Matt Groening, creator of *The Simpsons* and *Futurama*
Chris Hayes, MSNBC host
Kazuo Ishiguro, Nobel Prize-winning author (*The Remains of the Day*)
Phil Jackson, NBA coach
Thomas Jefferson, U.S. president
Charles R. Johnson, novelist (*Middle Passage*)
Rashida Jones, actor
Martin Luther King, Jr., civil rights leader
John Lewis, civil rights activist, U.S. House of Representatives
Terrence Malick, filmmaker, director
Yann Martel, author (*Life of Pi*)
Deepa Mehta, director, screenwriter (*Fire*)

Iris Murdoch, author (*Under the Net*)
Robert Parris Moses, educator, civil rights leader
Stone Phillips, broadcaster
Susan Sarandon, actor
Susan Sontag, author, MacArthur Fellow
David Souter, Supreme Court justice
Alex Trebek, host of *Jeopardy*
George F. Will, journalist, author
Juan Williams, journalist

PHILOSOPHY MAJORS AND THE GRE

Philosophy majors score higher than *all other majors* on the verbal reasoning and analytic writing sections of the GRE.

	Verbal Reasoning	Quantitative Reasoning	Analytic Writing
Philosophy	160	154	4.3
Average	149.97	152.57	3.48

Educational Testing Service, 2017 GRE Scores, between July 1, 2013 and June 30, 2016.

SALARIES

According to recent surveys by PayScale, a major source of college salary information, philosophy majors can expect to earn a median starting salary of $44,800 and a median mid-career salary of $85,100. As you might expect, most of the higher salaries go to STEM graduates (those with degrees in science, technology, engineering, mathematics). But in a surprising number of cases, salaries for philosophy majors are comparable to those of STEM graduates. For example, while the philosophy graduate earns $85,100 at mid-career, the mid-career salary for biotechnology is $82,500; for civil engineering, $83,700; for chemistry, $88,000; for industrial technology, $86,600; and for applied computer science, $88,800. Median end-of-career salaries for philosophy majors (10 to 19 years' experience) is $92,665—not the highest pay among college graduates, but far higher than many philosophy-is-useless critics would expect.[viii]

Another factor to consider is the increase in salaries over time. On this score, philosophy majors rank in the top 10 of all majors with the highest salary increase from start to mid-career. Philosophy's increase is pegged at 101 percent. The major with the highest increase: government at 118 percent. Molecular biology is the fifth highest at 105 percent.[ix]

SALARY POTENTIAL FOR BACHELOR DEGREES

Major	Median Early Pay	Median Mid-Career Pay
	(0 to 5 yrs. work experience)	(10+ yrs. work experience)
Mechanical Engineering	$58,000	$90,000
Applied Computer Science	$53,100	$88,800
Information Technology	$52,300	$86,300
Civil Engineering	$51,300	$83,700
Business and Finance	$48,800	$91,100
Biotechnology	$46,100	$82,500
Business Marketing	$45,700	$78,700
Philosophy	**$44,800**	**$85,100**
History	$42,200	$75,700
Advertising	$41,800	$84,200
General Science	$41,600	$75,200
Telecommunications	$41,500	$83,700
English Literature	$41,400	$76,300
Marine Biology	$37,200	$76,000

PayScale, "Highest Paying Bachelor Degrees by Salary Potential," *College Salary Report: 2017-2018*, https://www.payscale.com/college-salary-report/majors-that-pay-you-back/bachelors

And among liberal arts majors, philosophy salaries are near the top of the list. All liberal arts majors except economics earn lower starting and mid-career pay than philosophy does.

MEANING

In all this talk about careers, salaries, and superior test scores, we should not forget that for many students, the most important reason for majoring in philosophy is the meaning it can add to their lives. They know that philosophy, after two-and-one-half millennia, is still alive and relevant and influential. It is not only for studying but also for living, that is, for guiding our lives toward what's true and real and valuable. They would insist that philosophy, even with its ancient lineage and seemingly remote concerns, applies to your life and your times and your world. The world is full of students and teachers who can attest to these claims. Perhaps you will eventually decide to join them.

SALARY POTENTIAL FOR LIBERAL ARTS BACHELOR DEGREES

Major	Median Early Pay	Median Mid-Career Pay
	(0 to 5 yrs. work experience)	(10+ yrs. work experience)
Economics	$54,100	$103,200
Philosophy	**$44,800**	**$85,100**
Political Science	$44,600	$82,000
Modern Languages	$43,900	$77,400
Geography	$43,600	$72,700
History	$42,200	$75,700
English Literature	$41,400	$76,300
Anthropology	$40,500	$63,200
Creative Writing	$40,200	$68,500
Theatre	$39,700	$63,500
Psychology	$38,700	$65,300
Fine Art	$38,200	$62,200

PayScale, "Highest Paying Bachelor Degrees by Salary Potential," College Salary Report: 2017-2018, https://www.payscale.com/college-salary-report/majors-that-pay-you-back/bachelors

RESOURCES

American Philosophical Association, "Who Studies Philosophy?" http://www.apaonline.org/?whostudiesphilosophy.

BestColleges.com, "Best Careers for Philosophy Majors," 2017, http://www.bestcolleges.com/careers/philosophy-majors/.

The University of North Carolina at Chapel Hill, Department of Philosophy, "Why Major in Philosophy?" http://philosophy.unc.edu/undergraduate/the-major/why-major-in-philosophy/

University of California, San Diego, Department of Philosophy, "What Can I Do with a Philosophy Degree?" https://philosophy.ucsd.edu/undergraduate/careers.html.

University of Maryland, Department of Philosophy, "Careers for Philosophy Majors," http://www.philosophy.umd.edu/undergraduate/careers

Forbes, "That 'Useless' Liberal Arts Degree Has Become Tech's Hottest Ticket," 29 July 2015, https://www.forbes.com/sites/georgeanders/2015/07/29/liberal-arts-degree-tech/#5fb6d740745d

TopUniversities.com, "What Can I Do with a Philosophy Degree?" 2 March 2015, https://www.topuniversities.com/student-info/careers-advice/what-can-you-do-philosophy-degree

Notes

i   Federal Reserve Bank of New York, "The Labor Market for Recent College Graduates," 11 January 2017, https://www.newyorkfed.org/research/college-labor-market/college-labor-market_compare-majors.html.

ii T. Rees Shapiro, "For Philosophy Majors, the Question after Graduation Is: What Next?" Washington Post, 20 June 2017.

iii Carolyn Gregoire, "The Unexpected Way Philosophy Majors Are Changing the World of Business," Huffpost, 3 January 2017, https://www.huffingtonpost.com/2014/03/05/why-philosophy-majors-rule_n_4891404.html.

iv Shapiro.

v   David Silbersweig, "A Harvard Medical School Professor Makes a Case for the liberal arts and Philosophy," Washington Post, 24 December 2015.

vi Shapiro.

vii American Philosophical Association, "Who Studies Philosophy?" (accessed 14 November 2017), http://www.apaonline.org/?whostudiesphilosophy.

viii PayScale, "Highest Paying Bachelor Degrees by Salary Potential," College Salary Report: 2017-2018, https://www.payscale.com/college-salary-report/majors-that-pay-you-back/bachelors.

ix PayScale; reported by Rachel Gillett and Jacquelyn Smith, "People with These College Majors Get the Biggest Raises," Business Insider, 6 January 2016, http://www.businessinsider.com/college-majors-that-lead-to-the-biggest-pay-raises-2016-1/#20-physics-1.

Glossary

analogical induction An argument making use of analogy, reasoning that because two or more things are similar in several respects, they must be similar in some further respect.

availability error Relying on evidence not because it's trustworthy but because it's memorable or striking.

civil disobedience Deliberate lawbreaking designed to bring about change in a law or government policy.

confirmation bias The act of seeking out and using only evidence that confirms our views.

conscientious objection A refusal to comply with a directive or legal order for reasons of personal morality.

counterspeech Any speech that tries to counter or undermine hateful or discriminatory messages.

cultural relativism The view that right actions are those sanctioned by one's culture.

deductive argument An argument intended to give logically conclusive support to its conclusion.

divine command theory The view that right actions are those commanded by God, and wrong actions are those forbidden by God.

Dunning-Kruger effect The well-researched phenomenon of being ignorant of how ignorant we are.

enumerative induction An inductive argument pattern in which we reason from premises about individual members of a group to conclusions about the group as a whole.

ethics The study of morality using the methods of philosophy.

evidence Something that makes a statement more likely to be true.

fake news Deliberately false or misleading news stories that masquerade as truthful reporting.

false consensus effect The tendency to overestimate the degree to which other people share our opinions, attitudes, and preferences.

fighting words Intimidating face-to-face speech aimed directly at a specific person and likely to cause an immediate violent reaction against the speaker.

harassment Unwelcome speech directed at a person or group of persons that repeatedly undermines or interferes with their freedom or privacy.

hate speech Hateful, abusive, or discriminatory speech directed against a person or group because of their race, religion, sexual orientation, gender identity, ethnicity, or national origin.

illusion-of-truth effect A phenomenon in which you come to believe that a false claim is actually true simply because it is familiar.

individual racism Person-to-person acts of intolerance or discrimination.

inductive argument An argument intended to give probable support to its conclusion.

inference to the best explanation A form of inductive reasoning in which we reason from premises about a state of affairs to an explanation for that state of affairs.

institutional or structural racism Unequal treatment that arises from the way organizations, institutions, and social systems operate.

mere exposure effect The idea that just being exposed repeatedly to words or images (even without registering them consciously) can induce a favorable or comfortable feeling toward them, whether or not there is any good reason for doing so.

microaggressions Commonplace slights or insults conveyed intentionally or unintentionally by words or actions to disadvantaged groups.

moral absolutism The belief that objective moral principles allow no exceptions or must be applied the same way in all cases and cultures.

moral objectivism The idea that at least some moral standards are objective.

moral relativism The view that moral standards are not objective but are relative to what individuals or cultures believe.

moral statement A statement asserting that an action is right or wrong (moral or immoral) or that something (such as a person or motive) is good or bad.

morality Beliefs about right and wrong actions and morally good and bad persons or character.

motivated reasoning Reasoning for the purpose of supporting a predetermined conclusion, not to uncover the truth.

no platforming The policy or practice of barring someone from speaking on campus because of their expressed opinions.

principlism A moral theory consisting of multiple moral principles that must be weighed and balanced against each to reach a moral judgment.

protest A public demonstration of dissent, disapproval, or resistance against policies, actions, or ideas deemed to be morally wrong or unjust.

punishable incitement Speech in which the speaker intentionally incites an immediate and specific act of violence or other illegal conduct.

racial discrimination Unfavorable treatment of people because of their race.

racial prejudice Antipathy toward a racial group based on a faulty view of that group.

racism The belief that some races are inferior in important ways or are otherwise deserving of dislike or hostility.

safe space An environment or atmosphere on campus thought to be a refuge or haven for students.

speech code A campus regulation that restricts, forbids, or punishes what is generally considered protected speech.

subjective relativism The view that right actions are those sanctioned by a person.

trigger warning Statement from a teacher alerting students to course material that might be traumatizing, stigmatizing, offensive, or disturbing.

true threat Statement through which the speaker "means to communicate a serious intent to commit an act of unlawful violence to a particular individual or group of individuals. The speaker need not actually intend to carry out the threat."

uncivil disobedience Lawbreaking protest that (unlike civil disobedience) shuns publicity, evades lawful penalty, is morally offensive, or potentially violent.

Index